STUDIES IN HISTORY, ECONOMICS AND PUBLIC LAW

Edited by the
FACULTY OF POLITICAL SCIENCE
OF COLUMBIA UNIVERSITY

NUMBER 511

THE IDEA OF PROGRESS IN AMERICA, 1815-1860

BY

ARTHUR ALPHONSE EKIRCH, JR.

THE IDEA OF PROGRESS
IN AMERICA, 1815-1860

BY

ARTHUR ALPHONSE EKIRCH, JR., Ph.D.

NEW YORK
PETER SMITH
1951

Printed in the United States of America

To

My Father and My Mother

PREFACE

THE idea of progress is one of those vague concepts which have been cherished, at least until recently, by a large portion of the modern occidental world. Formerly the subject of much philosophical theorizing by intellectuals, the idea in the nineteenth and twentieth centuries has also penetrated to the generality of the people. It has been withdrawn from the exclusive scrutiny of the philosophers to become accepted as a part of the ideology of industrial civilization. Traditionally the idea has been advocated and believed in as a vision of the future, but it also has been invoked as a useful justification and rationalization for the events of the past. Lending itself to varied interpretations and to many uses, it has served divergent interests and classes.

While its influence has been generally recognized, the historical treatment of the idea of progress has been confined mostly to a discussion of the leading philosophical treatises on the subject. In this fashion the history of the idea in Europe has been outlined, but in the United States the literature of progress has been a subject of concern only with regard to its incidental or biographical aspects. The need for a more definite analysis of the American conception of the idea of progress was first indicated by Professor Charles A. Beard, in 1932, in his Introduction to the American edition of J. B. Bury's history of the idea in Europe. Since then it has received the attention of several students of American intellectual history, but no attempt has been made to present a thorough survey of the concept for any extended period of American history.[1] This study, therefore, is an effort to portray the American faith in progress during an important period of our history and to analyze the idea in the terms of the interests and groups which it served or promised to serve.

[1] However, since the completion of this study, the history of the complementary concept, the idea of civilization, has been published. See: Charles A. and Mary R. Beard, *The American Spirit: A Study of the Idea of Civilization in the United States* (New York, 1942).

In collecting the data, an extensive range of published material was surveyed and analyzed. The obscure magazine article and the forgotten academic address, as well as the formal treatise, were admitted as witnesses to the widespread popularity of the concept of progress. With an idea so vague in its meaning and at the same time so persuasive in its philosophy, the search for the written evidences of its affirmation could have been virtually endless. However, although no systematic search of the newspaper files of the period seemed practicable, it is felt that those materials analyzed are representative and that their further increment would not alter the essential outlines of this study.

The gathering of the data was carried on mostly in the libraries of Columbia University, in the New York Public Library, and in the Library of the Union Theological Seminary in New York. Several weeks were spent at the Library of Congress, and material from the New York Historical Society and from the Harvard University Library was also used. To the members of the staffs of all of these libraries I am under an obligation for their efficiency and courtesy in making available the diffuse material necessary to this study.

My initial interest in the idea of progress as a subject for research was the result of its suggestion by Professor Merle Curti, now at the University of Wisconsin, in his seminar at Columbia University. To Professor Curti's invaluable advice, numerous readings of the manuscript, and general interest and enthusiasm I owe a deep debt of appreciation. The manuscript was also read by Professors John A. Krout, Herbert W. Schneider, Ralph L. Rusk, Allan Nevins, and Henry Steele Commager of Columbia University. To each one of these men I am indebted for many helpful suggestions and for much valuable criticism.

For their work in typing the manuscript, I wish to thank my sister, Miss Kathryn L. Ekirch, and especially Miss Irene Schaefer, who typed the pages in their final form.

Finally, I am particularly grateful to my wife, Dorothy Gustafson Ekirch, for her patience and help while the manuscript was being prepared for the press.

TABLE OF CONTENTS

CHAPTER I

THE HERITAGE OF THE IDEA

THROUGH the course of its long and important history the idea of progress has been defined and interpreted in various ways. This idea that " civilization has moved, is moving, and will move in a desirable direction " has been compared with the concepts of Fate, Providence, or personal immortality. Like those ideas it is believed in not because it is held to be good or bad, nor because it is considered to be true or false. In the words of J. B. Bury, the leading historian of the concept of progress, " belief in it is an act of faith." Bury accordingly included progress among those ideas not dependent for their fulfillment upon man's will.[1] And in this opinion he was supported by many of the European philosophers of the concept. However, in the United States, as we shall see, the American people felt that, although progress was indeed certain, it could nevertheless be impeded or accelerated by human will and effort. It was, therefore, not only a theory of the past or a prophecy of the future, but also an incentive to action. In other words, progress represented a measurable growth in the pursuit of knowledge and in the achievements of science as well as an advance in the ability of men to control for good their own lives and destinies.

This division of opinion over the meaning of progress complicates any effort to trace the idea back even to its approximate beginnings in the realm of time.[2] However, the historians and

1 J. B. Bury, *The Idea of Progress: An Inquiry into Its Origin and Growth* (first English ed. 1920; New York, 1932), pp. 1-7.

2 The meaning of progress has provoked much discussion in the extensive philosophical and sociological literature on the subject. For some examples, see: J. E. Boodin, " The Idea of Progress," *Journal of Social Philosophy,* IV (Jan., 1939), 101-120; and his, *The Social Mind: Foundations of Social Philosophy* (New York, 1939), ch. 14; Allan Nevins, *The Gateway to History* (Boston and New York, 1938), ch. 9, and p. 239; Lewis Mumford, *Technics and Civilization* (New York, 1934), pp. 182-185; H. W. Schneider, *Science and Social Progress* (Lancaster, Pa., 1920), pp. 24-26; F. J. Teggart, *Theory of History* (New Haven, 1925), Part II, ch. 8, and pp. 222-223; W. D. Wallis, *Culture and Progress* (New York, 1930), Part III.

philosophers have for the most part agreed that the concept in its fullest exposition is of a relatively modern origin. Bury in his history concluded that the idea was discovered neither by the Greeks nor by the philosophers of the Middle Ages.[3] Although he noted that Francis Bacon and other sixteenth century thinkers were on the threshold of formulating an idea of progress, the concept was, according to Bury, in reality fostered by the Cartesian philosophy of the seventeenth century. While Bury credited the idea of the progress of knowledge to Fontenelle, he maintained that the entire concept was first proclaimed in explicit form early in the eighteenth century by the French philosopher, the Abbé de Saint-Pierre. Influenced by the philosophy of Locke in England and by the Encyclopedists in France, the dogma of progress was finally given to all the civilized world by the exponents of the eighteenth century enlightenment.

During the nineteenth century the idea of progress has been promoted by philosophers like Hegel, Comte, Spencer, and Marx, and by the Darwinian theory of evolution.[4] Also given

3 For the remainder of this paragraph and for the general history of the European idea of progress, see Bury, *op. cit., passim*; and also: J. J. Thonissen, " Quelques Considérations sur la Théorie du Progrès Indéfini ..." in *Mémoires Couronnés et Autres Mémoires Publiés par l'Académie Royale...de Belgique*, Tome IX (Bruxelles, 1859), *passim*; Robert Flint, *Historical Phillosophy in France...* (New York, 1894), *passim*; Jules Delvaille, *Essai sur l'Histoire de l'Idée de Progrès...* (Paris, 1910), *passim*; J. O. Hertzler, *Social Progress* (New York and London, 1928), chs. 2-3; Wallis, *op. cit.*, Part II; Preserved Smith, *A History of Modern Culture* (New York, 1930-1934), II, ch. 7; H. E. Barnes, *An Intellectual and Cultural History of the Western World* (rev. ed.; New York, 1941), ch. 20; H. E. Barnes and Howard Becker, *Social Thought from Lore to Science* (Boston and New York, 1938), I, ch. 13.

Delvaille, Flint, Hertzler, Wallis, and Barnes all trace the idea of progress back further into ancient times than does Bury. See also: A. O. Lovejoy and George Boas, *Primitivism and Related Ideas in Antiquity* (Baltimore, 1935), chs. 8, 12.

4 The general characteristics of the idea of progress in the nineteenth century have been commented upon by, for example: W. R. Inge, *The Idea of Progress* (Oxford, 1920), p. 9, and *passim*; Crane Brinton, *English*

an immense impetus by the rise of technology, it has however, been set back by the spread of war. Therefore, in our times Charles A. Beard, a distinguished American critic of Bury's definition, has concluded that progress is not inevitable but that it is dependent on human will and effort.[5] Proponents of this view are strong in the faith that the powers of education and of science can make a better world in the future, even if it be granted that the past has not been altogether progressive.

The idea enjoyed, then, a position in the intellectual heritage of the world long before the birth of the United States. An important factor in the philosophy and ideology of Western Europe, it was also carried across the Atlantic to the New World, where it prospered in a rich and fertile environment. In America the successful development of a seemingly limitless expanse of land and resources made the people peculiarly susceptible to a belief in so dynamic an idea as that of progress. While their concept of the idea may rightly be considered a part of the European culture pattern transmitted to and modified by the New World, the impact of the American environment made it inevitable that the American people should interpret the idea of progress in the light of their own interests and experience.

Although it has been maintained that some of the ancient and medieval philosophers moulded their optimism into a notion of progress, it is not the foreshadowings of the idea in antiquity but rather the explicit formulation of the idea in France, Germany, and England in the eighteenth and early nineteenth centuries that is pertinent to this study of the American concept of progress during the period from 1815 to 1860.

Political Thought in the Nineteenth Century (London, 1933), pp. 295-304; Carl Becker, *Progress and Power* (Stanford, Calif., 1936), pp. 2-3; Jacques Barzun, *Darwin Marx Wagner: Critique of a Heritage* (Boston, 1941), *passim.*

5 C. A. Beard, "Introduction" to the Am. ed. of Bury's *Idea of Progress* (New York, 1932), p. xl, and *passim*; see also Beard's "The Idea of Progress," ch. I in *A Century of Progress,* ed. C. A. Beard (New York, 1933), pp. 3-19.

The conditions in eighteenth-century Europe, heralding the collapse of a feudal order before the advent of the industrial revolution and of modern capitalism, were especially favorable to the reception of the idea of progress. Satisfaction with the old order yielded to discontent and then to an optimism over what the future portended.[6]

In France an eighteenth-century philosopher especially under the influence of the concept of progress during this period of change was the enlightened liberal, M. de Condorcet, whose *Outlines of an Historical View of the Human Mind* has been recognized as the first book to treat the idea "with explicit fulness."[7] Familiar with the thought of his predecessors, Saint-Pierre and Turgot, Condorcet in turn influenced later theorists of progress, particularly the French socialists and the English utilitarians.[8] Like so many of the leaders of the revolutionary movement in France, he held a keen interest in the future of the American Republic. Since the United States also owed a debt to the French philosophers of the enlightenment, it was most appropriate that Condorcet's sketch of progress should be published in Philadelphia in 1796, one year after it had first appeared in France and England.[9]

In Condorcet's work the idea of progress became the intellectual force and explanation of the more idealistic aspects of the French Revolution. Especially interested in the possibilities for improvement and in the capacity for progress of the masses of

6 J. S. Schapiro, *Condorcet and the Rise of Liberalism* (New York, 1934), pp. 55-56, 234 ff.; Carl Becker, *The Heavenly City of the Eighteenth-Century Philosophers* (New Haven, 1932), pp. 136-137; A. O. Hansen, *Liberalism and American Education in the Eighteenth Century* (New York, 1926), pp. 1-22; Kingsley Martin, *French Liberal Thought in the Eighteenth Century* (London, 1929), pp. 277-298.

7 J. B. Bury, *Selected Essays*, ed. Harold Temperley (Cambridge, 1930), p. 27.

8 Schapiro, *op. cit.*, p. 262.

9 M. de Condorcet, *Outlines of an Historical View of the Progress of the Human Mind* (tr. from the French; Phil., 1796). This work was also published in Baltimore in 1802, but the Philadelphia edition is used in this study.

the people, he claimed that the progress of the race was subject to the same general laws which governed individual improvement. In the manner of Locke, he attributed all human knowledge to the fact that human beings were capable of receiving sensory experiences from their environment. And from an application of this theory to the masses of the people, he concluded, along with Lamarck, that there was a continuity and growth in the progress of the human intellect from generation to generation.[10] The course of civilization, Condorcet believed, could be divided into ten epochs or stages, but before proceeding with his own survey, he announced the historical nature of his *Outlines*:

> From these observations on what man has heretofore been, and what he is at present, we shall be led to the means of securing and of accelerating the still further progress, of which, from his nature, we may indulge the hope.
>
> Such is the object of the work I have undertaken; the result of which will be to show, from reasoning and from facts, that no bounds have been fixed to the improvement of the human faculties; that the perfectibility of man is absolutely indefinite; that the progress of this perfectibility, henceforth above the controul of every power that would impede it, has no other limit than the duration of the globe upon which nature has placed us.[11]

Condorcet's survey of past history exhibited the transformation of an agricultural society into one increasingly affected by scientific and technological progress. His hopes of future progress were based on the attainment of an equality among men and nations and on the achievement of a real improvement in the condition of men through the growing power of science and education.[12] Written during the French Revolution while

10 *Ibid.*, pp. 9-10; see also: John Morley, *Critical Miscellanies* (London, 1886), II, 229.

11 Condorcet, *op. cit.*, p. 11.

12 *Ibid.*, pp. 251, 250-293.

its author was under the proscription of the government, Condorcet's book absorbed the revolutionary fervor, but it also argued eloquently for a society in which violence would be unnecessary. In the language of one authority, Condorcet contributed to the idea of progress: (1) that it was a natural law, (2) an emphasis, shared by Turgot, upon the social aspects of man, and (3) the development of the idea of an unlimited future perfectibility for the race.[13]

In England during the eighteenth and early nineteenth centuries the idea of progress attracted the attention of several writers whose influence also extended to America.[14] During this period the industrial revolution was giving an increasing sense of material reality to the dogma of progress. Adam Smith, the great expositor of the economic liberalism under which the revolution flourished in England, revealed in his writings that he was actuated by the possibility of a future improvement of society.[15] It is true, however, that Smith in his general philosophy had been much influenced by David Hume, the Scotch historian and philosopher, who gave only a partial acceptance to the idea of progress.[16] On the other hand, a less qualified belief in progress was expressed by Hume's fellow Scotch philosopher, and a contemporary of Smith, Adam Ferguson. In his *Essay on the History of Civil Society,* first published in England in 1767, and often republished in both England and America, Ferguson affirmed a faith in the future progress of

13 Schapiro, *Condorcet,* pp. 265-266.

14 For a general discussion, see: Lois Whitney, *Primitivism and the Idea of Progress in English Popular Literature of the Eighteenth Century* (Baltimore, 1934), *passim*; R. S. Crane "Anglican Apologetics and the Idea of Progress, 1699-1745," *Modern Philology*, XXXI (Feb., May, 1934), 273-306, 349-382.

15 G. B. Strong, *Adam Smith and the Eighteenth Century Concept of Social Progress* (Chicago, 1932), *passim*; H. J. Laski, *Political Thought in England from Locke to Bentham* (New York and London, 1920), ch. VII; Delvaille, *Essai,* Livre VII.

16 In addition to the citations in Note 15, see: Bury, *The Idea of Progress,* pp. 219-220.

society if men preserved it from corrupt government.[17] Mentioning the analogy of the rise of vegetables from shoots and of animals from infancy, he concluded: " This progress in the case of man is continued to a greater extent than in that of any other animal. Not only the individual advances from infancy to manhood, but the species itself from rudeness to civilization." [18]

A disciple of progress who exercised a direct influence in America was Joseph Priestley, the English scientist and writer. An outcast in England because of his radical sympathies with the French Revolution, he came to the United States in 1791, remaining until his death thirteen years later. In his *Essay on the First Principles of Government,* first published in 1768, Priestly affirmed that the individual was able to profit by the experience of the past and "that the human species itself is capable of a similar and unbounded improvement; whereby mankind in a later age are greatly superior to mankind in a former age, the individuals being taken at the same time of life." [19] Believing that the "great instrument in the hand of divine providence, of this progress of the species towards perfection, is *society,* and consequently *government,*" he predicted continual progress in the arts and sciences, with knowledge becoming more and more subdivided as it became more perfectly known.[29] Priestly anticipated Bentham in his application of the criteria of utility to the acts of government, and he also advocated the establishment of religious and civil liberty as necescessary prerequisites for progress and happiness. Of the opinion that the time in which he wrote was one of advancement and

17 Adam Ferguson, *An Essay on the History of Civil Society* (7th ed., Boston, 1809), Parts V and VI.

18 *Ibid.,* p. 1; W. C. Lehmann, *Adam Ferguson and the Beginnings of Modern Sociology* (New York, 1930), chs. IV and V; pp. 117-118, 147-152.

19 Joseph Priestley, *An Essay on the First Principles of Government and on the Nature of Political, Civil, and Religious Liberty. . .* (2nd ed.; London, 1771), p. 1; Leslie Stephen, *History of English Thought in the Eighteenth Century* (3rd ed.; New York, 1927), II, 256.

20 Priestly, *An Essay,* pp. 2-4.

openmindedness, he declared that, " whatever was the beginning of this world, the end will be glorious and paradisical, beyond what our imaginations can now conceive." [21]

Perhaps the most explicit treatment of the idea of progress
in eighteenth-century England was made by the philosophical
anarchist, William Godwin, in his *Enquiry Concerning Political Justice,* published toward the close of the century in both
England and the United States.[22] During the period of the
French Revolution Godwin enjoyed a great vogue among his
radical contemporaries and among the romantic poets like
Shelley.[23] On the other hand, among conservatives in both England and America in the early part of the nineteenth century,
Godwin's name became a symbol for all the radical and revolutionary tendencies which they feared had been inaugurated by
the French Revolution.[24] In his work Godwin explored the
means of finding a beneficent social state in which the rights of
the individual might also be preserved.[25] Repudiating in the
manner of Locke the idea of innate principles and instincts, he
proclaimed that man is perfectible and susceptible of perpetual
improvement.[26] Although he believed that the progress of truth
was certain, he admitted with regret that it was also gradual
because established institutions, and especially governments,

21 *Ibid.,* pp. 4-5, 13, 76, 293-299. A contemporary of Priestley, and second
only to him in his sympathy with the American colonies, Richard Price also
expressed a belief in progress. See his *Observations on the ... American
Revolution* (London, 1785), pp. 1-8, 84-85; and *The Evidence for a Future
Period of Improvement* (London, 1787), pp. 5-6, 29 ff.

22 William Godwin, *Enquiry Concerning Political Justice, and Its Influence
on Morals and Happiness* (Phil., 1796). The first of several English editions
was published in 1793.

23 H. N. Brailsford, *Shelley, Godwin, and Their Circle* (New York and
London [1913]), *passim;* Crane Brinton, *The Political Ideas of the English
Romanticists* ([London], 1926), *passim;* Bury, *op. cit.,* pp. 224 ff.

24 Leslie Stephen, *History of English Thought,* II, 264 ff.

25 Godwin, *Enquiry,* p. 21.

26 *Ibid.,* pp. 46, 49, 87.

were always the enemies of change and progress.[27] No less sanguine than Condorcet over the possibilities in science and education, Godwin however went further and advocated the abolition of all government and the end of the monopoly of private
property.[28] Like Condorcet he even looked forward to a time
when propagation would cease and men would live forever![29]

A more generally important English philosopher was Jeremy
Bentham, the exponent of the utilitarian philosophy and the
opponent of the theory of natural rights. Much of Bentham's
writings was not revealed until long after his death in 1832,
but during the 1830's and 1840's his views on property and
legislation were published in the United States.[30] Bentham believed that the protection and preservation of property was
necessary for the progress of society,[31] but he also warned

> To reject all innovation is to reject all improvement: In
> what a condition should we be, if we had followed such a
> principle up to this time? For what exists now, had its begin-
> ning; whatever is now *establishment*, was once *innovation*.
> Those who approve a law to-day because of its antiquity,
> would have blamed it once for being new.[32]

Bentham enjoyed a wide influence in America not only through
his own ideas but also through those of his early disciples like
Owen and Brougham. By his concept of utility he offered to the
rising industrial and middle classes a more satisfactory theory
of progress than the revolutionary interpretation of the doctrine

27 *Ibid.*, pp. 199-200.

28 *Ibid.*, pp. 107, 161 ff.

29 *Ibid.*, p. 385; Condorcet, *op. cit.*, pp. 289-291.

30 Jeremy Bentham, *Principles of Legislation* ... with notes ... by John
Neal (Boston, 1830); *Theory of Legislation*, ed. R. Hildreth (2 vols. Boston,
1840); *Benthamiana* (Phil., 1844).

31 Bentham, "Principles of the Civil Code," *Theory of Legislation*
(Hildreth), I, 134-149.

32 Bentham, *Principles of Legislation* (Neal), p. 287; *Theory of Legislation* (Hildreth), I, 88; also *Benthamiana*, pp. 52-53, 252-254.

propounded by the French philosophers of the eighteenth century or by English radicals like Godwin.[33]

A particular example of the continuing European influence on the American idea of progress from 1815 to 1860 may be found in the articles in the American periodicals of the period reviewing the extensive European literature on the philosophy of history. Minor English historical works dealing with the philosophical implications of history were reviewed in America with reference to the significance of their theme for the larger concept of the progress of civilization.[34] The important works of the German idealist school were, in the same period, also evaluated in the light of their contributions to a philosophy of history and to a theory of progress. Herder's belief in progress by the broken curves of the rise and decline of nations, Kant's hope of progress for the individual by the achievement of a reign of peace under a universal state, Friedrich Schlegel's romantic faith in natural progress, Fichte and Hegel's subjection of individual progress to the welfare of the state were facets of the German philosophy of history.[35] Fragments of

33 Crane Brinton, *English Political Thought in the Nineteenth Century*, pp. 25-26; see also: Elie Halévy, *The Growth of Philosophic Radicalism* (New York, 1928), Part II, *passim*.

By neglecting the effect of his views on property, Paul A. Palmer, perhaps, slights the influence of Bentham in America. See his article, " Benthamism in England and America," *Am. Political Science Rev.*, XXXV (Oct., 1941), 855-871.

34 See, for example, the following works and reviews: James Douglas, *The Advancement of Society* (Hartford, 1830); *Bib. Rep.*, III (July, 1831) 306-319; W. Cooke Taylor, *The Natural History of Society*... (2 vols., New York, 1841); S. Q. Rev., I (April, 1842), 301-317; Thomas Arnold, *Introductory Lectures on Modern History* (New York, 1845); *North Am. Rev.*, LXIII (Oct., 1846), 334-357.

For a famous work influential at the close of our period, see Henry Thomas Buckle's, *History of Civilization in England* (2 vols., New York, 1858-1861). On the idea of progress, see especially vol. I, ch. 4.

35 For an analysis of the concept of progress entertained by these philosophers, see: Bury, *op. cit.*, ch. 13; Robert Flint, *The Philosophy of History in France and Germany* (New York, 1875), Book II, chs. 4, 5, 7, 9, 11; Delvaille, *Essai*, Livre, VIII; Barnes and Becker, *Social Thought*, pp. 481 ff.

these German writings on the progress of civilization were translated and·published in America especially by Frederic H. Hedge, the Unitarian minister and transcendentalist, in his *Prose Writers of Germany* (1848).[36] Citing many of the philosophies of history from that of Vico to that of Schlegel, an American writer in 1844 declared: " The Philosophy of History thus becomes the exposition of the progress of humanity . . ." [37]

The German philosophy of progress was also received in the 1830's in the New World through the medium of French translations or in the writings of French disciples. Especially important in this regard, and also for his study of the· Scottish realists, was the French apostle of an eclectic philosophy, Victor Cousin. Cousin's famous lectures on the history of philosophy, delivered in Paris in 1828, were republished in the United States in 1832 and again in 1852.[38] Cousin believed that modern philosophy dated from Descartes' well known *Discourse on Method* in 1637 and that since that time it had been progressive. More interested in synthesizing the systems of other philosophers than in establishing one of his own, Cousin announced that " Human science, like humanity itself, should be progressive; and a real progress in sciences is made, only

36 F. H. Hedge (ed.), *Prose Writers of Germany* (4th ed., New York and London, 1856), pp. 77, 247, 394-395, 402-403, 453-454.

For some reviews discussing the German concept of progress, history, and religion, see: North Am. Rev., XXXVI (April, 1833), 418-448; *Meth. Q. Rev.*, XXIV (July, 1842), 383-420; *S. Q. Rev.*, V (April, 1844), 265-311; *Presby, Q. Rev.*, III (June, 1854), 1-28.

37 " Schlegel's Philosophy of History," *S. Q. Rev.*, III (April, 1843), 283.

38 Victor Cousin, *Introduction to the History of Philosophy*, tr. from the French by H. G. Linberg (Boston, 1832) ; *Course of the History of Modern Philosophy*, tr. by O. W. Wright (2 vols.; New York, 1852).

For the interesting work of a Scotch-Irish disciple of Cousin, which also seems to anticipate some of Comte's philosophy and system, see: [P. E. Dove], *The Theory of Human Progression* (London, 1850; Boston, 1851). A copy of the London ed. in the New York Public Library bears the autograph of George Bancroft.

when a new work represents all that preceded it. . . ." [39] In discussing Cousin's idea of universal history, an American reviewer declared in 1832:

> Humanity is a grand topic. It is not an immoveable picture, but a continued action of life and reality, whose periods and eras are all connected by the wisest relations, evolving the most beneficent effects. Nor is this all, for this immense development of created mind is but a single manifestation of that infinite and eternal mind, in whose essence all others are contained.[40]

A contemporary of Cousin at the Sorbonne in Paris was the French statesman, Francois P. Guizot, whose published lectures, the *General History of Civilization in Europe,* enjoyed an extensive notice and many editions in the United States. At the outset in defining civilization Guizot noted " that the first idea comprised in the word *civilization* . . . is the notion of progress, of development. It calls up within us the notion of a people advancing, of a people in a course of improvement and melioration." Guizot further remarked:

> Two elements, then, seem to be comprised in the great fact which we call civilization;—two circumstances are necessary to its existence — it lives upon two conditions — it reveals itself by two symptoms: the progress of society, the progress of individuals; the melioration of the social system, and the expansion of the mind and faculties of man.[41]

American reviewers adopted Guizot's thesis that civilization

39 Cousin, *op. cit.* (Linberg ed.), p. 330; see also the Wright ed., I, 211-212.

40 [Mrs. W. Minot], "Cousin's Philosophy," *North Am. Rev.*, XXXV (July, 1832), 33.

41 F. P. Guizot, *General History of Civilization in Europe* (3rd Am. ed. from the 2nd Eng. ed., with notes by C. S. Henry; New York, 1842), pp. 23, 25, and Lecture I; see also: Robert Flint, *Historical Philosophy in France*, p. 503.

had been progressive with approval and enthusiasm.[42] One of the earliest of these writers observed in 1839:

> The chief value of history lies in its faithful representations of the progress of human improvement. The great facts in the annals of the world are pregnant indications of a progressive intellectual and moral movement, under a wise and righteous superintendence; and it is reading history with eyes that see not, to overlook the significance of the world's vicissitudes, and suffer the thought to adhere in the rigid surface of a bare narration.[43]

Guizot's fellow French historian, Alexis de Tocqueville, made the development of civilization in the New World the theme of his famous treatise *Democracy in America*. In this work, published soon after his visit to the United States in 1831, he identified the idea of progress with the growth of equality and of democracy. "Democratic nations," he wrote, "care but little for what has been, but they are haunted by visions of what will be . . ."[44] Moreover, the principle of equality seemed to suggest to the Americans the idea of indefinite perfectibility, and this idea, Tocqueville observed, exercised an influence "even on men who, living entirely for the purposes of action and not of thought, seem to conform their actions to it, without knowing anything about it."[45] Of the opinion that the vast reservoir of Western lands were the principal bulwark for the maintenance of American prosperity and free institutions, Tocqueville was, however, fearful of the implications of their extravagant exploitation. Such exceptional prosperity, he warned, would create envy, mistrust, and regret in the future: "The Americans contemplate this extraordinary and hasty

42 See for example: *S. Q. Rev.*, III (Jan., 1843), 1-17; *ibid.*, n. s. II (Feb., 1857), 393-405; *Christian Rev., VIII* (Dec., 1843), 535-567.

43 [John W. Yeomans], "European Civilization," *Biblical Repertory*, XI (Jan., 1839), 114.

44 Alexis de Tocqueville, *Democracy in America* (New York, 1841), II, 78.

45 *Ibid.*, II, 34.

progress with exultation; but they would be wiser to consider it with sorrow and alarm." [46]

An interest in the idea of progress was also expressed by other European philosophers whose writings were known in the United States. George Combe, the popular Scottish phrenologist, arrived in the United States in 1838 with the impression that the science of phrenology " would contribute powerfully to the advancement of civilization in that country . . ." In his *Notes on the United States* (1841), he accused Tocqueville of not being properly optimistic over the future of America. Applying Guizot's definition of the progress of civilization to the New World, he concluded that in America the " progress of civilization has been steady and rapid . . ." [47] James McCosh, the Scottish philosophical writer, who was to become the President of Princeton in 1868, published in 1850 his influential *Method of Divine Government*. In this volume McCosh systematically identified the whole philosophy of progress with the designs of Providence and the teachings of the Christian religion. The fall of man, he felt, did not preclude his ultimate redemption, and the sins and misery of the world were but the prelude of its eventual renovation. McCosh distrusted all radical Utopian programs, but he admitted that there was progress in the world and that there was an indicated future improvement. As yet however, progress had not been extended from the sciences and the arts to the character of the individual, and this, he stated would be accomplished only through the will of God— the effective agency in all true progress. [48]

In the field of science the progress of the first half of the nineteenth century was summed up at great length by the

46 *Ibid.*, I, 435. See also the comments in: *North Am. Rev.*, XLIII (July, 1836), 178-206; *Christian Rev.*, IV (June, 1839), 284-303.

47 George Combe, *Notes on the United States of North America during a Phrenological Visit in 1838-9-40* (Phil., 1841), I, xvi; II, 103-104, 241 ff., 255.

48 James McCosh, *The Method of the Divine Government, Physical and Moral* (first pub. in Edinburgh, 1850; 8th ed. same as 4th ed. of 1855; New York [186]), pp. 172 ff., 470 ff.

famous German naturalist and traveller, Alexander von Humboldt. Early in the century Humboldt had visited America and had spent some time with Thomas Jefferson. Later his interest in the New World was returned by the favorable reception in the United States of his *Cosmos: A Sketch of a Physical Description of the Universe*. Humboldt presented this work as a study of physical phenomena not only in their bearing on the material wants of life but also in their " general influence on the intellectual advancement of mankind . . ." [49] He traced this progress through the course of history, maintaining the principle of the unity of the human race and the capacity for improvement of all nations in some degree.[50]

The philosophies of progress developed by these European thinkers were, of course, known in America. Their treatises were found in the libraries of American intellectuals, and many of the volumes were republished in the United States. Americans went abroad and returned home bringing back their gleanings of European culture. Europeans came to the New World as visitors, settlers, and propagandists. However, the problem of gauging the European influence on the American concept of progress in our period is a part of the general problem of the transfer of ideas and culture between Europe and America.[51] Since this is a subject in need of much further research, only an indication can be given regarding the influence of European thought upon the American idea of progress.

The American theory of progress in the early years of the Republic may be considered a product of the philosophy of the eighteenth-century enlightenment transplanted to the virgin soil of a new nation. During their lives many of the American peo-

---

49 Alexander von Humboldt, *Cosmos; A Sketch of a Physical Description of the Universe* (tr. from the German by E. C. Otté; New York, 1850), I, 23, and Introd. *passim*.

50 *Ibid.*, I, 350-358, II, 352-356.

51 For some indication, see: H. M. Jones, " The Influence of European Ideas in Nineteenth-Century America," *Am. Lit.*, VII (Nov., 1935), 241-273; Orie Long, *Literary Pioneers: Early American Explorers of European Culture* (Cambridge, Mass., 1935), *passim*.

ple had seen the thirteen colonies enjoy a tremendous expansion in population, wealth, and territory. Their own dynamic role in pushing forward the frontier of settlement and in achieving independence from England made such a concept as that of progress congenial to their tastes and experience. In contrast to the "worn-out, effete" monarchies of Europe, it was felt that in the United States the advantages of youth were combined with a superior form of republican government. With a continent opened to the enterprise of its citizens, the faith of a Condorcet or of a Godwin in the powers of science and of human reason to effect progress, was shared by the American philosophers in the first decades of the Republic.

Benjamin Franklin, during the years of his long life from 1706 to 1790, had witnessed many progressive changes in American society. Equally at home on both sides of the ocean, Franklin in the last years of his life related his hopes of future world progress to the advance of science and to the growth of the American political experiment.[52] Writing during the 1780's to Joseph Priestley and to John Lathrop, he expressed his regrets that he would not live to see the fruits of the rapid progress being made by science.[53] In 1788, five years before Godwin voiced the hope that men might live forever, Franklin wrote that, " if the art of physic shall be improved in proportion with other arts, we may then be able to avoid diseases, and live as long as the Patriarchs in Genesis . . ."[54] Before the French Revolution, Franklin, writing to the Chevalier de Chastellux, ventured to predict: " Establishing the liberties of America will not only make that people happy, but will have some effect in diminishing the misery of those, who in other parts of the world

[52] See the treatment by Macklin Thomas, *The Idea of Progress in the Writings of Franklin, Freneau, Barlow, and Rush* (Ms. Ph.D. thesis, 1938, Univ. of Wisconsin).

For the thought of another contemporary disciple of progress, see: James Wilson's, *Works*, ed. Bird Wilson (Phil., 1804), I, 30, 142-143, 164-165.

[53] Benjamin Franklin, *Writings*, ed. A. H. Smyth (New York and London, 1905-1907), VIII, 10; IX, 651.

[54] *Ibid.*, IX, 651.

groan under despotism . . ." [55] When the United States itself was undergoing the transformation in its form of government which culminated in the adoption of the Constitution, Franklin in a letter of 1786 to Jonathan Shipley of England wrote:

> You seem desirous of knowing what Progress we make here in improving our Governments. We are, I think, in the right Road of Improvement, for we are making Experiments. I do not oppose all that seem wrong, for the Multitude are more effectually set right by Experience, than kept from going wrong by Reasoning with them. And I think we are daily more and more enlightened; so that I have no doubt of our obtaining in a few Years as much public Felicity, as good government is capable of affording.[56]

During those years around the turn of the century in 1800 Franklin's faith in the progress of the United States was exemplified by a group of patriotic orators and poets who saw in America a land of progress, freedom, and destiny. In the words of a typical Fourth of July orator: " The sun of the old world is setting; of the new just beginning to rise." [57] The same optimistic confidence in the future of the New World was voiced by the poet of the American Revolution, Philip Freneau,[58] and

55 *Ibid.*, VIII, 416.

56 *Ibid.*, IX, 489.

57 Samuel Stillman, *An Oration delivered July 4, 1789* (Boston, 1789), p. 29; see also: Samuel Austin, *An Oration pronounced at Worcester* (Worcester, 1798), p. 42; Elihu Palmer, *The Political Happiness of Nations* (photostat copy in the Columbia Univ. Library; [New York, 1800]), *passim*; Charles Paine, *An Oration pronounced July 4, 1801* (Boston, [1801]), *passim*.

Also the comments by: Joseph Priestley in his Letter of Oct. 4, 1796, quoted in Edgar F. Smith, *Priestly in America, 1794-1804* (Phil., 1920), p. 92; Thomas Low Nichols, *Forty Years of American Life* (London, 1864), I, 39, 63; II, 17-18, 27-28; Henry Adams, *History of the United States of America* (New York, 1889-1891), I, 16, 73, 156-184.

58 See for example: Philip Freneau, "Ode to the Americans" (1798), in *Poems*, ed. F. L. Pattee (Princeton, 1902-1907), III, 203-207; and his "America Independent" (1778), *ibid.*, I, 271-282; see also: Macklin Thomas, *The Idea of Progress*, *passim*; and Lewis Leary, *That Rascal Freneau* ([New Brunswick, 1941]), chs. 3 and 4.

by his fellow American bard, Joel Barlow, who was the more explicit in his exposition of progress. A student at Yale and a chaplain in the American army during the Revolutionary period, Barlow began, soon after the conclusion of that struggle, to write an American epic on the theme of the grand accomplishment of Columbus. In his poem he represented the consequence of Columbus' discovery in the form of a vision in which the great explorer was soothed by the knowledge that his work had not been in vain. Barlow throughout his poem professed a strong faith in progress as the design of Providence. From the advances already made in the arts and sciences by the United States, and with the return of peace, he predicted an enormous worldwide melioration in the future. In the words of the seraph of the vision, addressing Columbus:

> See, thro' the whole, the same progressive plan,
> That draws for mutual succour, man to man,
> From friends to tribes, from tribes to realms ascend,
> Their powers, their interests and their passions blend;
>
> .   .   .   .   .
>
> Till tribes and states and empires find their place,
> And one wide interest sways the peaceful race.[59]

A conservative in his youth, Barlow was one of the famous group of Connecticut Federalist poets, the Hartford Wits. However, he later forsook much of his early Puritan and Federalist background in his enthusiasm for the democratic spirit of the age. In 1788 he left America for what was to be a seventeen-year stay in Europe. Happy in his new surroundings, Barlow in *Two Letters to the Citizens of the United States . . . Written from Paris in the Year 1799* expressed the faith in progress typical of the early French Revolutionary philosophy.

---

59 Joel Barlow, *The Vision of Columbus* (Hartford, 1787), pp. 240-241; see also the interesting footnote in which Barlow cites Richard Price's *Observations on . . . the American Revolution* as a corroboration for his own faith in progress: *ibid.*, pp. 241-244; and see: T. A. Zunder, *The Early Days of Joel Barlow* (New Haven, 1934), ch. 10; Leon Howard, *The Connecticut Wits* (Chicago, 1943), pp. 142 ff., 313 ff.

After stressing the isolation of America and its vast expanse of vacant lands—the guarantee of its character as an agricultural nation—he announced that he looked forward to a future in which science, education, and democracy would unite to create a nation in which peace and progress would rule.[60] Then in 1807 he expanded his *Vision of Columbus* with the publication of a long epic poem, *The Columbiad*. This latter poem furnished an added illustration of the transformation effected by Barlow's experience in France. For his older faith in the Divine will of God as the motivating cause of human progress, Barlow now substituted his enthusiastic belief in the power of science and of human reason. In the Preface he declared that his object was to encourage a love of liberty, peace, and republican principles. Admitting that he could not " expect that every reader, nor even every republican reader, will join me in opinion with respect to the future progress of society and the civilization of states," he, however, stated that " there are two sentiments in which I think all men will agree : that the event is desirable, and that to believe it practicable is one step towards rendering it so." [61]

Barlow in his writings was influenced by the ideas of his friend Thomas Paine, an enthusiastic disciple of the principles of the French Revolution. Characteristic of the Revolution for a time at least was the idea of a progressive crusade destined to culminate in the perfectibility of man and in the confederation of all nations. In the United States Paine, the pamphleteer of the American Revolution, hailed the French struggle as an example of the spread of American principles. Writing in 1791 in reply to Edmund Burke's attack on the French Revolution, Paine emphasized the fact that in a world of change " the opinions of men change also." Opposed to the idea that the future

60 Joel Barlow, *Two Letters to the Citizens of the United States* (New Haven, 1806), pp. 14, 27-28, 46-51.

61 Barlow, *The Columbiad* (Phil., 1809), I, Preface, viii-ix; see also: II, 167.
Compare Book IX of *The Vision of Columbus* with Book X of *The Columbiad*, noting especially the deletion of the religious terms in the latter.

was bound to the prejudices of the past, he rejoiced that " The opinions of men with respect to government are changing fast in all countries. The revolutions of America and France have thrown a beam of light over the world, which reaches into man." [62] In contrast to the wasteful cost of the English monarchy, Paine wrote:

> I see in America the generality of people living in a style of plenty unknown in monarchical countries; and I see that the principle of its government, which is that of the *equal Rights of Man,* is making a rapid progress in the world. . . .
>
> From the rapid progress which America makes in every species of improvement, it is rational to conclude that, if the governments of Asia, Africa and Europe had begun on a principle similar to that of America, or had not been very early corrupted therefrom, those countries must by this time have been in a far superior condition to what they are.[63]

The enthusiasm of Thomas Paine for the principles of the French Revolution was not shared by the conservative Federalist elements in the United States. And with the transformation of the early idealism and radicalism of the Revolution into the conquering nationalism of Napoleon, liberals were also forced to turn from France in their hopes for future world progress. Some indication of the further effect of the French Revolution on the American concept of progress may be discovered in the correspondence on the subject maintained by John Adams and Thomas Jefferson after the close of their active political careers. John Adams, the Federalist and conservative, was a staunch opponent from its inception of the philosophy and actions of the French Revolutionary movement. Familiar with the writings of Condorcet, Adams took pains to deprecate both his originality

62 Thomas Paine, "Rights of Man" (1791-1792), *Writings,* ed. M. D. Conway (New York and London, 1894), II, 359; see also: V. E. Gibbens, "Tom Paine and the Idea of Progress, *Pa. Mag. of Hist. and Biog.,* LXVI (April, 1942), 191-204.

63 *Ibid.,* II, 367, 402.

and greatness.[64] Believing that Europe was toward the close of the eighteenth century " advancing by slow but sure steps towards an amelioration of the condition of man in religion and government, in liberty, equality, fraternity, knowledge, civilization, and humanity," Adams in a letter of 1813 to Jefferson went on to say: " The French Revolution I dreaded, because I was sure it would not only arrest the progress of improvement, but give it a retrograde course, for at least a century, if not many centuries." [65] Skeptical of the extravagant optimism of the early nineteenth century and doubtful that the science of government had yet made much advance,[66] Adams nevertheless on the whole retained his early faith in the progress of science and in the future of America.[67]

The political opponent of Adams on almost all public questions, Thomas Jefferson combined an international outlook with a liberal faith that the United States would be the theatre of the world's future progress.[68] Jefferson did not become discouraged by the periodic retrograde motions which seemed to occur at times like the Napoleonic period, but in 1816, in a letter to John Adams, he predicted:

64 John Adams, *Works*, ed. C. F. Adams (Boston, 1850-1856), X, 57; Adams' letters in: Thomas Jefferson, *Writings* (Memorial ed.; Washington, 1907), XIV, 14-15, 320-321.

65 Adams' letter in Jefferson, *Writings* (Mem. ed.), XIII, 314.

66 Adams, *Works*, X, 174-176, 50; see also Jefferson's reply in his *Writings* (Mem. ed.), XIV, 393.

67 See Adams' varying expression in: "A Defence of the Constitutions of Government of the United States" (1787-1788), *Works*, IV, 283; "To the Young Men of Philadelphia" (1798), *ibid.*, IX, 188; Letters to Jefferson (June 28, 1813 and May 19, 1821), *ibid.*, X, 43-46, 398; and (Nov. 15, 1813), in Jefferson, *Writings* (Mem. ed.), XIV, 6.

68 See the contemporary estimate by A. H. Everett, "Character of Jefferson," *North Am. Rev.*, XL (Jan., 1835), 188, 199. The most detailed study is by E. T. Martin, *Thomas Jefferson and the Idea of Progress* (Ms. Ph.D. thesis, 1941, Univ. of Wisconsin); see also: C. M. Wiltse, *The Jeffersonian Tradition in American Democracy* (Chapel Hill, 1935), pp. 78, 86, 92, 140, 203.

We are destined to be a barrier against the returns of ignorance and barbarism. Old Europe will have to lean on our shoulders, and to hobble along by our side, under the monkish trammels of priests and kings, as she can. What a colossus shall we be, when the southern continent comes up to our mark! What a stand will it secure as a ralliance for the reason and freedom of the globe! I like the dreams of the future better than the history of the past.[69]

No one in the New World had been more zealous than Jefferson in giving practical effect to some of the liberal ideas of the eighteenth-century enlightenment. Although he recognized that progress often lagged, he maintained his belief that science and education in a democratic society would be the bulwarks of future progress.[70] Writing in 1818 to Dr. Benjamin Waterhouse, Jefferson gave a characteristic expression of his faith in the future:

When I contemplate the immense advances in science and discoveries in the arts which have been made within the period of my life, I look forward with confidence to equal advances by the present generation, and have no doubt they will consequently be as much wiser than we have been as we than our fathers were, and they than the burners of witches.[71]

The faith in progress of the founding fathers like Franklin and Jefferson not only continued to prevail in the period of our survey, but it also became a dogma of widespread mass appeal. With the fall of Napoleon and with the close of the War of 1812 in America, the people of the United States were once more free to pursue the development of their own continent. " In 1815 for the first time Americans ceased to doubt the path they were to follow. Not only was the unity of their nation

69 Jefferson in Adams' *Works*, X, 223.

70 For Jefferson's varied comments on the idea of progress, see: *Writings*, ed. P. L. Ford (New York and London, 1892-1899), VII, 415; IX, 169, 387, 429-430; X, 42, 188-189; *Writings* (Memorial ed.), XVI, 74-76; Henry Adams, *History of the United States*, I, 179.

71 Jefferson, *Writings*, ed. P. L. Ford, X, 103.

established, but its probable divergence from older societies was also well defined."[72] While Europe seemed to be fastened in the grip of a political and economic reaction, American independence was now assured. Although the return of peace was followed by a depression lasting until 1820, there was no lack of confidence in the eventual prosperity of the nation. That democracy would grow with the physical expansion of the country seemed also certain. The year 1815 therefore marked the beginning of a period in American history in which new forces of great significance to the idea of progress were unleashed.[73]

However, in spite of the generally favorable conditions prevailing in the United States of 1815 for the growth in popularity of the idea of progress, certain exceptions may be noted. Some of the old Federalists and their descendants still took a pessimistic view of the democratic tendencies which had been growing since the time of Jefferson's capture of the presidency. Also foremost among groups hostile to the idea of radical or inevitable improvement were some of the leading church sects in America. Calvinism remained with its low view of human nature and its adherence to the idea of predestination. The vogue of revivalism and the growth of evangelistic sects meant in part an emphasis on life in the world to come and culminated during the early 1840's in the Millerite's gospel of the approaching end of the world. Throughout the period Catholicism received from among the immigrants many adherents to its auth-

---

72 Henry Adams, *History of the United States*, IX, 220.

73 Although the historians of the Middle Period in American history have on the whole neglected the idea of progress, there are important exceptions: C. A. and M. R. Beard, *The Rise of American Civilization* (new ed.; New York, 1937), I, 444-460, 737-751; II, 831; V. L. Parrington, *The Romantic Revolution in America, 1800-1860* (Main Currents in American Thought, vol. II; New York, 1927), Introd. and *passim*; R. H. Gabriel, *The Course of American Democratic Thought* (New York, 1940), *passim*.

On its connection with the frontier spirit, see: F. J. Turner, *Rise of the New West* (New York, 1906), p. 107; Carl Becker, "Kansas," in *Essays in American History dedicated to Frederick Jackson Turner* (New York, 1910), pp. 89 ff.; F. L. Paxson, *When the West Is Gone* (New York, 1930), p. 39.

oritarian and generally backward-looking ideology and to its otherworldly outlook. This spread of Catholicism also strengthened the conviction of the nativists that the immigrants were a menace to American progress. Among the poorer classes of farmers and workers the occasional depressions fostered in some measure the feeling that progress was not automatic or inevitable. Intellectuals and reformers, distressed by the ruthless materialism of so much of American progress, sometimes withdrew into an attitude of hopeless pessimism. In the South the necessity of defending slavery imparted in many quarters a generally conservative, backward-looking philosophy of life opposed to the concept of progress entertained in the other parts of the nation. These influences on American thought were, to be sure, not the major note, but they interposed a conservative interpretation which had its effects in modifying the idea of progress.

More positive and dynamic in their influence upon the idea were those aspects of the American scene which gave reality to American optimism in the period from the close of the War of 1812 to the outbreak of the Civil War. In the the United States during these decades the material environment and intellectual atmosphere were alike favorable to a philosophy of progress. The ever-expanding frontier and the abundant resources of the youthful nation provided for a rapidly increasing population. Growing from some eight million people in 1815 to over thirty million in 1860, the generous natural increase was augmented by a rising tide of migration from Europe. The comparatively modest numbers of immigrants arriving at first were increased during the latter part of the 1840's. Then during the 1850's the new arrivals, especially from Ireland and Germany, came at an average annual rate of over a quarter of a million.

It was also during these decades that the industrial revolution took strong root and began to flourish in America. In New England cotton manufacturing vied with foreign trade for the dominant position, and in the South the promise of the cotton gin was realized in the processing and marketing of larger crops. These were the decades in which the first railroads were built. In 1844 the telegraph was perfected, and like the canals and railways, it helped to bring the various parts of the country closer together. Throughout the period a vast area of Western lands was also available to settlement, and as the people moved west from the seaboard, immigrants came from Europe to fill their places or go west at their side. Except for the long depression beginning in 1837 and some minor economic crises, the period was one of general prosperity. Since all did not share equally in this material prosperity, the period was also one of growing class and sectional conflicts with the protests against the evils of the rising industrial system exemplified in the numerous reform movements of the day.

During the 1820's democracy took a step forward with the liberalization of some of the state constitutions and with the emergence of a small group of labor parties in New York and Pennsylvania. When Andrew Jackson was elected President in 1828, American political democracy with a more nearly universal manhood suffrage had come to prevail in most of the states of the Union. The workingmen and small farmers were assured a voice in political affairs. If they did not gain full control, they at least secured some attention and deference from the statesmen of the nation. The Jacksonian era of political and social reform in the thirties was succeeded by the great decade of fads and isms in the forties. And then in the fifties the energies of the reformers were drained off into the slavery struggle, climaxed by the Civil War and the triumph of Northern industrial society.

Culturally the period also witnessed a great advance. The public school system, under state control and leadership, was established in response to the demands of working men, humanitarian reformers and philanthropists. Helping to fulfill the ideal of an educated population, the lyceum spread " culture " to the interested audiences. Magazines and newspapers grew in numbers and in popularity. The colleges became less exclusive, and some at least came to be more free of religious domination. In keeping with these material evidences of culture a national literature and a national art were developed during the period.

The reality provided by this material and cultural advance also served to strengthen the old idea that America enjoyed an especial and urique position in the world. The American people, imbued with a strong faith in the efficacy of their own physical and intellectual achievements, universalized their experience into a general theory of progress to which the rest of the world was expected to accede. In the eyes of the Americans the older civilization of Europe was already in a state of decay. Confident of their own future in the " era of good feeling " and of youthful nationalism prevailing after 1815, they emphasized the difference between the Old and the New World with the proclamation of the Monroe Doctrine in 1823. Later during the forties and fifties the concept of a peculiar American mission, under the slogans of manifest destiny and of Young America, became transformed into a rationalization for territorial expansion in those regions considered necessary for the westward movement of the Republic. But in its more idealistic aspects the concept of a unique American destiny embraced the hope that democracy, through the force of its peaceful example, might become the form of government for the world. And in religious circles this same faith was related to the spread of Christianity under American auspices. The belief in American institutions, in conjunction with the prosperity of its society, fostered a sentiment of nationalism which was only temporarily interrupted by the Civil War. It also helped to provide the proper material and intellectual setting for the mass reception of the idea of progress. With the concrete evidences of material advancement on every side, progress was the faith of the common man as well as of the philosopher. Sometimes considered as an inevitable law of destiny or of Providence, it was also regarded as an aspiration to be attained by human will and effort.

During the period of our survey the formal definitions of progress embraced the traditional concept of advance and melioration. In contrast to a violent or revolutionary change, progress was considered to involve a regular and gradual process of growth. The concept of intellectual and moral improvement was used to distinguish the idea from those mere material and physical advances which might involve a change without true individual and social betterment.[74] As defined in Europe by generations of intellectuals, it came to be treated as a purely philosophical idea. However, in America the unique experience and concrete achievements of the people helped to give the concept a dynamic reality. No longer only a philosophical theory, but also a demonstrable fact, the idea in the United States of the Middle Period was delivered from the cloister of the scholar into the hands of the people. We shall see, moreover, that the idea of progress was sufficiently vague in its meaning and congenial in its portent to be susceptible of use in justifying even contradictory tendencies in the age of which it was a dominant, if not the most widely cherished, idea.

74 For these formal definitions of progress, see the various editions of the *Dictionaries,* edited by Noah Webster, and by Joseph E. Worcester, in the period from 1815 to 1860.

CHAPTER II

THE PROMISE OF THE AMERICAN POLITICAL EXPERIMENT

THE philosophy of progress developed by early European and American writers proved especially adaptable to the American faith in the idea that the United States were destined to carry out a political experiment in democratic government. The roots of the idea of a unique American mission extended far back in its history. From the time of its discovery America had been celebrated as a land of destiny. With the success of the American Revolution a sharp break seemed to be made with the past. The feudal remnants of primogeniture and of an established church were overthrown. Launched on its new course, the confidence of the young Republic in the future progress of democracy was strengthened by the host of patriotic orators and writers who reminded the American people that the Revolution and the Declaration of Independence had made possible that freedom and liberty which would henceforth be the guide-star for the future progress of democracy.[1] This idea of the promise of the American political experiment received one of its best expressions in the writings of the patriotic and popular historian of the Middle Period, George Bancroft. Bancroft, who felt that, in 1776, " the hour of revolution was at hand, promising free-

1 See for example: J. H. Hammond, "An Oration delivered in the Presbyterian Church on the Fourth of July, 1829, Columbia, South Carolina," unpublished Ms. in the Hammond Papers, vol. I (Library of Congress); A. H. Everett *An Oration...on the 5th of July, 1830* (Boston, 1830), pp. 31-35, and *passim*; Philip Lindsley, "An Address on the...Centennial Birthday of George Washington" (1832), *Works* (Phil., 1866), III, 227-262; J. R. Ingersoll, *An Address...Lafayette College* (Phil., 1833), *passim*; F. H. Hedge, *An Oration...before the Citizens of Bangor* (Bangor, 1838), *passim*; Parke Godwin, "The Course of Civilization," *Dem. Rev.*, VI (Sept., 1839), 208-217; "The Progress of Society," *ibid.*, VIII (July, 1840), 67-87; O. A. Brownson, *An Oration before the Democracy of Worcester* (Boston and Worcester, 1840), *passim*; James De Peyster Ogden, *Lecture on National Character* (New York, 1843), *passim*.

dom to conscience and dominion to intelligence," wrote in his
History:

> The authors of the American Revolution avowed for their
> object the welfare of mankind, and believed that they were in
> the service of their own and of all future generations. Their
> faith was just; for the world of mankind does not exist in
> fragments, nor can a country have an isolated existence.   All
> men are brothers; and all are bondsmen for one another. All
> nations, too, are brothers, and each is responsible for that
> federative humanity which puts the ban of exclusion on none.
> New principles of government could not assert themselves in
> one hemisphere without affecting the other. The very idea of
> the progress of an individual people, in its relation to
> universal history, springs from the acknowledged unity of
> the race.[2]

Bancroft was giving expression to the popular idea that the
American Revolution had been a struggle waged for the purpose of achieving the natural rights of man. The Revolution
was not considered merely a selfish battle for political independence, but it was hoped that, by the force of the American example, the principles of freedom would be extended to all the
world. In the period after 1815 a belief in progress also meant
a patriotic confidence in the future of America. Following in
the path of the United States, the peoples of South America
were revolting against their Spanish rulers, and the success of
their efforts, in turn, seemed to give an assurance of support
to the democratic Republic in the North. In contrast to the despotism and poverty of Europe, just emerging from the strain
of the Napoleonic Wars, the liberty and prosperity of the New
World offered an obvious indication of future progress. It was
believed that the United States, the foremost nation of the
Western hemisphere, would soon become an important world
power, guiding other peoples to democracy.

2 George Bancroft, *History of the United States* (Boston, 1834-1874),
IV (1853), 5-6.

During the 1820's the speeches and writings of prominent American citizens reflected this idea that the world's hope of future progress rested on the advances being made in the two American continents. Their orations were delivered primarily to celebrate in patriotic fashion another anniversary of the Fourth of July, but along with their rhetoric, they voiced the prevailing assumption that America was different and progressive.[3] This contrast between Europe and America, underlined by the Monroe Doctrine, was also well illustrated in the two volumes published in the 1820's by Alexander H. Everett, the brother of Edward Everett. In his *Europe* (1822) Everett showed how the reactionary spirit following the French Revolution was impeding the advance of civilization and democracy.[4] The future of civilization therefore seemed to rest on the progress being made in the New World. And in the second of his works, *America* (1827), he gave expression to a widespread belief in his declaration that " The discovery of America furnished, in fact, to the friends of improvement, the point d'appui . . ." [5] This same faith in the future of the New World was the theme of the famous four volumes of *Travels* written by

3 H. S. Legaré, " An Oration . . . Fourth of July, 1823," *Writings,* ed. by his sister (Charleston, 1845-1846), I, 257-269; A. G. Greene, *An Oration* (Providence, 1823), pp. 5, 15; Edward Everett, " First Settlement of New England " (1824), *Orations and Speeches* (Boston, 1850-1859), I, 45-72; and " The Circumstances Favorable to the Progress of Literature in America " (1824), *ibid.,* I, 9-44; Daniel Webster, "An Address . . . Bunker Hill . . . 1825," *Writings and Speeches* (National ed.; Boston, 1903), I, 235-254; Samuel Young, *A Discourse . . . July 25, 1826* (Ballston Spa, 1826), pp. 5, 65-70; Joseph Blunt, "An Anniversary Discourse . . . Dec. 13, 1827," *Speeches, Reviews, Reports* (New York, 1843), pp. 1-28; Eber Wheaton, *Oration delivered July 4, 1828* (New York, 1828), pp. 15-17.

See also: James Monroe, " Seventh Annual Message " (Dec. 2, 1823), in J. D. Richardson, *A Compilation of the Messages and Papers of the Presidents* (Washington, 1896-1899), II, 219; J. Q. Adams, Letters to R. C. Anderson and to C. J. Ingersoll, May 27 and June 19, 1823 in his *Writings,* ed. W. C. Ford (New York, 1913-1917), VII, 441-442, 485-487; *North Am. Rev.,* III (May, 1816), 77-106; *ibid.,* XXV (July, 1827), 112-153.

4 A. H. Everett, *Europe* (Boston, 1822), chs. 1, 10.

5 Everett, *America* (Phil., 1827), pp. 337, 21-22, and ch. 10.

Timothy Dwight, the patriotic and conservative President of Yale College, and published posthumously in 1821 and 1822. Dwight called the attention of his readers on both sides of the ocean to the unique progress and prospects offered by the American environment:

> The scene is a novelty in the history of man. The colonization of a wilderness by civilized men, where a regular government, mild manners, arts, learning, science, and christianity have been interwoven in its progress from the beginning, is a state of things of which the eastern continent, and the records of past ages, furnish neither an example nor a resemblance.[6]

However, in the United States the idea of an idealistic political mission soon became a part of a program of territorial conquest under the standards of manifest destiny and Young America. Progress in the spirit of the enlightenment was changed over into the more ruthless nineteenth-century pattern, but the idea itself remained and proved useful. The dogma of national progress now provided the verbalization of expansion —an expansion not only in territory but also in material prosperity and in cultural advantages. Buoyed up by the success of their experiment at home, the American people even became imbued with a confidence in their mission to spread political democracy abroad. To the actuality and ideology of American expansionism the idea of progress lent a comforting aura of historic inevitability and of righteous respectability.[7]

First to feel the effects of this expanding white civilization were, of course, the American Indians, who were gradually being pushed from their lands by the westward movement of

6 Timothy Dwight, *Travels in New-England and New-York* (New Haven, 1821-1822), I, 16, and Preface; IV, 510-527; see also: C. E. Cuningham, *Timothy Dwight, 1752-1817: A Biography* (New York, 1942), ch. 10; Leon Howard, *The Connecticut Wits*, pp. 224-228.

7 The ideology of American expansionism has been analyzed in great detail, but without an adequate recognition of the role of the idea of progress, by A. K. Weinberg, *Manifest Destiny: A Study of National Expansionism in American History* (Baltimore, 1935), especially chs. 3-7.

the American frontier. For a time the scheme of moving the Indians to lands west of the Mississippi seemed to offer a practical solution to their problem. Jedidiah Morse, an orthodox New England clergyman, also famous as the " father of American geography," in his detailed Report on Indian Affairs, published in 1822, urged the government to undertake the civilization of the Indians by sending them to prepared settlements in the West. Morse and some of the leaders of the Christian missionary societies believed that the Indians possessed the capacity for making progress in the arts of civilized life if only they were given government aid and an education.[8]

However, in most of the arguments for the removal of the Indian tribes to lands beyond the Mississippi, little concern was expressed in regard to any possible future progress of the Indians. Instead the emphasis was placed on the advantages to the white man which would result from the displacement of the noble savage, and the idea of progress was invoked, especially by Southern and Western writers, to give a rationalization of inevitable justice to the forced migration. A contributor to the *Southern Review* in 1828 observed: " We can perceive neither justice, nor wisdom, nor humanity, in arresting the progress of order and science, that unproductive and barren wastes may be reserved for the roaming barbarian." [9] And in the same year a writer in the *Western Monthly Review,* deplored the failure of the Indians to learn the white man's arts. Urging the abandonment of the reservation policy, he argued: "As separate and independent communities, with institutions of their own, they will always tend toward barbarism. As citizens of the United States, many of them might become valuable to themselves and to others." [10] Lewis Cass, Governor of Michigan Territory,

8 Jedidiah Morse, *A Report to the Secretary of War ... on Indian Affairs* (New Haven, 1822), pp. 81-84; see also: "North American Indians. Progress in Civilization," *Missionary Herald,* XXV (Feb., 1829), 57-58.

9 *Southern Rev.,* II (Nov., 1828), 545.

10 *West. Monthly Rev.,* II (Nov., 1828), 330.

in discussing the "Removal of the Indians" for the *North American Review* of 1830, noted that the decline of a barbarous people was necessary to the progress of civilization.[11] President Jackson himself, in his Second Annual Message to Congress, defended the removal of the Indian tribes as an inevitable step in progress. He declared:

> Humanity has often wept over the fate of the aborigines of this country, and Philanthropy has been long busily employed in devising means to avert it, but its progress has never for a moment been arrested, and one by one have many powerful tribes disappeared from the earth.[12]

During the 1830's and 1840's the claim that the Indians were doomed to extinction by the inevitable laws of progress continued to be advanced to justify the removal policy. Joel R. Poinsett, a South Carolinian statesman and diplomat devoted to learning, provided one of the most elaborate of these arguments in his *Inquiry into the Received Opinions of Philosophers and Historians, on the Natural Progress of the Human Race from Barbarism to Civilization* (1834). Poinsett denied that hunter or shepherd tribes advanced through the various stages of progress. Also believing that civilization and advancement were reserved only for certain races like the Caucasian, he included the American Indians in his historical survey of the world's unprogressive races. Poinsett asserted that so far the Indians had resisted all humane efforts to transfer them to lands beyond the Rockies, and he predicted that:

> so long as this barrier shall check the enterprize of our rapidly increasing population, the Indians may remain in safety in the land marked out for their retreat; but wherever our people pass beyond those mountains, the hunting Tribes must retreat

11 Lewis Cass, "Removal of the Indians," *North Am. Rev.*, XXX (Jan., 1830), 64, 77.

12 Andrew Jackson, "Second Annual Message" (Dec. 6, 1830), in Richardson, *Messages and Papers of the Presidents*, II, 520-521.

before the advance of civilization, or perish under the shade of the white man's settlements.[13]

Less pessimistic over the future of the Indians, Lewis Henry Morgan, the father of American anthropology, nevertheless expressed the belief that the Indians' passion for the hunter state precluded their progress toward civilization. In his history of the Iroquois, published in 1851, Morgan placed the key to the Indians' lack of progress upon their ignorance of the white man's "love of gain." He pointed out that, despite their many admirable traits,

> There was, however, a fatal deficiency in Indian society, in the non-existence of a progressive spirit. The same rounds of amusement, of business, of warfare, of the chase, and of domestic intercourse continued from generation to generation. There was neither progress nor invention, nor increase of political wisdom. Old forms were preserved, old customs adhered to.[14]

Although unprogressive in their own society, Morgan felt that the Indians were not impervious to the influences of the white man's civilization. Therefore, differing from those who foresaw only the extinction of the Indians, Morgan advocated stimulating "the desire for improvement, which now prevails among them," in order "to initiate them into the arts of civil-

13 J. R. Poinsett, *An Inquiry . . . on the Natural Progress of the Human Race from Barbarism to Civilization* (Charleston, 1834), pp. 39-40, and *passim*.
See also: Jaspar Adams, *The Moral Causes of the Welfare of Nations* (Charleston, 1834), pp. 25-26; Charles Caldwell, *Thoughts on the Spirit of Improvement* (Nashville, 1835), p. 4; James Hall, *Notes on the Western States* (Phil., 1838), pp. 195-196; W. A. Caruthers, *A Lecture delivered before the Georgia Historical Society* (Savannah, 1843), p. 35; "The North American Indians," *S. Q. Review*, V (Jan., 1844), 132-133; H. V. Johnson, *The Probable Destiny of our Country* (Penfield, 1847), p. 6.

14 L. H. Morgan, *League of the Ho-Dé-No-Sau-Nee or Iroquois* (Rochester, 1851), p. 142; see also: B. J. Stern, *Lewis Henry Morgan: Social Evolutionist* (Chicago, 1931), p. 64, and *passim*.

ized life, and to prepare them eventually for exercising those rights of property, and rights of citizenship, which are common to ourselves." [15]

Although they were perhaps in the minority, many influential persons defended the capacity for progress of the once noble savage.[16] Statesmen, anxious to justify the removal policy, praised the progress made by the Indians in their new abodes.[17] On the other hand, Horace Greeley's *New Yorker* blamed the bad treatment of the Indians by vagabond whites as responsible for " the fallacy which holds the Red Man incapable of social and political improvement . . ." [18] Ralph Waldo Emerson, in sympathy with " the painful efforts of the red men to redeem their own race from the doom of eternal inferiority," protested to President Van Buren that the removal policy would interrupt their nascent progress and fasten a blot on the record of the American government.[19]

Henry R. Schoolcraft, a popular writer on the subject of his explorations among the Indians, was also one of those who believed that they possessed the capacity for progress. Although Schoolcraft felt that the Indians were still in a state of barbarism or of early civilization, he was confident of the ability of the missionary and school teacher to effect their reclamation. He reported in 1846, in his *Notes on the Iroquois,* that

> it is gratifying to know that they are at least able to live upon their own means; and their condition and improvement is (certainly within the ear of the temperance movement among

15 Morgan, *op. cit.,* p. 452.

16 Grant Foreman, *The Five Civilized Tribes* (Norman, 1934), chs. 3, 13, 26, and *passim.*

17 See for example: H. L. White, *Register of Debates,* 23 Cong., 2 Sess., Senate (Feb. 4, 1835), p. 304; John Tyler, " Fourth Annual Message " (Dec. 3, 1844), in Richardson, *Messages and Papers,* IV, 348.

18 " The Indians," editorial in *New Yorker,* I (Aug. 6, 1836), 313.

19 R. W. Emerson, " Letter to Martin Van Buren ... A Protest against the Removal of the Cherokee Indians ..." (1838), *Complete Works* (Cent. ed.; Boston and New York, 1903-1906), XI, 89-96.

them,) decidedly progressive and encouraging. They have reached the point in industrial progress, where it is only necessary to go forward.[20]

After having made a detailed survey of Indian affairs for the federal government in the 1850's, Schoolcraft concluded that despite their opposition to the removal policy, there had resulted a "progressive improvement in the Indian character." [21]

The Indians were, of course, only one of many obstacles in the path of American westward expansion. Also in conflict with the American pursuit of manifest destiny were the British interests in Oregon and the Mexican interests in Texas. The presidential campaign of 1844 had revolved around the issues of the acquisition of Oregon and of Texas, and in the controversy occasioned by these questions reference was made to the idea of progress by both sides in support of their respective positions. In the debate on the resolution to give notice to Great Britain terminating our participation in the joint occupation of the Oregon territory, both expansionist Congressmen from the North Central states and their critics from the South viewed their arguments as in accord with the true idea of progress. Edward D. Baker, Whig Congressman from Illinois and later one of Oregon's first United States Senators, urged the needs of future generations, and in his interpretation of American history he observed: " We had a continent before us in which to spread our free principles, our language, our literature, and power; and we had a present right to provide for this future progress." [22] William Allen, the Democratic Senator from

20 H. R. Schoolcraft, *Notes on the Iroquois* (New York, 1846), pp. 9, 3-20.

21 Schoolcraft, *Information Respecting the History, Condition, and Prospects of the Indian Tribes of the United States* (Archives of Aboriginal Knowledge, vol. VI; Phil., 1860), p. 512; see also the comments by N. H. Parker in his *Iowa as It Is in 1856* (Chicago and Phil., 1856), pp. ix-x; and *The Minnesota Handbook, for 1856-7* (Boston, 1857), p. 50.

22 E. D. Baker, *Cong. Globe*, 29 Cong., 1 Sess., House of Rep. (Jan. 3, 1846), p. 136.

Ohio, also denounced English imperialism. With the occupation of Oregon he believed that the United States, no longer subordinate to England, would become the foremost nation in the world, " leading it on to that social regeneration, which promises the delivery of mankind from the miseries of antiquated monarchy.[23] Edward A. Hannegan, the Democratic Senator from Indiana, attempted to show the futility of resist-ing the occupation of Oregon and the workings of inevitable progress. Then he also invoked the lessons of history to explain that

> the spirit of resistance to progress, which we witness here now, is as ancient as our country is old. It has been seen at an early day, in opposition to the settlement of Kentucky struggling to confine our republic without the Alleghanies; in vehement opposition to the purchase of Louisiana and Florida; in uncharitable efforts to repel Texas.[24]

These expansionists from the Northwest were answered by Southern Congressmen, who were opposed to the prospect of losing the British cotton market in a war over territory unsuited to slavery. Not denying altogether some of the advantages which the acquisition of Oregon might give the United States, Robert M. T. Hunter, Congressman from Virginia, nevertheless expressed his fears over the effects of a war on the future prosperity and freedom of America. Believing that the " genius of our institutions is pacific," Hunter declared that the United States were destined " to minister to the progress and the universal peace and happiness of mankind by the beneficent example of a free and happy people . . ." [25] In like vein John C. Calhoun of South Carolina addressed the Senate.

23 William Allen, *ibid.*, 29 Cong., 1 Sess., Senate (Feb. 10 and 11, 1846), Appendix, p. 839.

24 E. A. Hannegan, *ibid.*, 29 Cong., 1 Sess., Senate (Feb. 16, 1846), Appendix, p. 310.

25 R. M. T. Hunter, *ibid.*, 29 Cong., 1 Sess., House of Rep. (Jan. 10, 1846), Appendix, p. 91.

He declared his opposition to any war over Oregon for certain practical and material reasons, including the disastrous effect it would have on the improving commercial relations between the United States and England. Then he continued:

> But I have still higher reasons. I am opposed to war as a friend to human improvement, to human civilization, to human progress and advancement. . . . Civilization has been spreading its influence far and wide, and the general progress of human society has outstripped all that had been previously witnessed. . . . All this progress, all this growth of human happiness, all this spread of human light and knowledge, will be arrested by war. And shall we incur a result like that which must be produced by a war, for Oregon? And this work is at yet but commenced; it is but the breaking of the dawn of the world's great jubilee. It promises a day of more refinement, more intellectual brightness, more moral elevation, and consequently of more human felicity, than the world has ever seen from its creation.[26]

In his speech, Calhoun had to defend himself against the charge of inconsistency because of his earlier approval of the annexation of Texas—a policy which many in the North denounced as insuring the perpetuation of slavery. For example, William Ellery Channing, the Unitarian minister, in his letter to Henry Clay in 1837, had stigmatized the agitation for Texas as a scheme to spread slavery, and he had warned the American people that they were " a restless people prone to encroachment, impatient of the ordinary laws of progress, less anxious to consolidate and perfect than to extend our institutions."   Although he admitted the truth of the prevalent notion " that more civilized must always exert a great power over less civilized communities in their neighbourhood," he urged that it " be a power to enlighten and improve, not to crush and destroy." [27]

26 J. C. Calhoun, *ibid.*, 29 Cong., 1 Sess., Senate (March 16, 1846), p. 505.

27 W. E. Channing, " On the Annexation of Texas to the United States " (A Letter to the Hon. Henry Clay . . . August 1, 1837), *Works* (Boston, 1855), II, 205, 210.

When the struggle over Texas culminated in the Mexican War, the hostilities and ensuing territorial expansion were alternately praised and condemned in the name of progress. James K. Polk, the war president, in his Annual Messages to Congress carefully noted the material progress and prosperity of the nation:

> The progress of our country in her career of greatness, not only in the vast extension of our territorial limits and the rapid increase of our population, but in the resources and wealth and in the happy condition of our people, is without an example in the history of nations.[28]
>
> So successful have been all branches of our industry that a foreign war, which generally diminishes the resources of a nation, has in no essential degree retarded our onward progress or checked our general prosperity.[29]

Of a different opinion, Theodore Parker, the famous clergyman and abolitionist, in reviewing Polk's Message for December, 1846, admitted that war was to be expected in a barbarian state. However, Parker declared: "Every war in this age retards the progress of mankind." [30] Also opposed to the war Alexander H. Stephens, Southern Whig and later vice-president of the Confederacy, denounced the struggle as a war of conquest. He then announced that he looked for true progress and national greatness in the advance of knowledge and in the cultivation of domestic industry:

> in a word, the progress of civilization and everything that elevates, ennobles, and dignifies man. This, Mr. Chairman, is not to be done by wars, whether foreign or domestic. Fields

28 J. K. Polk, "Second Annual Message" (Dec. 8, 1846), in Richardson, *Messages and Papers*, IV, 472.

29 Polk, "Third Annual Message" (Dec. 7, 1847), *ibid.*, IV, 554.

30 [Theodore Parker], "The Mexican War," *Mass. Q. Rev.*, I (Dec., 1847), 9-10.

of blood and carnage may make men brave and heroic, but seldom tend to make nations either good, virtuous, or great.[31]

In an attempt to justify the war, the explanation was evolved that certain unfortunate nations were doomed by the inexorable law of progress. Thus the fate of the Mexicans was explained by alluding to their unprogressive condition. In an editorial in 1847 on " Machinery and Its Results," *The Subterranean,* a New York labor journal, expressed the opinion that machinery accounted for the difference between the degrees of progress enjoyed by the two nations. Contrasting the " penury and want " existing in Mexico with the " wealth and abundance " in the United States, the writer concluded: " Here the progress of the people in all that elevates the race, in all that ministers to the comfort of mankind, is unprecedented in the world's history." [32] A few months later the *Scientific American* observed: " Civilization is a progressive work—there is no standing still —its principle is continual advancement. The nation that ceases to go forward must certainly go back." [33] In a more explicit fashion F. O. J. Smith, a former Congressman, and a railroad lawyer associated with Morse in the commercialization of the telegraph, contributed in 1848, under the title " Progress," an article to Hunt's *Merchants Magazine* in which he pictured the commercial advantages of an expansionist policy. Smith believed that the United States " in the great drama of events which Progress has in view " were destined to subject those nations which had

hitherto been shut up in ignorance and mental stupidity, and prostrated by the physical debility incident thereto, to the

31 A. H. Stephens, *Cong. Globe,* 29 Cong., 1 Sess., House of Rep. (June 16, 1846), Appendix, p. 950; see also: *Niles' Register,* LXX (May 30, 1846), 195, quoting the *New York Courier and Enquirer's* insertion from the *Courier des Etats Unis,* a French journal pub. in New York; and George Rogers, *An Address on our Destiny* (New York [1846?]).

32 *Subterranean,* IV (May 8, 1847), 2.

33 *Sci. Am.,* II (July 31, 1847), 357; see also: " The Conquest of California," *S. Q. Rev.,* XV (July, 1849), 413-414.

influences of her own higher, active energies, and by which
are being carried forward the whole human race to perfect-
ability of enjoyments from COMMERCE, AGRICULTURE, MANU-
FACTURES, the ARTS and SCIENCES.[34]

During these years of expansion at the expense of the Indians
and Mexicans, Americans proudly discussed their progressive
mission. The material growth of the nation, its territorial acquisitions, and its future prospects were argued by the
articulate citizens of various groups and professions. Their
articles and addresses were couched in terms of the highest
patriotism, and the doctrine of progress was invoked to give a
cloak of idealism to what was more bluntly called manifest
destiny. Statesmen like Lewis Cass, Caleb Cushing, Levi
Woodbury and William H. Seward praised the republican form
of government and rejoiced that the tendencies of the age indicated an extension of American democracy to other lands.[35]
Clergymen and educators related America's destiny to the
spread of its political and religious liberty.[36]

34 F. O. J. Smith, "Progress," Hunt's *Merchants Mag.*, XVIII (March,
1848), 260; for some different views, see: T. G. Cary, "Destiny Progress,"
ibid., XVIII (April, 1848), 391-394; "Internal Commerce of the West,"
ibid., XIX (July, 1848), 19, 40.

35 Lewis Cass, *Address ... before the Association of the Alumni of Hamilton
College* (Utica, 1830), pp. 5-7; and *A Discourse ... before the American
Historical Society* (Washington, 1836), *passim*; Caleb Cushing, *An Oration
... Amherst College* (Boston, 1836), pp. 13-14; and *An Oration on the
Material Growth and Territorial Progress of the United States* (Spring-
field, 1839), *passim*; Levi Woodbury, "Historical Inquiries..." (1837),
Writings (Boston, 1852), III, 149-150; and "On Some of the Peculiar
Traits of American Character" (1845), *ibid.*, III, 191-216; W. H. Seward,
"The True Greatness of our Country" (1844), *Works* (new ed.; Boston
and New York, 1884), III, 11-24.

36 C. E. Stowe, "Advantages and Defects of the Social Condition in the
United States of America," *Am. Bib. Repos.*, 2 ser., I (Jan., 1839), 130-
161; R. J. Breckinridge, *A Discourse on ... the American Mind* (Baltimore,
1837), *passim*; and "Fragments of a Discourse Concerning the Progress of
Liberty," *Spirit of the Nineteenth Century*, II (July, 1843), 369-383; J. W.
Fowler, *Society, Its Progress and Prospects* . . . (Utica, 1843), *passim;*
Gamaliel Bailey, Jr., *American Progress* (Cincinnati, 1846), *passim.*

This enthusiasm on the part of the clergymen and the states-men was repeated by writers in some of the popular journals of the period. In the *Democratic Review* for 1839 a writer devel-oped the thesis that America was " destined to be *the great na-tion* of futurity . . . We are the nation of human progress, and who will, what can, set limits to our onward march?" [37] A ver-satile author, a contributor to many periodicals, and a vigorous nationalist in his writings, Cornelius Mathews, in the first num-ber of his own magazine begun in 1840, exulted that America was a new land, in which " custom hath lost its sway, and Time and Change are the champions against the field." [38] Orestes A. Brownson, the radical reformer of the 1830's, writing in 1842 for the popular *New York Mirror,* praised " Young America " as an example of the truth that " We are THE PEOPLE OF THE FUTURE . . ." [39] Walt Whitman, the future poet, in a newspaper editorial in 1846 announced that, " Thirty years from this date, America will be confessed the *first nation* on the earth." From the progress of American democracy, Whitman felt

> we are to expect the great FUTURE of this Western world! a scope involving such unparalleled human happiness and na-tional freedom, to such unnumbered myriads, that the heart of a true *man* leaps with a mighty joy only to think of it! God works out his greatest results by such means; and while each popinjay priest of the mummery of the past is babbling his alarm, the youthful Genius of the people passes swiftly over era after era of change and improvement, and races of human beings erewhile down in gloom or bondage rise gradually toward that majestic development which the good God doubt-less loves to witness . . . [40]

37 " The Great Nation of Futurity," *Dem. Rev.,* VI (Nov., 1839), 426-427.

38 Cornelius Mathews, " Political Life," *Arcturus,* I (Dec., 1840), 5.

39 O. A. Brownson, "Young America," *New York Mirror,* XX (Oct. 22, 1842), 338.

40 Walt Whitman, "American Futurity" (Nov. 24, 1846), in *The Gather-ing of the Forces,* ed. Cleveland Rogers and John Black (New York and London, 1920), I, 4-5, 27.

That the promise of the American political experiment also attracted the attention of the poets is suggested by the example of William Cullen Bryant. The editor of the New York *Evening Post* for almost a half-century after 1829, Bryant also found the time to commemorate the future of the United States in his verse. During the 1830's and 1840's, before the approach of the Civil War and the failure of democracy abroad had dimmed his optimism, he expressed an implicit faith in progress. Often given to a kind of tolerant meditation over the destiny of the world, Bryant, however, seemed to see in his native land the prospects of a happier future. From Italy in 1834, he addressed his American homeland, declaring:

> O thou,
> Who sittest far beyond the Atlantic deep,
> Among the sources of thy glorious streams,
> My native Land of Groves! a newer page
> In the great record of the world is thine;
> Shall it be fairer? Fear, and friendly Hope,
> And Envy, watch the issue, while the lines,
> By which thou shalt be judged, are written down.[41]

The older countries of Europe, Bryant felt, were jealous of their youthful rival, but in her natural resources and political freedom America enjoyed all the advantages for the future. In his famous poem, " Oh Mother of a Mighty Race," written in 1846, he predicted:

> Thine eye, with every coming hour,
> Shall brighten, and thy form shall tower;
> And when thy sisters, elder born,
> Would brand thy name with words of scorn,
> Before thine eye,
> Upon their lips the taunt shall die.[42]

---

[41] W. C. Bryant, "Earth" (1835), *Life and Works*, ed. Parke Godwin (New York, 1883-1884), III, 241; see also: "The Fountain" (1839), and "Noon" (1844), *ibid.*, III, 282, 315.

[42] Bryant, "Oh Mother of a Mighty Race" (1847), *ibid.*, IV, 19.
For a good instance of Bryant's later pessimism in regard to the idea of progress, see his letter to the Rev. Orville Dewey (August 15, 1854), *ibid.*, II, 77-78.

When revolution broke out in Europe during the year 1848, many persons in America believed that a great step forward in the progress of democracy was in the process of achievement.[43] From the time of their own independence Americans had distrusted the ancient monarchies of the Old World. In the period of our survey, in article and address, various Americans interpreted progress in terms of the gains of democracy and liberty over European despotism.[44] Elaborating upon this literature an obscure writer, George Sidney Camp, published in 1841 a work on *Democracy,* in which he contrasted the monarchical and aristocratic with the democratic forms of government. In a chapter devoted to a discussion of " The permanency of democratic government and the eventual prevalence of democratic principles," Camp expressed the American belief that,

> If there be a tendency in the species towards progressive improvement, if there be a dispensation over us which points to the eventual realization, in the affairs of men, of those principles of rectitude existing in the Divine Mind, we must be continually approximating to this consummation of political justice.[45]

However, the revolutionary movements of 1848 had hardly begun when they were suppressed, and American sympathizers were forced to transfer their enthusiasm into apologies and ex-

43 J. G. Gazley, *American Opinion of German Unification, 1848-1871* (New York, 1926), *passim*; A. J. May, *Contemporary American Opinion of the Mid-Century Revolutions in Central Europe* (Phil., 1927), *passim*.

44 See for example: " On the Progress of Political and Literary Opinions on the Continent of Europe," *West. Monthly Rev.,* III (Nov. and Dec., 1829), 266 ff., 280 ff.; " The Prospect of Reform in Europe," *North Am. Rev.,* XXXIII (July, 1831), 178; William Maclure, *Opinions on Various Subjects* (New Harmony, 1831-1837), I, 279; Joseph Blunt, " Address before the New York Historical Society 1839," *Speeches,* p. 195; " Revolutions in Europe," *Meth. Q. Rev.,* XXVIII (April, 1846), 181; " Our Country," *Sci. Am.,* II (July 3, 1847), 325; Carlos D. Stuart, "America vs. England," *Nineteenth Century,* I, no. 1 (1848), 101-102; " The French Republic," *S. Q. Rev.,* XIV (July, 1848), 240-241.

45 G. S. Camp, *Democracy* (New York, 1841), p. 162.

planations. Parke Godwin, writing in the Fourierist *Harbinger* for September 1848, admitted that violent revolutions always failed to achieve progress, but he did not despair: "We know that the demonstrations of science sustain the instincts of the heart, and that no hopes of the Future can be so impetuous and so wild as to outrun its swift coming realities."[46] Charles A. Dana, foreign correspondent for the *Tribune* during the period of the revolutions, concluded his series of despatches with an admission of their failure everywhere, and the question:

> What, then, is the good produced by the Revolution? Briefly it consists in the opening wide the way of progress —in the putting of society face to face with the questions on which its fate depends, and in the rousing of many minds to solve them. Of positive results it has little to show— nothing in comparison with the evils by which it has been attended. But all evil is temporary. Good is permanent and renews itself forever.[47]

To some of the clergymen surveying the collapse of the revolutionary movements, the events of 1848 seemed to indicate the necessity of a return to more personal and spiritual values. Orville Dewey, a Unitarian minister, regarded the revolutions of 1848 as "a distinct step in the progress of the world," but, feeling that progress was gradual, he also believed that they could only be considered as a preparation for a future era of self government.[48] Frederic H. Hedge, Unitarian minister and transcendentalist, discounted the revolutions because he felt that, "From political revolutions there is nothing to be hoped. The obstacles in the way of social progress are such as no pol-

---

46 Parke Godwin, "Revolutions in Europe," *Harbinger*, VII (Sept. 9, 1848), 148.

47 C. A. Dana, "Balance-Sheet of the Revolution," *New York Weekly Tribune*, VIII (Feb. 24, 1849), 1; for a more pessimistic view, see: Margaret Fuller Ossoli, *Memoirs*, ed. R. W. Emerson, W. H. Channing, and J. F. Clarke (London, 1852), III, 266-267.

48 Orville Dewey, "The Crisis of Freedom in the Old World and the New," *Chr. Ex.*, XLVI (Jan., 1849), 6, and *passim*.

itics can remove." [49] Viewing the reaction following the revolutions as only temporary, Charles Hawley, a Presbyterian clergyman, exhorted:

> Oh, never let us despair of the final triumph of truth and freedom. There is a deathless spirit abroad upon the world, which despots can never conquer. There is a flame kindled which blood can never quench. The day of universal light and liberty is approaching with the certainty of a comet to the sun. This must be, in the destined progress of the gospel. What Christianity has done for us, it will do for the world. The movement is as sure as the providence of God.[50]

Consolation for the failure of the European revolutions was also found in a review of America's own prospects. In the December, 1848, issue of *Graham's Magazine* Joseph R. Chandler, one of the editors, soon to be elected to Congress as a Clay Whig, made a survey of the events just passed. Chandler rejoiced that American institutions were not endangered, and he maintained that a true republic " is for all men, and for all times; and never since the first gathering of people into a political body was there such a foundation for national greatness and diffused individual happiness, as is laid in this country." [51] William W. Greenough, a Boston merchant, after noting the connection of American prosperity with the success of her institutions abroad, declared in his address on July 4, 1849:

> There never has been a constitution or government, which admitted such an indefinite and unlimited extension of territory or population, as our own—nay, more, which so required extension for success. To this people applies with peculiar force, the observation of Humboldt: " It is with nations as

---

49 F. H. Hedge, " The Nineteenth Century," *ibid.*, XLVIII (May, 1850), 375.

50 Charles Hawley, *The Advantages of the Present Age* (Rochester, 1850), p. 13.

51 J. R. Chandler, " Reflections on Some of the Events of the Year 1848," *Graham's Mag.*, XXXIII (Dec., 1848), 324.

with nature which knows no pause in progress and development, and attaches her curse on all inaction." [52]

In a similar vein, a month later, a contributor to a Western reform journal decided that the events of the year 1848 made it manifest "that it belongs to the United States to stir up free principles over the world . . ." Confident in the expectation of a future material and scientific advance in the United States, and arguing that it was a world of change, the author urged: "As Americans we should have respect also for the great principle of PROGRESS." [53]

Of the many uprisings in 1848 the struggle of Hungary for independence from Austria was one which particularly stirred the American people. By the summer of 1849 Hungarian resistance had collapsed, but late that year Lewis Cass, veteran Democratic expansionist, introduced a resolution in the Senate calling for an inquiry into the " expediency of suspending diplomatic relations with Austria." This resolution was immediately attacked by those senators who opposed any intervention in European affairs, but Cass maintained that the progress of science had broken down the barriers between nations, and he upbraided the opponents of his resolution for opposing the progress of the age.[54] For the opposition, Henry Clay, the advocate of American self-sufficiency, replied with a criticism of Cass' interpretation of the idea of progress. Clay then went on to declare:

> Ah, I am afraid it is progress in foreign wars. I am afraid it is progress in foreign conquest—in territorial aggrandizement. I am afraid it is progress as the disturbers of the possessions of our neighbors, throughout this continent, and throughout the islands adjacent to it. If that be the progress

52 William W. Greenough, *The Conquering Republic* (Boston, 1849), p. 34.

53 "The Position of America," *New Constitution*, I (Aug. 4, 1849), 221, 223.

54 Lewis Cass, *Cong. Globe*, 31 Cong., 1 Sess., Senate (Jan. 4, 1850), Appendix, p. 58.

which the honorable Senator wishes to effect, I trust that it will be long before this country engages in any such object as that; at least, at the expense of the peaceable portion of the world.[55]

To both the protests of Austria and the entreaties of Kossuth, Daniel Webster, the American Secretary of State, responded in the general terms of the idea of progress. When Austria remonstrated against the unneutral attitude of the United States, Webster answered with a defense of American institutions and the announcement that

the country in all its interests and concerns, partakes most largely in all the improvements and progress which distinguish the age. Certainly, the United States may be pardoned, even by those who profess adherence to the principles of absolute government, if they entertain an ardent affection, for those popular forms of political organization which have so rapidly advanced their own prosperity and happiness, and enabled them in so short a period, to bring their country, and the hemisphere to which it belongs, to the notice and respectful regard, not to say the admiration, of the civilized world.[56]

With the conclusion of the Hungarian revolt, Louis Kossuth, its leader, went into exile, and then later in 1849 he visited America, seeking funds to finance further revolution. Speaking at a banquet in honor of the Hungarian visitor, Daniel Webster portrayed his country as a land of liberty deserving its independence, but in place of urging material support, he offered the cheerful observation that " the progress of things is unquestionably onward. It is onward with respect to Hungary; it is onward everywhere. Public opinion, in my estimation at least, is making great progress." [57]

55 Henry Clay, *ibid.*, 31 Cong., 1 Sess., Senate (Jan. 7, 1850), p. 116.

56 Daniel Webster, " The Secretary of State to Mr. Hulsemann " (1850), *Writings*, XII, 170.

57 Webster, " Speech at the Kossuth Banquet Washington, January 7, 1852," *ibid.*, XIII, 461.

In the midst of the excitement aroused in behalf of Kossuth, Francis Bowén, the editor of the *North American Review,* in its issue for January, 1850, took the unpopular stand that the Hungarian revolt was in reality only a struggle of the Magyar ruling class to hold its power against the other races of Hungary. Bowen condemned the Magyar institutions as antiquated and out of step with the improved civilization of the nineteenth century. Ridiculing Kossuth's claim of the reforms effected by the Hungarian Diet, Bowen declared:

> Even of late years, when ideas of progress and democratic reform had pushed their way even into Hungary, the great question at the Diet did not relate to the mode of embodying these ideas into legislative acts, but to doubt whether the king, at the close of the session, would wear the Hungarian surcoat or the Austrian royal mantle; and whether he would make his speech in Magyar or in German.[58]

Although Bowen lost a chance for a professorship in history at Harvard because of the opinions advanced in his article, the popular enthusiasm for Kossuth's cause did not long continue. When Lewis Cass, maintaining his interventionist position, early in 1852 introduced a resolution expressing sympathy with Hungarian independence,[59] his scheme was bitterly denounced by the members of the Whig party in Congress. Jacob W. Miller, Senator from New Jersey, declared: " The Senator from Michigan (Mr. Cass) says we cannot stand still; yet he neglects to tell us whither we shall go. The friends of progress expected something more bold and decided from that Senator . . ." Then, alluding to Washington's " Farewell Address," he continued:

> That policy which caused us to stand still and look with national indifference upon the exciting conflicts of interest

58 [Francis Bowen], " The War of Races in Hungary," *North Am. Rev.,* LXX (Jan., 1850), 104, and *passim.*

59 *Cong. Globe,* 32 Cong., 1 Sess., Senate (Feb. 10, 1852), Appendix, pp. 158-159.

and ambition, of tyranny and of liberty, which grew out of the
first French Revolution, has accomplished more during the
last ten years for the real progress of free institutions than
will ever be attained by *filibustering interveners* and locomotive politicians to the world's end; and if, in the coming storm
which now threatens Europe, the statesmen of this country
can muster moral courage enough to stand unmoved by its
fury, we shall prove to mankind that our house is founded
upon a rock.[60]

As a substitute for Cass' resolution, one calling for non-inter-
vention was offered. In defending this measure John Bell, the
Whig Senator from Tennessee, expressed his concern over the
effects of European "ultraisms" on American progress. Denouncing the unneutral conduct of the United States in the
Hungarian affair, he concluded his speech with the satirical
comment:

> Now, sir, from these proceedings we may form some esti-
> mate of the true character and extent of that moderation and
> sober discretion of the American people and of their represen-
> tatives, of the present times and generation, so confidently re-
> lied upon to keep us in the faith and in the counsels of the
> fathers of the Republic. Truly, we have before us a most not-
> able and instructive example and illustration of the progress
> of the age.[61]

Opponents of the notion that the advancement of civilization
might be furthered by American intervention in European
struggles for liberty, urged an attention to domestic concerns.
In this regard they depicted the progress which would result
from the passage of a Homestead bill, providing free land to
settlers. The principles of this bill had previously been advocated and related to the idea of progress by radical groups in a

60 J. W. Miller, *ibid.*, 32 Cong., 1 Sess., Senate (Feb. 26, 1852), Appendix,
pp. 212-213.

61 John Bell, *ibid.*, 32 Cong., 1 Sess., Senate (April 13, 1852), Appendix,
p. 445.

National Reform Association,[62] and during the 1850's the question was also agitated in Congress. In a speech censuring Kossuth and the philosophy of intervention, Presley Ewing, Whig Representative from Kentucky, praised the Homestead bill as one of the harmless developments of the idea of progress, affirming:

> I love progress of the right sort—that progress which has been for fifty years an American idea. There was in that idea of an " ocean-bound Republic " at least something patriotic, something which stirred the heart and appealed to the pride of every lover of his country. I love, natural, American progress, the development of true principles, in all their consequences, the advance of true happiness and true greatness. But let us not turn back and attempt, what I fear is a hopeless task, to regenerate the old, worn-out, *effete* institutions of Europe.[63]

Also opposed to the " Kossuth infatuation," William R. Smith, Whig Representative from Alabama, declared that the Homestead bill would further the domestic progress of the nation, aiding both farm laborers and unemployed mechanics. Announcing that the bill was "intimately connected" with the idea of progress, Smith went on to say:

> Its spirit is the spirit of progress—true American progress, which looks for the greatest good to the greatest number. . . .
> I beg to say . . . that I see a vast difference between progress at home and progress abroad. The progress which I favor,

---

62 See for example: *Young America! Principles and Objects of the National Reform Association, or Agrarian League* (Young America Extra no., pamphlet in the New York Public Library, no date) ; " Freedom of the Soil," *Subterranean*, IV (July 25, 1846), 2 ; " The Land Question," *Q. Journal and Rev.*, I (Oct., 1846), 289-302; John Pickering, *The Working Man's Political Economy* (Cincinnati, 1847), ch. 20, and *passim*; " Poverty and Misery, versus Reform and Progress," *Dem. Rev.*, XXIII (July, 1848), 27-30; see also: H. S. Zahler, *Eastern Workingmen and National Land Policy, 1829-1862* (New York, 1941), *passim*.

63 Presley Ewing, *Cong. Globe*, 32 Cong., 1 Sess., House of Rep. (April 24, 1852), Appendix, p. 532.

is the progress of AMERICA *at home*, regardless of the concerns of the other portions of the earth.[64]

With the stimulus provided by the acquisition of Oregon, the Mexican cession, and the revolutions of 1848, the decade before the Civil War witnessed a great many appeals connecting the idea of progress with America's destiny. Expansionist sentiment in this decade became crystalized in the program of Young America, a radical group within the Democratic party who favored an aggressive foreign policy. In the months leading up to the election of 1852 the Young America faction was not without political influence.[65] Opposed to its interventionist principles, President Millard Fillmore, a conservative Whig, in his Third Annual Message warned that wars and revolutions designed to spread liberty might only result in its destruction. Affirming his belief that "We live in an age of progress, and ours is emphatically a country of progress," Fillmore invoked the force of the concept of progress against those who mistook

> change for progress and the invasion of the rights of others for national prowess and glory. The former are constantly agitating for some change in the organic law, or urging new and untried theories of human rights. The latter are every ready to engage in any wild cursade against a neighboring people, regardless of the justice of the enterprise and without looking at the fatal consequences to ourselves and to the cause of popular government.[66]

In 1853 Fillmore was succeeded by Franklin Pierce, who set the tone for further expansionist sentiments in his inaugural

64 W. R. Smith, *ibid.*, 32 Cong., 1 Sess., House of Rep. (April 27, 1852), Appendix, p. 517; for a different view see: John Allison, *ibid.*, 32 Cong., 1 Sess., House of Rep. (April 20, 1852), Appendix, p. 432.
Andrew Johnson in his well-known appeal for the Homestead bill also invoked the idea of America's progressive destiny, *ibid.*, 35 Cong., 1 Sess., Senate (May 20, 1858), pp. 2265-2273.

65 Merle Curti, "Young America," *Am. Hist. Rev.*, XXXII (Oct., 1926), 34-55.

66 Millard Fillmore, "Third Annual Message" (Dec. 6, 1852), in Richardson, *Messages and Papers*, V, 181.

address, in which he told his listeners: " But if your past is limited, your future is boundless." [67] Some of his fellow Democrats, mindful of the collapse of the liberal movement in Europe in 1848, now transferred their interest in intervention to the Latin American nations of the Caribbean. Lewis Cass feared that American security was menaced in this region. A staunch upholder of the idea that the scientific progress of the age had made national isolation impossible, he proclaimed that the United States must expand or become a dependency of Europe, and he declared that the Gulf of Mexico should be an American lake.[68] Caleb Cushing, another ardent Democratic expansionist, argued that Mexico and perhaps Cuba lay in the path of American destiny. Confronting his opponents with the inevitability of this progressive destiny, he declared:

> let them tell me by what arguments they justify the beginnings of that advancement, and its progress thus far,—nay, let them tell me by what rule of right we stand anyhere in America? Where is Powhatan? Where Massasoit? Where Sassacus? Is not the occupation of any portion of the earth by those competent to hold and till it, a providential law of national life? Can you say to the tide that it ought not to flow, or the rain to fall? I reply, *it must!* And so it is with well-constituted, and, therefore, progressive and expansive nations. They cannot help advancing; it is the condition of their existence.[69]

67 Franklin Pierce, " Inaugural Address " (March 4, 1853), *ibid.*, V, 199.

68 Lewis Cass, *Cong. Globe*, 32 Cong., 2 Sess., Senate (Jan. 15, 1853), Appendix, pp. 90-95; for some milder statements connecting Cuba and the idea of progress, see: "Cuba," *Putnam's Monthly*, I (Jan., 1853), 3-16; M. S. Latham, "Rights of Neutrals—Cuba," *Cong. Globe*, 33 Cong., 1 Sess., House of Rep. (June 14, 1854), Appendix, p. 954.
For a scholarly argument, tying American expansion to the operation of the laws of progress, see: [George F. Holmes], "Relations of the Old and the New Worlds," *De Bow's Rev.*, XX (May, 1856), 521-540.

69 Caleb Cushing, "Address at Meeting of Virginia Agricultural Society 1858," quoted in C. M. Fuess, *The Life of Caleb Cushing* (New York, 1923), II, 225; for a hostile account of this speech, see editorial: " Cushing on Progress," *New York Weekly Tribune*, XVIII (Nov. 6, 1858), 2; see also

These arguments were carried to an extreme by J. F. H. Claiborne, a retired Democratic Congressman, in his biography of John A. Quitman, Mississippi soldier and statesman. Claiborne especially defended Quitman's connection with the Lopez filibustering expedition against Cuba, remarking in regard to the government's opposition:

> We proceed upon the theory that the condition of a republic is repose. What an error! That is the normal condition of absolutism. The law of a republic is progress. Its nature is aggressive.
>
> We are in the restless period of youth; the law of the age is progress; let our flag be given to the winds, and our principles go with it wherever it is unfurled. Conquest is essential to our internal repose. War sometimes becomes the best security for peace.[70]

Although more restrained in their views, expansionist sentiments were also voiced by some of the Whig leaders of the 1850's. Placing less emphasis on territorial annexation, their program envisioned the progress which would result from the commercial development of the world's backward areas. Horace Greeley, the leading Whig editor of the country, on the occasion of the Fourth of July, 1852, explained " the unswerving law of Man's progress " as:

> first emancipation from the control of natural wants, the subjugation of natural forces, and with these the gradual establishment of political and social liberty and gradual elevation in the scale of intelligence, virtue, religion. . . .

Cushing's earlier speech, "The Nation's Progress" (1853), in *A Library of American Literature*, ed. E. C. Stedman and E. M. Hutchinson (vol. VI, New York, 1888), pp. 31-32.

70 J. F. H. Claibourne, *Life and Correspondence of John A. Quitman* (New York, 1860), II, 111, 113; see also: [George Fitzhugh], "Love of Danger and of War," *De Bow's Rev.*, XXVIII (March, 1860), 305; for a different view, see: S. S. Nicholas, "Manifest Destiny" (1858), *Conservative Essays Legal and Political* (Phil., 1863), pp. 38-47.

—Such, then, is the moral of this Anniversary; at home, the increase and diffusion of Liberty by Industry, Science, Education; abroad, to do unto others as we would have others do to us, and to give aid and comfort and support everywhere to nations struggling to be free! [71]

Opposed to the policy of conquering more territory, Greeley in an editorial of 1853, entitled "True and False Progress," instead advocated a railroad to the Pacific and a steamship line to China.[72] William H. Seward, Whig Senator from New York, later chiefly responsible for the purchase of Alaska, shared Greeley's interest in developing our trade with the Pacific Ocean regions. In his argument for a mail line to China, Seward remarked that such questions were customarily discussed under the assumption of man's free will. Although he rejected the extreme reliance of some on manifest destiny, Seward declared:

> that sometimes, when I take on outside position and review the thickly recurring changes through which we have passed, it seems to me that our course has been shaped, not so much by any self-guiding wisdom of our own, as by a law of progress and development impressed upon us by nature herself.[73]

A concrete example of this American interest in the Pacific was furnished by the dispatch of an American expedition to Japan and the China Seas in 1852 under the command of Commodore Matthew C. Perry. In the *Narrative of the Expedition* published four years later by Congress, Perry made an eloquent plea, urging the United States to pursue an imperialistic policy in the Far East. Arguing that the growth of American commerce made national isolation impossible, Perry declared: "In the developments of the future, the destinies of our nation must

71 "Moral of the Fourth of July," *New York Weekly Tribune*, XI (July 10, 1852), 2.

72 *Ibid.*, XII (April 9, 1853), 2; see also: Edward Everett, "Stability and Progress" (1853), *Orations and Speeches*, III, 230.

73 W. H. Seward, *Cong. Globe*, 33 Cong., 1 Sess., Senate (June 29, 1854), p. 1566; for two addresses by Seward at this time, on the subject of American destiny and progress, see: *Works*, IV, pp. 122 ff., 166 ff.

assume conspicuous attitudes; we cannot expect to be free from the ambitious longings for increased power, which are the natural concomitants of national success." [74] In answer to the charge that this policy might lead to a series of territorial aggressions and annexations, Perry replied that, " after all, these events in the history and fate of nations are doubtless directed by an overruling Providence, and probably we could not, if we would, change their course, or avert our ultimate destiny." [75]

This quest for new lands and markets to satisfy the material expansion of the nation, supported by references to the dogmas of progress and destiny, led to a fatalism in which even aggressive war was condoned as a step in the fulfillment of America's progressive mission. This was indicated in the discussion of progress and the Mexican War. It was explicitly argued by Herschel V. Johnson, Senator from Georgia, in his defense of the war. Admitting the evils of war, he, however, declared that " it has also been made, by the Allwise Dispenser of events, the instrumentality of accomplishing the great end of human elevation and human happiness." Full of confidence that in the advance of civilization the whole of North America was destined for freedom, he concluded his speech in favor of a vigorous prosecution of the war against Mexico with the statement that:

> The results of war and the developments of science are but the echoes of the voice of prophecy. The one opens the door for civilization, and the other sends its ministers by the power of steam, and speeds them upon the wing of the " seraphic lightening." [76]

74 M. C. Perry, " Remarks of Commodore Perry upon the Expediency of Extending Further Encouragement to American Commerce in the East," *Narrative of the Expedition . . . to the China Seas and Japan* (House Ex. Doc. no. 97, 33 Cong., 2 Sess., II, 177-178).

75 *Ibid.*, pp. 177-178.

76 H. V. Johnson, *Cong. Globe*, 30 Cong., 1 Sess., Senate (March 16, 1848), Appendix, pp. 379-380.

The interpretation of war as a step in the advance of civiliza- tion raised a problem in the minds of believers in peaceful prog- ress. In a famous address, delivered on the occasion of the fifth anniversary of the Massachusetts Peace Society, in 1820, Josiah Quincy, a staunch Federalist and pacifist, analyzed the causes of war and the prospects of permanent peace. Quincy assumed that man as an individual and as a species was suscep- tible of improvement, and that some progress had already been effected, especially with regard to lessening the horrors of war. The question which Quincy posed, therefore, was whether or not the admitted degree of improvement offered any guarantee that the possibility of future wars could be virtually elimin- ated?[77] Despite the recent Napoleonic struggles, Quincy was encouraged by the relatively peaceful advancement of the United States in this period. Even in Europe he saw signs of that progress through which he expected war to be eliminated, and he told his audience:

"Revolutions go not backward!" Neither does the moral and intellectual progress of the multitude. Light is shining where once there was darkness; and is penetrating and purify- ing the once corrupt and enslaved portions of our species. It may, occasionallly, and for a season, be obscured; or seem retrograde. But light, moral and intellectual, shall continue to ascend to the zenith until that, which is now dark, shall be in the day; and much of that earthly crust, which still adheres to man, shall fall and crumble away, as his nature becomes elevated.[78]

Among some of the reformers of the period the idea was entertained that war was essentially a barbarous institution. While perhaps necessary in earlier ages, it was viewed as in- compatible with modern progress. Henry Ware, Jr., a promi- nent Unitarian clergyman, expressed this feeling when he wrote in the *Christian Examiner* for 1843

[77] Josiah Quincy, *Address...Massachusetts Peace Society* (Cambridge, 1821), pp. 6-7, 12.

[78] *Ibid.*, pp. 25-26.

that nothing so essentially irrational as war, so intrinsically barbarous, so inimical to the true interests of an advancing civilization, and to the doctrines and laws, the spirit, purposes, and promises of Christianity, can hold its place against the well-concerted, preserving assaults of reason, humanity, and faith.[79]

And when war was threatened between England and the United States over Oregon, Parke Godwin, the Associationist, observed that although war could not as yet be always avoided, it was a resort incompatible with an intelligent people. He rejoiced that a new era seemed to be dawning, in which " Brute force is retiring before the energy of enlightened intellect," and in which all classes of men " are adjusting their relations and habits to a better order of civil existence." [80] Not so optimistic, in 1852 when a war loomed in Europe, Henry Thoreau, the transcendental individualist, made the bitter comment:

> We are told today that civilization is making rapid progess; the tendency is ever upward; substantial justice is done even by human courts; you may trust the good intentions of mankind. . . . Does the threatened war between France and England evince any more enlightenment than a war between two savage tribes, as the Iroquois and Hurons? Is it founded in better reason? [81]

Among the pacifists and opponents of any further extension of slavery, the Mexican War particularly aroused opposition. In his *Tribune* for 1846 Horace Greeley, " convinced that all War, whether between Nations, Classes or Persons, is fatally hostile to true Progress and Human well-being," declared that

79 Henry Ware, Jr., " Notice of the Progress of Peace Principles," *Chr. Ex.*, XXXIII (Jan., 1843), 306; see also: J. H. M. " Channing on War," *ibid.*, XXVII (Sept., 1839), 72-88.

80 Parke Godwin, " The Oregon Question," *Harbinger*, I (June 14, 1845), 11; see also his "Annexation," *Putnam's Monthly*, III (Feb., 1854), 194.

81 Henry Thoreau, " Journal " (Feb. 26, 1852), *Writings* (Boston and New York, 1906), IX, 321-322; for a similar expression, see: A. Hall, "Civilization," *Regenerator*, n. s., II (Feb. 7, 1848), 339.

" the work of the true Reformer is one of Creation, not Destruction; for when the good or even the better is made manifest, the bad and the relatively defective will surely pass away." [82] Also opposed to all war, Charles Sumner, a leader in the peace movement, in a speech on the Fourth of July, 1845 delivered a sensational indictment of the motives for war, especially denouncing the prospect of fighting over Oregon and Mexico. Although Sumner realized that progress was slow, in a world still at peace he felt able to rejoice that " Auspicious omens in the history of the Past and in the present cheer us for the future." [83] Then in 1849 Sumner wrote to his brother regarding the peace movment:

> Most clearly do I see that this cause is destined to a triumph much earlier than many imagine ... If the friends of progress in Europe would aim at the armies and navies, direct all their energies at these monster evils, all else that can reasonably be desired will soon follow. It is the armies and navies that are the stays and props of arbitrary power, of unjust decrees, of martial law. Why not sound the idea in the ears of Europe? [84]

During the fifties other reformers also connected the two ideals of peace and progress. A leader in the crusade for world peace and for arbitration, the internationally famous Elihu Burritt, " the learned blacksmith," had a firm faith in Christian progress and in its ability to achieve world peace through universal brotherhood.[85] At the time of the Crimean War Burritt

82 " Prospectus for 1846," *New York Weekly Tribune*, V (June 13, 1846), 5; see also: "The Foreign News," *ibid.*, VII (May 13, 1848), 5; "Our Position in the War," *ibid.*, XIV (Jan. 13, 1855), 2.

83 Charles Sumner, *The True Grandeur of Nations* (Boston, 1845), p. 75, and *passim*.

84 Charles Sumner, "To George Sumner, July 17, 1849," *Memoir and Letters*, ed. E. L. Pierce (Boston, 1893), III, 44.

85 Elihu Burritt, *Miscellaneous Writings* (2nd. ed.; Worcester, Mass., 1850), pp. 60-62, 89-96, and *passim*; *Thoughts of Things at Home and Abroad* (Boston and New York, 1854), pp. 266-269, and *passim*.

wrote to President Pierce, urging him to use American power and neutrality to prevent " a conflict which threatens to involve the progress and civilization of the age in a bloody abyss of ruin!" [86] Also sympathetic to the peace cause, Gerritt Smith, well known abolitionist and reformer, during his term in Congress early in the fifties, delivered an address on the " Evils of War." In the course of his speech, in which he opposed an appropriation for the United States military academy, Smith affirmed that the progress of the nineteenth century had been largely the result of the era of comparative peace succeeding the Napoleonic Wars, and he announced:

> I believe, sir, in the progress of the human race. I delight to dwell upon the idea of an ever-growing civilization. Hence, it is, that I am afflicted at every demonstration of the war spirit. For the spirit of war is the spirit of barbarism—and, notwithstanding the popular idea to the contrary, war is the mightiest of all the hindrances to civilization.[87]

During the period of our survey the concept of an American political mission changed. The faith of the early Republic in the general progress of democracy through the peaceful workings of the American example became transformed into a dogma of expansion—political and material. Against the opposition to expansion offered by the Indians and by the Mexicans, the concept of progress was used to prove that backward peoples must yield to the force of civilization or be crushed in its advance. To the expansionist's slogan of manifest destiny the idea of progress imparted a kind of historic background and a vision of a better future for all—conquerors and conquered alike. Although there was a widespread interest in the European revolutionary movements of 1848, the American concept of the idea

86 Burritt, " Journal " (April 2, 1854), quoted in Merle Curti, *The Learned Blacksmith: The Letters and Journals of Elihu Burritt* (New York, 1937), p. 87.

87 Gerritt Smith, *Cong. Globe*, 33 Cong., 1 Sess., House of Rep. (Jan. 18, 1854), Appendix, p. 59.

of progress was not altered drastically by the fortunes of democracy abroad. Europe was considered hopeless; its revolutions had failed. On the other hand, the American Revolution had been successful. And so, despite the sympathetic speeches of the interventionists, the thoughts of the people remained rooted in a contemplation of the possibilities for progress at home. When expansionism, carried to an extreme, implied the threat of war, the philosophy of violence was justified as necessary to fulfill the progress of civilization. Against this apologia for war, the idea of progress was also invoked to urge the necessity of world peace. Vague in itself, the dogma of progress was thus a convenient intellectual rationalization, susceptible of use in justifying other equally vague ideas.

CHAPTER III

THE RESOURCES FOR MATERIAL EXPANSION

MUCH of the impetus for the idea of an American mission was provided by the tremendous resources available for material expansion and development in the United States during the period from 1815 to 1860. During these decades, before the Civil War and the final triumph of industrialism, progress in terms of material growth and accumulation was still evaluated with regard to the prosperity of mercantile capitalism. Expansion in this so-called Middle Period was not confined primarily to an intensive development of home industry, but the criteria of economic progress were also based on the rise of foreign commerce and on the speed with which the Great American West was exploited. During this period a great gain was made not only in the acquisition of new raw materials and markets but also in the rapid increase of the population. Expansion westward to the Pacific uncovered areas rich in natural resources, awaiting development by a growing population. To provide the necessary labor force, the large natural increase at home was augmented by the vast numbers of immigrants coming from Europe. Discouraged by the toils and privations of life in the Old World, they came to America in the hope of sharing in its abundant material resources. When the growing numbers of Catholic immigrants came to be considered a menace to American advancement, the religious interests in the United States rose to emphasize the Protestant nature of the national progress. Seemingly threatened by the wave of materialism, the church tempered its support of the new tendencies with an emphasis on moral progress. However, the Protestant churches also sent their missionaries after the pioneers and traders, and Christian people rejoiced that in an era of material progress the church was also making gains.

The resources for material expansion included, then, both the land and the people. During the Middle Period the problem of how the land should be used and of whether or not the growth of population should be encouraged provoked an endless diversity of opinion. The Great American West was the seat of these vast natural riches and also the source of much of the controversy which they aroused. Political and religious interests were directly affected by the expansion of the American people and of the American frontier; and the contemporary term, Christian Republicanism, was used to cover the new civilization in all of the varied aspects of its development.

The concept that man's progress depended on the fullest use of the natural resources of his environment was a popular idea in the young republic. During the 1820's this philosophy was given a practical application in the programs for internal improvements suggested for the Federal government's adoption. President John Quincy Adams was an important advocate of these undertakings, and he was also the statesman who expressed most strongly his conviction that they were vital and necessary to the further progress of civilization in the United States. Adams believed that a "progressive improvement in the condition of man is apparently the purpose of a superintending Providence " and that a great step in the progress of man had been taken with the Protestant Reformation.[1] Already endowed with this natural and historical heritage, he wished to see the American people further strengthen themselves through a comprehensive scheme of self-improvement, stimulated by the aid and intervention of the Federal government. To this end, in his First Annual Message to Congress in 1825, he declared:

> The great object of the institution of civil government is the improvement of the conditions of those who are parties to the social compact . . . Roads and canals, by multiplying and facilitating the communications and intercourse between dis-

1 J. Q. Adams, *An Address . . . on the Fourth of July, 1821* (Cambridge, 1821), p. 5; *An Oration Addressed to the Citizens of the Town of Quincy, on the Fourth of July, 1831* (Boston, 1831), p. 38.

tant regions and multitudes of men, are among the most important means of improvement. But moral, political, intellectual improvement are duties assigned by the Author of Our Existence to social no less than to individual man. For the fulfillment of those duties governments are invested with power, and to the attainment of the end—the progressive improvement of the condition of the governed—the exercise of delegated powers is a duty as sacred and indispensable as the usurpation of powers not granted is criminal and odious.[2]

Adams was driven from the White House in the election of 1828 by Andrew Jackson, and a few years later in 1837, in looking back upon his work, he wrote to a friend:

> I fell, and with me fell, I fear never to rise again, certainly never to rise again in my day, the system of internal improvements by National means and National energies—The great object of my life therefore as applied to the administration of the Government of the United States has failed—[3]

Adams, however, continued to regard the civilization of his day as representing an advanced stage of progress, and he maintained this view in an oration on the progress of society to civilization, which he delivered in 1840 in Boston, New York, Brooklyn, and Baltimore and which he later revised as a magazine article for the *American Whig Review*.[4] In 1825 one of his specific recommendations to Congress had been the appropriation of funds for the establishment of an astronomical observatory, and in 1843, toward the close of his career, he travelled to Cincinnati to deliver the address at the dedication of the local Astronomical Society's observatory. On that occasion he reiterated his faith in progress, and he told his listeners that,

2 Adams, "First Annual Message" (Dec. 6, 1825), in Richardson, *Messages*, II, 311.

3 Adams, Letter to Charles W. Upham, Feb. 2, 1837, in "Ten Unpublished Letters of John Quincy Adams, 1796-1837," ed. E. H. Tatum, *Huntington Lib. Q.*, IV (April, 1941), 383.

4 Adams, "Society and Civilization," *Am. Whig Rev.*, II (July, 1845), 80-89; the oration is cited in the Beards' *The American Spirit* (New York, 1942), pp. 153-154.

"Among the modes of self-improvement, and social happiness, there is none so well suited to the nature of man, as the assiduous cultivation of the arts and sciences." [5]

The issue of internal improvements, to which John Quincy Adams devoted so much of his energy, was a question that also divided both the geographic sections and the political parties of the entire nation. In the halls of Congress, from the representatives of regions without the natural means of cheap transportation, there came a strong demand for government funds. Therefore, at a time when the Constitution was being invoked against federal aid for the construction of roads, Tomlinson Fort, Democrat from Georgia, replied in 1829:

> The framers of the constitution did not attempt a code of laws, but a constitution. They knew the age they lived in, and had they been required to do so, it was beyond the wisdom of man to devise laws suited to the progressive wants of this expanding nation . . . No, sir: the march of knowledge, and the spread of institutions, beneficial to mankind, forbade it.[6]

Then when an interest in railroads began to turn public attention from turnpikes, Congressmen noted the change. In 1836 Taylor Webster, a Jacksonian Democrat from Ohio, advocated the abandonment of the Cumberland Road for a railroad because he felt that transportation was undergoing a revolution, in which

> The general adoption of railways will accomplish all that is desirable; and, viewed in this light, the connexion of the great Eastern and Western sections of the Union by a railway is of the utmost importance. The improved mode and increased facilities of intercommunication are among the prominent events which characterize this age.[7]

5 Adams, *An Oration delivered before the Cincinnati Astronomical Society* (Cincinnati, 1843), p. 62.

6 Tomlinson Fort, *Register of Debates*, 20 Cong., 2 Sess., House of Rep. (Jan. 26, 1829), p. 269.

7 Taylor Webster, *ibid.*, 24 Cong., 1 Sess., House of Rep. (June 29, 1836), p. 4543; see also: S. P. Carson, *ibid.*, 21 Cong., 1 Sess., House of Rep. (March 25, 1830), p. 669.

The optimism of some of the Congressmen over the material expansion of the nation was re-echoed in the popular periodical literature of the twenties and thirties. Writers in the *North American Review* argued that domestic improvements were the object of every enlightened government. Therefore, despite the great natural resources of the United States, it was only a part of wisdom to encourage the American people to devote their skill to the greater development and improvement of their heritage.[8] In the editorials of the *New York Mirror* internal improvements were discussed as patriotic enterprises, and to its columns James Kirke Paulding, the novelist, contributed an article in which he expressed the popular opinion that " In no country are such extremes of time and space brought together as in ours, nor have such quick changes ever been exhibited to view." [9] In the year before the depression of 1837 the editorial columns of the *New Yorker* magazine exhibited both a pride in the nation's material progress and a fear for its moral condition.[10] Before the *New Yorker's* misgivings were confirmed by the panic and depression, one writer voiced the opinion that, although the world was undoubtedly growing wiser, " its progress in virtue by no means keeps pace with its advances in knowledge." [11] In like vein contributors to the *Knickerbocker* weighed the merits of the nation's material growth.[12] In his capacity as the editor of the magazine for a short time, in 1833

8 " The New York Canals," *North Am. Rev.*, XIV (Jan., 1822), 231-251; " Internal Improvements," *ibid.*, XXIV (Jan., 1827), 1-23.

9 [J. K. Paulding], " Old Times in New York," *New York Mirror*, VIII (April 30, 1831), 337; see also: " Our Country," *ibid.*, VIII (Dec. 25, 1830 and April 23, 1831), 190, 335; " Improvements of the Age," *ibid.*, X (May 25, 1833), 375; " Improvements in the Western World," *ibid.*, XIV (July 16, 1836), 19.

10 " New York As She Is—," *New Yorker*, I (May 14, 1836), 121; " Our Country," *ibid.*, II (Oct. 15, 1836), 57.

11 " Cornering—," *ibid.*, II (Dec. 3, 1836), 169.

12 " On the Neglect of Moral Science," *Knickerbocker Mag.*, III (Feb., 1834), 95-96; " The Spirit of the Age," *ibid.*, VIII (Aug., 1836), 187-195; " Liberty vs. Literature and the Fine Arts," *ibid.*, IX (Jan., 1837), 1-2.

and 1834, Timothy Flint, disillusioned with his life in the West, lamented: "The physical improvements of the country have infinitely outbalanced the advance in morals." [13]

The over-expansion of internal improvements during this era was climaxed in 1837 by the beginnings of the disastrous depression foreseen by some of the critics of the spirit of speculation growing along with the Jacksonian prosperity.[14] The opponents of Jackson placed the onus of the depression on his destruction of the Bank of the United States,[15] but some of his supporters, in their denunciation of all monopolies, connected their hopes of progress with equal opportunities for everyone. The *Democratic Review* noted that the masses were not prosperous because the great resources and popular institutions of the country were subject to the power of the banks and paper money. With these privileges abolished it was believed that the advantages of science and of republican institutions would permit progress to "be diffused among all. And, as our natural resources are boundless, our nation will exhibit a picture of prosperity which will excite the world's admiration." [16] Orestes A. Brownson, at the time a radical supporter of the laboring class, also saw the real cause of the bad times in the privileges enjoyed by the upper class of society:

13 Timothy Flint, "Obstacles to American Literature," *ibid.,* II (Sept., 1833), 164; see also Flint's, "The Past—The Present—and The Future," *ibid.,* IV (Sept., 1834), 165-175; and *Lectures upon Natural History* (Boston, 1833), p. 341.

14 See: J. H. Perkins, "Dangers of the West," *West. Mess.,* II (Sept., 1836), 92-97; Samuel Osgood, "The Dark Side of Our National Prosperity," *ibid.,* II (Oct., 1836), 171-176; R. W. Emerson, "The Age," *Journals* (1836), IV, 137-138.

15 For a strong defence of commercial expansion, paper money, and the credit system, which attributed progress to their influence, see: H. S. Legaré, "Spirit of the Sub Treasury," *Register of Debates,* 25 Cong., 1 Sess., House of Rep. (Oct. 13, 1837), pp. 1541-1569, and *Writings,* I, 280-321.

See also the anti-Jackson satires: [Charles A. Davis], *Letters of J. Downing ... to His Old Friend, Mr. Dwight, of "The New-York Daily Advertiser"* (New York, 1834), *passim;* [James P. Kennedy], *Quodlibet* (Phil., 1840), *passim.*

16 "Thoughts on the Times," *Dem. Rev.,* VI (Dec., 1839), 462.

The result of the progress of civilization thus far, has not
been to elevate in any conceivable degree, the producing
classes, as such, but merely to increase the number of those the
producing classes must feed. The progress of science, the various implements and new inventions in the arts of production
and for abridging labor, and of which we hear such loud
boasts, have not as yet, so far as I can see, in the least light-
ened the burdens of working men and working women, properly so called; they have merely facilitated the means by which
a poor man, a producer, may pass to the class of the nonpro-
ducers, from one of the ridden to be one of the riders.[17]

Brownson was joined in his realistic appraisal of the causes
of the depression by the famous Unitarian leader, William
Ellery Channing,[18] who in his correspondence for the period
decried the faith of his age in the gospel of material progress.
Channing realized that a utilitarian spirit was inevitable in a
youthful country concentrating its energies and enterprise on a
supply of seemingly inexhaustible natural resources. " In such
an age," he wrote, "the idea of Property may be expected sometimes to take rank of Liberty." [19] Channing, however, was not
discouraged. He believed that the bad times heralded a revolutionary period from which an age more given over to spiritual
and cultural progress would emerge.[20] To his European corre-
spondents who complained that America was in default on its
debts, Channing replied that Europe must be patient because
the United States was the land of progress and the world's hope

17 O. A. Brownson, *Babylon Is Falling* (Boston, 1837), p. 14; see also:
William Leggett, "The Natural System," (From the *Plaindealer*, August
19, 1837), in *A Collection of the Political Writings of...Leggett* (New
York, 1840), II, 330-334; Samuel Young, "Views of...," *New Yorker*, III
(August 26, 1837), 363.

18 See the article by William Charvat, "American Romanticism and the
Depression of 1837," *Science and Society*, II (1937), 67-82.

19 W. E. Channing, *Memoir of William Ellery Channing, with extracts
from his correspondence and manuscripts*, ed. W. H. Channing (Boston and
London, 1848), III, 273.

20 *Ibid.*, III, 128, 275.

for the future.[21] Summing up his own expectations, Channing in a letter to his Unitarian colleague, James Freeman Clarke, wrote in April, 1837:

> Must not some tremendous social revolutions give the race a new start? Can we go on further under the present impulses of the social system? My spirit has groaned so much during what has been called our prosperity that I am not as much troubled as most by our present adversity. By all this I mean to utter no despondence. Our present, low, selfish, mercenary activity is better than stagnation of mind. Our present stage of society is one which must be passed through. A true civilization lies beyond it.[22]

Some observers of the depression were hopeful that a moral awakening might result from the bad times. Emerson, in his journal noted that the panic exposed a bankruptcy of principles as well as of property, and he wrote: " I see a good in such emphatic and universal calamity as the times bring. That they dissatisfy me with society." [23] Ministers like Horace Bushnell and George W. Burnap foresaw a happier future for religion with some of the national faith in purely material and practical values destroyed by the hard times.[24] However, in a lecture delivered before the Mercantile Library Association of Baltimore, Burnap defended trade as " the great means of civilizing and improving mankind," and he also declared that the merchant seeking his profits, and the general leading his army were " equally the instruments in the hands of a higher Power of ministering

21 *Ibid.*, III, 129, 269-270.

22 W. E. Channing to Clarke (April 22, 1837), in J. F. Clarke, *Autobiography, Diary, and Correspondence* (Boston and New York, 1891), p. 119; also p. 114.

23 R. W. Emerson, *Journals* (May 21, 1837), IV, 241; see also an article entitled " National Adversity," *S. Lit. Mess.*, VIII (Dec., 1842), 789-792.

24 Horace Bushnell, *An Oration . . . on the Principles of National Greatness* (New Haven, 1837), p. 4, and *passim*; G. W. Burnap, " Discourse on the Commercial Revulsions of 1837," *Miscellaneous Writings* (Baltimore, 1845), pp. 187-200.

to the gradual improvement of the world." [25] To the many members of his audience who were involved in financial distress and embarrassment, he offered the cheering advice that the depression would be only temporary because " The onward progress of a country like this can never be permanently repressed." [26]

Burnap's lecture was printed in Hunt's *Merchants' Magazine*, the journal of the commercial interests in the East, and during the depression other contributors to this magazine also urged an optimistic attitude toward business prospects. One writer predicted renewed material progress through an increase in the domestic production of the country. Undiscouraged by the over-expansion of the railroads, he maintained: " We, of this republic, are cast upon an age and in a country peculiarly adapted to advance the great object of internal improvement." [27] Daniel D. Barnard, a Whig Congressman, contributed to the first volume of the magazine its leading article, entitled : " Commerce as connected with the Progress of Civilization." In a note of introduction to Barnard's essay, the editor remarked : " No nation on earth is as eminently qualified, as the United States, by geographical position, internal resources, the spirit and indomitable enterprise of the people, for running a proud and successful career . . ." [28]

During these years of bad times the agricultural interests joined the commercial in expressions of optimism.[29] For the

25 Burnap, " The Social Influence of Trade . . . ," Hunt's *Merchants' Mag.*, IV (May, 1841), 415.

26 *Ibid.*, p. 424; see also Burnap's " The Influence of the Use of Machinery, on the Civilization, Comfort, and Morality of Mankind," *Am. Museum*, II (May, 1839), 349-364.

27 J. H. Lanman, " Railroads of the United States," Hunt's *Merchants' Mag.*, III (Oct., 1840), 295; see also his " Domestic Industry," *ibid.*, II (May, 1840), 353-365.

28 *Ibid.*, I (July, 1839), 3.

29 Henry Coleman, " Improvement," *New Eng. Farmer*, XVII (May 29, 1839), 374; "Agricultural Improvement," (From *Farmer's Cabinet*), in *New Eng. Farmer*, XVIII (Jan. 15, 1840), 241; " Improvement in Farms," *Am. Agriculturist*, I (Sept., 1842), 170; Edmund Ruffin, *Cultivator*, n. s. VIII (Feb., 1851), 91, cited in A. L. Demaree, *The American Agricultural Press, 1819-1860* (New York, 1941), p. 233.

farmer who desired to go West a writer, reviewing J. M. Peck's *A Gazeteer of Illinois* for the *North American Review,* advised that

> The operative farmer, who expects to till the soil with his own hands, may be assured, that the value of a year's wages will make him the owner of as much land as he can cultivate, as fertile as he can desire, which every year will be increasing in value; while he can settle his children around him, who will be here, by the way, aids to him in the acquisition of property, and not drawbacks upon his progress.[30]

Henry L. Ellsworth, in his *Report* as Commissioner of Patents in 1843, quoted an anonymous author who called attention to the steady progress of agriculture and urged its pursuit as a refuge from unemployment.[31] With the return of prosperous times the writers on agriculture continued to defend its claims to national attention, for, as one of them remarked in 1852, "Agriculture gives employment to more capital and labor in the United States than all other pursuits combined; and its progress marks, in a peculiar manner, the advancement of the republic in wealth, civilization and power." [32]

An important subject of concern among both the agricultural and the commercial interests during this period was the question of the tariff. For the free trade forces the classic argument was developed in the *Reports* made by Robert J. Walker, the Secretary of the Treasury under Polk, and the chief framer of the low tariff measure of 1846. Defending the philosophy and operation of this act, Walker in his *Report* of 1847 combined a prophecy of America's progressive destiny with a warning that:

---

30 *North Am. Rev.,* LI (July, 1840), 140.

31 H. L. Ellsworth, *Report of the Commissioner of Patents, for the Year 1843,* 28 Cong., 1 Sess., House Doc. no. 177, p. 133.

32 Daniel Lee, "Progress of Agriculture in the United States," *Report of the Commissioner of Patents for the Year 1852, Part II, Agriculture,* 32 Cong., 2 Sess., House Ex. Doc. no. 65, p. 1; see also: D. A. Wells, *The Yearbook of Agriculture* (Phil., 1856), p. 7.

This destiny we can never accomplish if commerce is restricted here, and our industry, instead of seeking for its products and fabrics the markets of more than a thousand millions of people, retires within our home market confined to twenty-one millions of people, and surrenders without an effort the markets and commerce of the world. A liberal commercial policy is essential to the fulfillment of this great destiny . . .[33]

Of American protectionist economists, one of the most influential was Henry C. Carey, son of the prominent publisher Mathew Carey. The younger Carey retired from the publishing firm in 1834 to study and write on economics and social science. His early works were arguments for laissez faire and free trade. In one of the most elaborate of these treatises Carey expressed his confidence that the material improvement of the earth's surface would also make possible a gradually improving moral and intellectual condition among its populations. He therefore urged that more attention be paid to the broader aspects of political economy as a science " which treats of those phenomena of society which arise out of the desire of mankind to maintain and improve their condition." [34]

In 1848, with the United States embarked on a low tariff policy, Carey revealed himself as a convinced protectionist in the publication of his *The Past, the Present, and the Future.* He denounced England's control of the world's markets, and he advocated an isolated, national self-sufficiency as the best means to progress. Full of praise for the American system of small land holdings and diversified ownership, and condoning our expansion and wars as peaceful and defensive, he rejoiced in the American economy of free enterprise in which " Every man determines for himself what he will do with his time and

33 R. J. Walker, *Letter from the Secretary of the Treasury transmitting His Annual Report . . .* (Dec. 9, 1847), 30 Cong., 1 Sess., House Ex. Doc. no. 6, p. 34; see also *Niles' Reg.,* LXXIII (Dec. 18, 1847), 255.

34 H. C. Carey, *Principles of Political Economy* (Phil., 1837-1840), III, 258; II, 465-466.

with his talents . . ." [35] From his observation of the effects on the American temperament of the increasing wealth, population, and generally peaceful course of the country, Carey drew the conclusion that no people have

> so universally confidence in themselves, and in the future. Hope animates all to industry, and stimulates the faculties for the invention of machinery for increasing the productiveness of labour, while prompting all to union for the promotion of works of public usefulness, of charity and benevolence.[36]

Carey also felt that an era of material progress and prosperity, by decreasing class antagonism at home and international antagonism abroad, would result in less need for government interference. To clarify this prediction, he explained:

> Civilization is marked by elevation and equality of physical, moral, intellectual, and political condition, and by the tendency towards union and harmony among men and nations. The highest civilization is marked by the most perfect individuality and the greatest tendency to union, whether of men or of nations.[37]

Carey believed that these conditions of progress were best fulfilled in the United States, and he therefore urged the nation to avoid foreign entanglements and to resist England's influence by a high tariff.[38] A proponent of the economic advantages of self-sustaining communities close to their sources of food, Carey was opposed to the westward migration of the American people. To support his plan, he called for the intensified cultivation of lands nearer home, concluding:

35 Carey, *The Past, the Present, and the Future* (Phil., 1848), pp. 223, and 134-135, 149, 233.

36 *Ibid.*, pp. 256-257.

37 *Ibid.*, p. 416.

38 *Ibid.*, pp. 426, 449, 469; see also: Carey's, *The Harmony of Interests, Agricultural, Manufacturing, and Commercial* (2nd ed.; New York, 1856), pp. 227-229, and *passim*.

The first and great desire of man is that of maintaining and improving his condition. With each step in the progress of concentration, his physical condition would improve, because he would cultivate more fertile lands . . . He would be less governed, better governed, and more cheaply governed: and all because more perfectly governed.[39]

A decade later Carey elaborated on this nationalistic system of material progress in his *Principles of Social Science,* in which he attempted to discover the relationship, under common universal laws, of the physical with the social sciences. In the inorganic world, Carey noted that matter was constant and indestructible, while in the organic world, characterized by change, man was distinguished from the animals by his " capacity for progress." However, he felt that progress was in proportion to the dissimilarity of the parts, and therefore some men tended to barbarism and some to civilization.[40] Proponent of a large population, laboring to develop the resources of the earth, Carey declared: " as man becomes more master of nature, and master of himself, the tendency towards improvement becomes more and more accelerated." [41]

The material progress of the nation was also outlined from time to time in the publication of various statistical summaries.[42] One of the more philosophical of these was Ezra C. Seaman's *Essays on the Progress of Nations,* published in 1846. Seaman, who shared Carey's protectionist views, was a relatively obscure lawyer. He seems to have been born in New York and later to have moved to Michigan. He believed that " man can, has, and does influence, his own destiny " but also that " he is governed by the stern laws of physical necessity, over which he can exer-

39 Carey, *The Past, the Present, and the Future,* pp. 473-474.

40 Carey, *Principles of Social Science* (Phil., 1858-1859), I, ch. 2; III, ch. 46.

41 *Ibid.,* III, p. 312 footnote.

42 See for example: George Tucker, *Progress of the United States* (New York, 1843); R. S. Fisher, *The Progress of the United States* (New York, 1854).

cise no influence whatever." [43] However, because the laws of nature tended to favor the diligent, industrious, and frugal types of persons, Seaman felt that there was an incentive to action within the limits fixed by man's destiny. Although the civilization of the United States was undoubtedly progressive, he warned that it might be declining in certain respects, and he therefore affirmed:

> My object is to analyze the elements and principles of civilization, together with the elements and principles of our social system, habits, customs, institutions, government, and national policy, both foreign and domestic; and to ascertain, as far as practicable, what parts of our system, institutions, customs and policy tend to advance, and what tend to retard us in the progress of civilization.[44]

He attributed man's lack of success in achieving that better life, which he believed was God's design, to his failure to use the resources of his nature and of the material world. Seaman also argued that the progress of industry, labor, and commerce all depended almost entirely on the improvements made in the mechanic arts, and he therefore concluded: " The whole history of civilization, is the history of the triumphs of man over the material world, and over the physical laws of nature." [45]

The material progress of the nation, so gratifying to the hopes of writers like Carey and Seaman, was also an important factor in conditioning the American attitude toward an increasing population. In a youthful land a large population was a necessary asset if the prosperity from the development of the natural resources of the nation was to continue and expand. American economists, beginning with Alexander H. Everett, in his *New Ideas on Population* (1823), accordingly took issue with the classical economists' pessimistic attitude toward the

43 E. C. Seaman, *Essays on the Progress of Nations* (Detroit, 1846), p. 33.

44 *Ibid.*, p. 47.

45 *Ibid.*, p. 59.

growth of population.[46] Henry C. Carey, in the opening chapters of his volume *The Past, the Present, and the Future* (1848), maintained the view that the larger the population the greater the progress of civilization. Deprecating the fear that the world's supply of food would eventually be exhausted, he wrote:

> Population asks only to be let alone, and it will take care of itself. Without its growth the power of union cannot arise, nor the love of harmony and of peace, essential to the promotion of the growth of wealth and to the cultivation of the best soils, without which the return to labour cannot be large. With its growth production increases, and the labourer is enabled to take as his reward a larger proportion, thus producing a tendency to equality of condition.[47]

Francis Bowen, a professor of philosophy at Harvard, in his popular text on political economy, first published in 1856, pointed out that the Malthusian theory of population took a gloomy view of the human race and of God's purposes. Critical of the civilization of the sparsely populated West, Bowen was of the opinion that " Cities and towns are the great agents and tokens of the increase of national opulence, and the progress of civilization."[48] Undismayed by the fear of a large population, he declared:

> In those facts which appear so alarming to the Malthusians, I see only indications of a beneficent arrangement of Providence, by which it is ordained that the barbarous races which

46 For Everett's connection of the idea of progress with a large population, see his *New Ideas on Population* (Boston, 1823), pp. 37-38, 42, 81-82; see also in this regard: G. J. Cady, " The Early American Reaction to the Theory of Malthus," *Journal of Political Economy*, XXXIX (Oct., 1931), 601-632; J. R. Turner, *The Ricardian Rent Theory in Early American Economics* (New York, 1921), p. 112.

47 Carey, *The Past, the Present and the Future*, p. 92, and chs. 1, 2, *passim*; and his *Principles of Social Science*, III, ch. 46.

48 Francis Bowen, *The Principles of Political Economy* (Boston, 1856), pp. 91, 95.

now tenant the earth should waste away and finally disappear, while civilized men are not only to multiply, but to spread, till the farthest corners of the earth shall be given to them for a habitation.[49]

Every ten years the amazing growth of the American people was recorded in a national census. In the published report of the census for 1860 the Superintendent in his Introduction observed:

> No more striking evidence can be given of the rapid advancement of our country in the first element of national progress than that the increase of its inhabitants during the last ten years is greater by more than 1,000,000 of souls than the whole population in 1810, and nearly as great as the entire number of people in 1820.[50]

That this growth was not entirely due to a natural increase of the domestic population, the writer felt, should only enhance the Americans' pride in the knowledge that their land was a favored destination of the European immigrants. " The great increase of population of our country," he declared, " is due to the fact that here, more than anywhere else, every man may find occupation according to his talents, and enjoy resources according to his industry." [51]

The emigrants from Europe were primarily attracted to the United States by the hope of sharing in America's freedom of enterprise and in the national prosperity.[52] Helping to mould a favorable European opinion of the opportunities available for the emigrant in the New World was the vast amount of optimistic literature about the United States—the enthusiastic ac-

49 *Ibid.*, p. 141, and ch. 11 *passim.*

50 United States Census, *Population of the United States in 1860* (Washington, 1864), Introd. by J. C. G. Kennedy, p. v.

51 *Ibid.*, p. xxvi.

52 On the motives of the immigrants, see: M. L. Hansen, *The Atlantic Migration, 1607-1860* (Cambridge, Mass., 1940), ch. 7; and his *The Immigrant in American History* (Cambridge, Mass., 1940), chs. 2, 3, 4.

counts of travellers, the guide books for immigrants, and the letters and diaries of pioneer settlers.[53] Such famous observers of the American scene as Harriet Martineau, George Combe, Alexis de Tocqueville, Charles Lyell, Fredrika Bremer, and Charles Mackay all noted the great material progress being made in the United States.[54] In the large reservoir of land and resources in the West they saw a guarantee of free institutions and of prosperity in the future.[55] Impressed by the apparent absence of poverty and by the material progress in the North, Charles Lyell, the English geologist, wrote in 1845 that " it would be impossible to find five millions in any other region of the globe whose average moral, social, and intellectual condition stands so high." [56] Lyell then went on to declare that these conditions were the characteristics of

> a progressive, as contrasted with a stationary, state of society ; —that they characterize the new colony, where there is abundance of unoccupied land, and a ready outlet to a redundant labouring class. They are not the results of a democratic, as compared with a monarchical or aristocratic constitution, nor

53 However, when some of the immigrants, who settled in the cities along the Atlantic coast, discovered that the bad conditions of Europe were being repeated in America, they rejected the idea of progress. In the case of the Irish in Boston, who did not share the optimism of some of these writers, see: Oscar Handlin, *Boston's Immigrants, 1790-1865* (Cambridge, 1941), ch. 5.

54 Harriet Martineau, *Society in America* (4th ed.; New York, 1837), II, 164, 369; George Combe, *Notes on the United States...* (Phil., 1841), I, 94; II, chs. 9, 11; Charles Lyell, *Travels in North America...* (London, 1845), I, 22-23, 73-75; Alexis de Tocqueville, *Democracy in America* (4th ed.; New York, 1841), I, 4, 270, and ch. 17; II, 33-48, 273, 279; Fredrika Bremer, *The Homes of the New World: Impressions of America* (New York, 1853), I, 190, 243-244, 539-541; II, 424, 530, 650-651; Charles Mackay, *Life and Liberty in America* (New York, 1859), Preface, pp. v-vi, 234, 261, and chs. 33, 34, 36.

55 For a dissenting view see: F. J. Grund, *The Americans, in Their Moral, Social, and Political Relations* (Boston, 1837), ch. 13; and his *Aristocracy in America* (London, 1839), II, 229-233, 250-251, and *passim.*

56 Lyell, *Travels in North America,* I, 74.

the fruits of an absolute equality of religious sects, still less of universal suffrage.[57]

American writers also published descriptive sketches and factual guides, relating the story of the progress of America and especially of the West. The Valley of the Mississippi was pictured as the new Eden to potential settlers from Europe or from the older states in the East. Robert Baird, a Presbyterian minister and author, in his emigrant's guide to the West, wrote in 1832 that for the settler in the Mississippi Valley, "A little effort, comparatively, will enable him to support his family, and live in comfort." [58] A Baptist clergyman, John M. Peck, in his popular *Guide for Emigrants,* declared:

> Probably there is no portion of the globe, of equal extent, that contains as much soil fit for cultivation, and which is capable of sustaining and supplying with all the necessaries and conveniences, and most of the luxuries of life, so dense a population as this great Valley.[59]

Judge James Hall, the founder of the *Western Monthly Magazine* and a leader in Western literary circles, in his well-known books on the West defended its claims for national attention, and he pictured the Mississippi Valley as the future center of American settlement and civilization.[60] Of this region, he wrote in 1848: "It is a new country, imbued with all the characteristics of a vigorous youth, and possessing extraordinary elements of expansion and improvement . . . Everything is grow-

---

57 *Ibid.,* I, 74-75.

58 Robert Baird, *View of the Valley of the Mississippi: or The Emigrant's and Traveller's Guide to the West* (Phil., 1832), p. 45.

59 J. M. Peck, *A Guide for Emigrants* (Boston, 1831), p. 13; see also the 2nd ed., *A New Guide for Emigrants to the West* (Boston, 1837), p. 17; and his *A Gazetteer of Illinois* . . . (2nd ed.; Phil., 1837), p. 328.

60 James Hall, *Letters from the West* . . . (London, 1828), pp. 9, 10, 67, 131, 163-165; *Notes on the Western States* . . . (Phil., 1838), pp. 46, 195-196; *The West: Its Commerce and Navigation* (Cincinnati, 1848), p. 12, and *passim.*

ing and changing, ripening and increasing . . ." [61] Enthusiastic predictions were also made in regard to the future prospects of the newer territories beyond the Mississippi.[62] In one of the many emigrant's guides for this region, a writer in his defence of Western optimism maintained:

> If we boast of our own works of improvement in the West, have we not on every hand a thousand proofs to sustain us? The former wild prairie, now a cultivated farm; the floating palaces upon the bosom of the river which but a little while ago rolled on undisturbed in its lonely beauty; the churches and school-houses that now stand where stood a few summers since the Indian's wigwam; the steam-cars, that fly across the land swifter than the light-footed Chippewa, the arrow from his bow, or the deer that he hunted,—are not all these proofs enough that we are justified in boasting of what we have accomplished? [63]

Some of the immigrant settlers themselves readily joined these writers in their expressions of hopeful enthusiasm over Western progress. In their "American letters" written to friends and relatives in Europe they discussed their own progress in their new homes.[64] An attempt at a balanced judgment was made in a volume first published in Norway in 1844, in which the writer concluded from his experiences in America:

61 Hall, *The West*, p. 28; see also the comments in *With Pen and Pencil on the Frontier in 1851: The Diary and Sketches of Frank Blackwell Mayer*, ed. B. I. Heilbron (Pub. of the Minn. Hist. Soc., Narratives and Documents, vol. I; Saint Paul, 1832), pp. 46, 73, 99.

62 J. B. Newhall, *Sketches of Iowa: or The Emigrant's Guide . . .* (New York, 1841), p. 12; D. S. Curtiss, *Western Portraiture, and Emigrant's Guide . . .* (New York, 1852), Preface and Introd., pp. 297-305; N. H. Parker, *Iowa As It Is in 1856* (Chicago and Phil., 1856), Introd. pp. ix-xv, and 62-70.

63 N. H. Parker, *The Minnesota Handbook for 1856-7* (Boston, 1857), p. 103.

64 For a good general treatment of this literature, see: T. C. Blegen, *Norwegian Migration to America, 1825-1860* (Northfield, Minn., 1931), *passim*.

Everyone, whether with or without money upon arrival, not only has made progress but also is making progress every year, although not in so high a degree as one might expect or desire. There is no evidence of want or poverty or of going backward. Well-paid work is available for all who are able and willing to use their powers and gifts and everyone enjoys the prospect of achieving a comfortable and an independent position.[65]

Another Norwegian writer of the forties, in commenting upon the sense of inferiority among the immigrants, noted that they felt " the need of progress " in order to keep up with the Americans.[66] However, a less enthusiastic Scandinavian author offered the dissenting opinion that for the typical emigrant, "America offers you, in all likelihood: more meat to eat, a greater area of land to cultivate, more exertion, less comfort, a shorter life; now choose." [67]

Divergent views over the chances for advancement in the New World may have depended somewhat on the anticipations and dreams entertained by the individual emigrants. In this regard an English settler in Wisconsin during the forties observed in one of his interesting letters to his father and mother that

some people form expectations of this cuntry before they come which would be impossible to realize in any cuntry in the world for I have thought sometimes that some people imagine that when they get to this country they will find fish

65 J. R. Reiersen, " Norwegians in the West in 1844: A Contemporary Account," tr. and ed. T. C. Blegen, ch. 10 of Reiersen's *Pathfinder for Norwegian Emigrants to the United North American States and Texas* (Christiania, 1844), pp. 110-125, in *The Norwegian-Am. Hist. Assoc. Studies and Records* (Minneapolis, 1926), I, 122.

66 Raeder, "America in the Forties, The Letters of Ole Munch Raeder," tr. and ed. G. J. Malmin, in *The Norwegian-Am. Hist. Assoc. Travel and Descriptive Series* (Minneapolis, 1929), III, 20; also pp. 83-90.

67 A. Budde, " Emigration as Viewed by a Norwegian Student of Agriculture in 1850," tr. by A. S. Bøe, pp. 43-57 in *The Norwegian-Am. Hist. Assoc. Studies and Records* (Northfield, Minn., 1928), III, 56.

in every pool of water, fruit on every tree and that wild fowl will come to them to be shot . . . I must say there is plenty of Fruit and fish and fowl but they are the same in this cuntry as in any other, *no catch no have* . . .[68]

In another letter, written in 1848, when the letters he received from England were filled with news of the Irish famine, this settler replied that although emigration depended on the individual, he himself was happy that he was not in England, perhaps, " to rouse my children at the sound of a bell from their beds and Drag them through the pelting storm of a Dark winters morning to earn a small pittance at a factory . . ." [69]

While the mass of the immigrants to the United States were motivated by their desire to achieve economic prosperity and security, their leaders were often political refugees, fleeing from the despotism of Europe to the democracy of America.[70] With this type of immigration in mind, Ralph Waldo Emerson, descended from a long line of Massachusetts clergymen, declared in 1851 :

> In the distinctions of the genius of the American race it is to be considered that it is not indiscriminate masses of Europe that are shipped hitherward, but the Atlantic is a sieve through which only or chiefly the liberal, adventurous, sensitive, *America-loving* part of each city, clan, family are brought. It is the light complexion, the blue eyes of Europe that come: the black eyes, the black drop, the Europe of Europe, is left.[71]

One of the most famous of these emigrants, and perhaps the one who best identified himself with American life, was Carl Schurz, who came to the United States in 1852, as an aftermath

68 Bottomley, *An English Settler in Pioneer Wisconsin: The Letters of Edwin Bottomley, 1842-1850*, ed. M. M. Quaife, in State Hist. Soc. of Wisconsin *Collections* (Madison, 1918), XXV, 90-91.

69 *Ibid.*, p. 185.

70 See for example: T. S. Baker, *Lenau and Young Germany in America* (Phil., 1897), pp. 46-81.

71 Emerson, *Journals* (1851), VIII, 226.

of the events of 1848. In his famous speech of 1859 in opposition to a Massachusetts law which discriminated against the naturalized citizen, Schurz argued that the greatness of America was derived from its varied races, its youth, and its extension of equality to all. Seeing America " as the great repository of the last hopes of suffering mankind," he went on to declare:

> New ideas are to be carried out by young nations. From time to time, violent, irresistible hurricanes sweep over the world, blowing the most different elements of the human family together, which by mingling reinvigorate each other, and the general confusion then becomes the starting-point of a new period of progress.[72]

Then after admitting that " The Anglo-Saxon spirit has been the locomotive of progress," Schurz warned that the locomotive also required the train of the other races which needed to be pulled along in the path of progress.[73]

Although these European immigrants helped to make possible much of the material expansion in the United States, and although their leaders contributed to the formulation of the American idea of progress, the aliens were also considered by some to represent a menace to American progress. Resented for their economic competition and because their customary Catholicism conflicted with prevailing American Protestantism, their persecution culminated by the decade of the fifties in the establishment of the Native American or Know Nothing party. However, the vogue of the anti-Catholic, anti-immigrant feeling was also widespread before the fifties, its rise being related to the arrival of the immigrants in great numbers especially after 1830.[74]

---

72 Carl Schurz, "True Americanism" (Speech delivered in ... Boston, April 18, 1859), in *Speeches, Correspondence, and Political Papers*, ed. Frederick Bancroft (New York and London, 1913), I, 54, 51.

73 *Ibid.*, I, 57.

74 For a detailed account of the nativist literature during this period, see: R. A. Billington, *The Protestant Crusade, 1800-1860* (New York, 1938), *passim.*

During the thirties popular works were published developing the thesis that Catholicism was incompatible with American free institutions. One of the most notorious of the anti-foreign propagandists was Samuel F. B. Morse, whose early achievements as an artist were later overshadowed by his recognition as the inventor of the telegraph. Under the pseudonym Brutus, Morse in 1834 wrote a series of articles for the *New York Observer* in which he maintained that the Catholic Church was a threat to the future progress of the American nation. Published in the following year as a book, these articles enjoyed a favorable reception and exerted an influence in Protestant circles. Morse believed that while Protestantism rested on the Bible, permitting a diversity of interpretation, and hence religious liberty, Catholicism taught that its dogma was unchangeable and infallible: " Innovation, repeal, reform, or progress can find no admittance into the Papal system, without destroying the fundamental principle on which the whole system rests." [75] Sharing the same views, William C. Brownlee, a strict Calvinist Presbyterian minister, who had migrated from Scotland in his youth, published several strongly anti-Catholic works. From his analysis of American progress, he concluded that it was in a great measure due to the strength of the Protestant religion and to the absence of Popery.[76]

During the 1840's and 1850's, in some of the essays and addresses which treated of the progress of America, serious concern continued to be voiced over the influx of the immigrants and Catholics. Often the hostility to them was justified by the argument that American progress was a result of the peculiar Anglo-Saxon character of the people.[77] Material success and

75 [S. F. B. Morse], *Foreign Conspiracy Against the Liberties of the United States* (New York and Boston, 1835), pp. 137-138, and *passim.*

76 W. C. Brownlee, *Popery An Enemy to Civil and Religious Liberty; and Dangerous to Our Republic* (New York, 1836), pp. 14-15, 120-121, and *passim.*

77 See, for example, the following addresses and articles: G. P. Marsh, *The Goths in New-England* (Middlebury, 1843), *passim* (reviewed by R. W. Haskins, "Human Destiny upon the Theatre of the American Con-

cultural refinement were both attributed to Anglo-Saxon influences. In the words of a writer in an obscure magazine published in 1849: " The Anglo-Saxon race is the wonder of the age; a people vicious and virtuous, they beat down all opposition by success." [78] One of the most vociferous of these opponents of Romanism was William G. Brownlow, itinerant Methodist preacher and Tennessee politician. In 1856, when the nativist American Party entered the presidential campaign, Brownlow, in calling for the election of Fillmore, the party's candidate, expressed the typical Know Nothing view that

> The civilization—the nationality—the institutions, civil and religious—and the mission of the United States, are all eminently American. Mental light and personal independence, constitutional union, national supremacy, submission to law and rules of order, homogeneous population, and instinctive patriotism, are all vital elements of American liberty, nationality, and upward and onward progress.[79]

The attitude expressed in much of the nativist writings was summed up in a volume, variously titled *The Progress and Prospects of America* or *A Voice to America,* which was published anonymously in 1855. Actually it was compiled and probably in part written by Frederick Saunders, the son of an English publisher, who came to America in 1837 to lobby for an international copyright, and who remained to become a writer

tinent," *Knickerbocker*, XXX (Nov., 1847), 399-407); Simeon North, *Anglo-Saxon Literature* (Utica, 1847), *passim;* " The Anglo-Saxon Race," *Am. (Whig) Rev.*, VII (Jan., 1848), 28-46; R. F. Stockton, "Address delivered at Elizabethtown, July 4, 1851," in S. J. Bayard, *A Sketch of the Life of... Stockton* (New York, 1856), pp. 82-83; W. J. Sasnett, " German Philosophy," *Q. Rev. of the Meth. Epis. Church South*, XII (July, 1858), 322-323; Two addresses before the Order of United Americans: Daniel Ullman, *The Course of Empire* (New York, 1856); and Erastus Brooks, *American Citizenship and the Progress of American Civilization* (New York, 1858).

78 G. Vale, "The Citizen of the World," *Independent Beacon* (New York, 1849), I, 645.

79 W. G. Brownlow, *Americanism Contrasted with Foreignism...* (Nashville, 1856), p. 9, and *passim*.

on the *Evening Post* and the librarian of the Astor Library in New York. In this volume of essays the view was expressed that the United States were destined to become " the refuge of the oppressed; the apostle of all truth; the freest, noblest, happiest, purest among the nations; the crown and culmination of human progress . . ." [80] Claiming that the progress of the country depended on the supremacy of its Anglo-Saxon elements, Roman Catholicism was denounced as an influence " opposed to all social and commercial progress." [81] Although no curb against immigration was advocated, it was felt that too much importance and too many privileges were accorded the alien. If the influence of the Catholic immigrants could be reduced to a minimum, the contributors to Saunders' volume were confident that the progress and expansion of the United States would be virtually limitless:

> We are to conquer, but not by the sword. We are to subjugate but not by violence. All nations are to come under the sway of our principles, but never are they to pass under any yoke. All is to be freedom and light, and the eye is to see as clearly as at noonday. Whatever is done, will be done in the direction of a single purpose: and that is the *emancipation of our race.*" [82]

The fear of the Catholic immigrant and the desire to convert some of the materialistic credos of American expansionism into moral and religious values were two important influences upon the philosophy of progress evolved in the Christian missionary movement of the period.[83] Imbued with a belief in America's

80 [F. A. Saunders], *The Progress and Prospects of America* (New York, 1855), p. 25; a 3rd ed. pub. in the same year and identical in content carried the title, *A Voice to America.* . . . See the card catalogues of the N. Y. P. L. and the Lib. of Cong.

81 *Ibid.,* p. 164.

82 *Ibid.,* p. 362; also pp. 306-307.

83 For the background of the missionary movement, see: P. G. Mode, *The Frontier Spirit in American Christianity* (New York, 1923); O. W. Elsbree, *The Rise of the Missionary Spirit in America, 1790-1815* (Williamsport, 1928); C. B. Goodykoontz, *Home Missions and the American Frontier* (Caldwell, 1939), chs. 6-7.

progressive destiny, the clergy leavened the concept of political and material expansionism with their appeals for progress by the spread of Christianity. Christian ministers and educators cited the spread of commerce and the advance of foreign missions to illustrate the progress being made toward achieving the millennium of the final and universal triumph of civilization and the Gospel. Wilbur Fisk, President of Wesleyan University, Connecticut, in an address published in the *Methodist Magazine* for 1831, rejoiced that the expansion of commercial intercourse and of religious enterprise was fast melting down " the strong national barriers that have so long retarded the progress of civilization and improvement . . ." [84] In a sermon of 1843, before the American Board of Commissioners for Foreign Missions, on *Progress, the Law of Missionary Work,* Thomas H. Skinner, a Presbyterian minister of New York City, argued against any retrenchment of missionary work, because since the church had taken up the missionary cause, he believed its condition had been " one of progressive prosperity." Confident that in the future this progress would be still more rapid, he maintained :

> The destined dominion of Christianity is universal. Its first victories, however glorious, will have no glory, comparatively, amid the splendors of those which it is yet to achieve. All nations are to be evangelized . . . And it is the highest degree probable, if not wholly beyond doubt, that the time for effecting this mighty triumph is short.[85]

Many of the clergymen and religious writers seemed to feel that the civilizing effects of foreign commerce were a great aid to the

84 Wilbur Fisk, " The Science of Education," *Meth. Q. Rev.,* XIII (Oct., 1831), 422; see also: Philip Lindsley, " Necessity of Revelation " (1830), *Works* (Phil., 1866), II, 413-436; Joseph Penney, *Claims of the Missionary Enterprise* (New York, 1836), pp. 12-17.

85 T. H. Skinner, *Progress, the Law of Missionary Work* (Boston, 1843), p. 25, and *passim*; see also: W. J. Armstrong, " The Gospel Triumphant " (1846), *Memoir and Sermons,* ed. Rev. Hollis Read (New York, 1853), pp. 383-394.

missionary movement of the church. In an article, typical of others expressing this general sentiment, a contributor to the *Quarterly Christian Spectator* declared:

> Commerce diffuses civilization, and excites everywhere the spirit of improvement. It diffuses civilization, by giving to savage tribes whom it visits, new ideas of comfort, and by thus forming them to habits of industry. It diffuses civilization by diffusing knowledge, and by imparting the improvements of the more intelligent and favored nations to those who are less so. It promotes the spirit of improvement, not only in these ways, but by bringing different nations into contact with each other, and compelling the ignorant to see their ignorance, and the uncivilized to acknowledge their inferiority.[86]

An especially popular field for the enterprise of American missionaries was the Sandwich Islands in the Pacific. In the pages of the *Missionary Herald* reports were printed of the progress being made in improving the dress, housing, and health of the natives. One correspondent felt able to write in 1854 that "Nakedness seldom appears in the streets, . . . and a public sentiment against going without clothes is evidently gaining ground. There is progress also in the comforts of home." [87] Although the expansion of commerce and the establishment of civilization were thus often considered the necessary bases for the flowering of Christianity, there was also the contrary opinion expressed by the writer who concluded:

86 " Encouragements to Effort, for the Speedy Conversion of the World," *Q. Christian Spec.*, VII (March, 1835), 4; see also: " The Aspect of the Age with Respect to Foreign Missions," *Bib. Rep.*, V (Oct., 1833), 449, 451 ff.; S. W. Coggeshall, " The Progress and Final Triumph of the Gospel," *Meth. Q. Rev.*, XX (Jan., 1838), 65-80; W. J. Sasnett, " The Relation of the Church to Missions," *Q. Rev. Meth. Epis., Church South,* VI (April, 1852), 250-251; J. E. Edwards, " Christ in History," *ibid.*, VIII (April, 1854), 263-264.

87 " Sandwich Islands:—Letter from the Evangelical Association," *Missionary Herald*, L (Nov., 1854), 339; see also: *ibid.*, XXXIV, 259; XXXV, 146; XXXVII, 151; XLII, 149; XLIII, 96; XLVI, 399; LVI, 293; (1838-1860).

Christian Missions are the grand reliance for the elevation of mankind in prosperity, in purity, and in happiness. Civilization has no boon to offer mankind which Christianity will not carry. Apart from Christianity civilization can proffer nothing of substantial good. Civilization has no inherent law of propagation whereby to diffuse its blessings; and its highest benefits often entail a curse.[88]

Added to the area of foreign missions was the vast field for home missionary work in the West. Developing the famous saying, " Westward the course of empire takes its way," a succession of Western clergymen and authors expressed their faith in the future progress of the frontier area. One of the most literary of these missionaries to the West was Timothy Flint, a former Congregational clergyman in New England, and a graduate of Harvard. From 1827 to 1830 the pages of Flint's *Western Monthly Review* contained articles devoted to detailing the progressive achievements and characteristics of the people of the Ohio Valley.[89] Looking further into the future a Utopian article in his magazine pictured life in an Oregon town at the mouth of the Columbia River in the year 1900. The writer predicted that balloons would be as common as ships, transporting passengers and mail to China, where a thousand Christian churches would flourish. At home the populace would be kept healthy by 5,000 advertised patent medicines, so that the mythical writer of the year 1900 might rejoice:

We now number the inhabitants west of our Rocky mountains by millions, the half being immigrants from China,

88 J. P. Thompson, " Christian Missions Necessary to a True Civilization," *Bibliotheca Sacra*, XIV (Oct., 1857), 847, and *passim*; see also: Greene, " The Promotion of Intellectual Cultivation and the Arts of Civilized Life in Connection with Christian Missions," *Missionary Herald*, XXXVIII (Nov., 1842), 439; " Evangelism," *Q. Rev. Meth. Epis. Church South*, XIV (Jan. and April, 1860), 56-69; 237-240.

89 " Progress of the West," *West. Monthly Rev.*, I (May, 1827), 25-27; " National Character of the Western People," *ibid.*, I (July, 1827), 133-139; " Present Population and Future Prospects of the Western Country," *ibid.*, I (Oct., 1827), 329-334; S. J. B., " Outline of an Essay on the Future Progress of Ohio," *ibid.*, III (Dec., 1829), 331-335.

Japan, and the islands of the sea. We have towns, villages, colleges, libraries, hospitals, charities, churches, legislative halls, orators, poets, and men of science. We have orchards, vineyards, and manufactories in the country. We see on every side, abundance, peace, contentment, in short every thing that can cheer, sustain, and elevate the human condition; every thing for improvement and enjoyment in this, our brief sojourn, and every thing that can gladden the heart, in better hopes beyond the grave.[90]

Like Flint, heeding the call of the West, Lyman Beecher, an established Presbyterian minister in Boston, in 1832 accepted the presidency of Lane Theological Seminary at Cincinnati. Returning East a few years later in quest of funds for his school, Beecher delivered his famous speech, *A Plea for the West,* in several cities along the Atlantic Coast. In his address he announced that predictions of a millennium for the United States were no longer chimerical:

There is not a nation upon earth which, in fifty years, can by all possible reformation place itself in circumstances so favorable as our own for the free, unembarrassed applications of physical effort and pecuniary and moral power to evangelize the world.[91]

Beecher also believed it to be " equally plain that the religious and political destiny of our nation is to be decided in the West," and he made a strong plea for saving the section from the perils of its own prosperity and from the influx of Catholic immigrants. To counteract these dangers, he recommended that more support be given by the Eastern churches for the schools and missions of the West.[92]

An equally famous New England clergyman, Horace Bushnell, took a somewhat different view of the West. Bushnell was

90 " National Independence," *ibid.,* I (Sept., 1827), 256-257, and *passim.*

91 Lyman Beecher, *A Plea for the West* (Cincinnati and New York, 1835), p. 10.

92 *Ibid.,* pp. 11-14, 30-56, 188-190, and *passim*; see also: J. H. Perkins, " Prospects of the West," *West. Mess.,* I (Nov., 1835), 318-323.

not unenthusastic over the material progress of the nation,[93] but he viewed the Mexican War, Negro slavery, and western migration with distrust. Preaching a discourse for home missions in 1847, he affirmed:

> *emigration, or a new settlement of the social state, involves a tendency to social decline.* There must, in every such case, be a relapse towards barbarism, more or less protracted, more or less complete. Commonly, nothing but extraordinary efforts in behalf of education and religion, will suffice to prevent a fatal lapse of social order.[94]

To redeem the West from barbarism and the peril of Catholic superstition, Bushnell urged a return to peace, the abolition of slavery, the promotion of railroads and telegraphs, and most especially the education of a great body of home missionaries.[95]

Dedicated to the cause of promoting the Gospel at home in the United States were the Congregational Monthly, *The Home Missionary,* and the American Home Missionary Society. In a discourse in behalf of the Society, Laurens P. Hickok, a professor of theology and a New School Presbyterian clergyman, called attention to the dangers of American material prosperity. He believed it was obvious that

> Never was such progress made, in the attainment of all that ministers to the material greatness of a nation, among any other people as in our country. Territory, population, industry, enterprise, wealth, power, all have accumulated beyond all former precedent. However, other nations have been endangered by rapid growth, we more.[96]

Declaring that the United States were essentially " a *Protestant*

93 Horace Bushnell, *A Discourse on the Moral Uses of the Sea* (New York, 1845), pp. 3-6, 10-12; and his *The Day of Roads* (Hartford, 1846), pp. 3, 12, 29-32.

94 Bushnell, *Barbarism the First Danger* (New York, 1847), pp. 4-5.

95 *Ibid.*, pp. 27-28, and *passim*; see also Bushnell's *Society and Religion* (San Francisco, 1856), pp. 6-11, 20-23.

96 L. P. Hickok, *A Nation Saved from Its Prosperity Only by The Gospel* (New York, 1853), p. 8, and *passim*.

and commercial people " [97] and that popular progress was " the law of American life," contributors to *The Home Missionary* went on to urge that the dangers of materialism and of Catholicism be overcome by " the school teacher, the tract distributor and home missionary . . ." [98]

This connection between Protestantism and progress was particularly developed in two discourses, entitled *The Railroad Jubilee,* delivered in Boston in 1851 by Thomas Starr King, a Unitarian clergyman, lecturer and writer. Popular in the East, and a rival of Henry Ward Beecher in his ability to attract large audiences, King nevertheless decided in 1860 to move to California. In the first of his two discourses delivered in Boston, he declared his belief that the world was entering an *"Industrial Age,"* in which " Worship is the only word that is deep enough to express the Anglo-Saxon relation to the mechanic powers and arts." [99] King also dwelt on the Providential mission of the railroads, binding the nation together, and he declared that God

> uses them to quicken the activity of men; to send energy and vitality where before were silence and barrenness; to multiply cities and villages, studded with churches, dotted with schools, and filled with happy homes and budding souls; to increase wealth which shall partially be devoted to his service and kingdom, and all along their banks to make the wilderness blossom as the rose.[100]

In the second of his two discourses King, in attributing much of the material progress made by the world to the influence of the Protestant Reformation, accused the Catholic Church of slighting " the importance and worth of the material side of civilization." [101] However, he also admitted that there was some truth in the Catholic charge that social and individual betterment were being neglected for material progress,[102] and he

97 " The Auspicious Era," *Home Missionary,* XXIII (March, 1851), 251.

98 " Popular Progress — Whither Are We Tending? " (*New York Recorder*), quoted in *Home Missionary,* XIX (Sept., 1846), 116-118.

99 T. S. King, *The Railroad Jubilee* (Boston, 1851), pp. 9-11.

100 *Ibid.,* p. 17.

101 *Ibid.,* p. 35.

102 *Ibid.,* pp. 30-38.

therefore warned: "There will never be a railroad to heaven
. . . Above the region of physical civilization is the domain
which the gospel rules . . ."[103]

With Western writers a particularly popular notion was the
concept of progress evolved from a union of democracy and
Christianity under the banner of "Christian Republicanism."
James D. Nourse, a Kentucky newspaper editor and author of
a volume on the philosophy of history, prefaced another work,
his *Remarks on the Past and its Legacies to American Society*
(1847), with the explanation that,

> In the prosecution of my favorite study of history, I have
> thought that I discerned two great events, towards which the
> movements of society and the arrangements of Providence
> have converged, in the ancient and modern worlds respec-
> tively:—the introduction of Christianity and the birth of the
> American Democracy . . .
>
> In the following pages I have attempted to trace the prog-
> ress of society down to that remarkable epoch, when the best
> products of the Christian civilization were transplanted to the
> virgin soil of America.[104]

Although he felt man was unfortunately in a fallen state,
Nourse expected Providence to raise him from the ruins
through the agency of the "Anglo-Norman race" and through
the establishment of a new seat of civilization in the Mississippi
Valley.[105]

---

103 *Ibid.*, p. 48; see also for some varied interpretations, during the 1850's,
of America's material and religious mission: T. S. King, "Patriotism"
(1851), *Patriotism and Other Papers* (Boston, 1864), pp. 29-54; P. F. Jones,
National Prosperity... (Utica, 1852), p. 10; Charles Wadsworth, *America's
Mission* (Phil., [1855]), *passim*; G. B. Taylor, "Society's Future," *Christian
Rev.*, XXII (July, 1857), 356-380; J. W. Scott, "Westward Movement of
the Center of Population, and of Industrial Power in North America,"
Hunt's *Merchants' Mag.*, XXXVI (Feb., 1857), 202.

104 J. D. Nourse, *Remarks on the Past and Its Legacies to American
Society* (Louisville, 1847), Preface, p. v.

105 *Ibid.*, pp. 32-34, 117-118, 175, 222-223; see also: J. F. Tuttle, "Three
Progressive Experiments in Human Government," *Bib. Repos.*, 3rd ser.,
I (Jan., 1845), 1-35.

Nourse's devotion to Christian Republicanism found further support in the writings of other Westerners who were not, however, such outspoken advocates of the manifest destiny of the English race. William D. Gallagher, the son of an Irish refugee, in his contributions to many Western periodicals, expressed a strong enthusiasm over Western prospects. Gallagher regarded Christianity as the decisive element of that modern civilization, the full fruits of which he saw gathered in his own Northwest area. In his book *Facts and Conditions of Progress in the North-West* (1850), he wrote:

> The new and glorious Experiment in Humanity, then, commences here, on the broad fields of the North West, which I have depicted—under Christianity, with that great agent, the Representative Principle, in the abiding faith that Progress is the order of man through the design of God . . . It does not lean for support upon the crutch of " Manifest Destiny," nor yet trust to light in the hands of that great but unsafe guide, about which the world has recently heard so much, the "Anglo-Saxon." [106]

One of the most eloquent apostles of Western progress was Elias L. Magoon, a New England-born Baptist minister, who held pastorates in Virginia and in Cincinnati before returning to the East. In 1849 Magoon published his *Republican Christianity*, a volume imbued with the spirit of the progressiveness of the age and with a confidence that God's purposes designed man " to fight the battles of the future now . . ." [107] To Hunt's *Merchants' Magazine*, he contributed in 1852 an article on " The Divine Use of Commerce " in which he called attention to " The celestial guide which rose on the view of the wise men in the east, led them westwards toward the sea, and has ever since been the polestar of human progress." [108] Then later in the decade he wrote an elaborate survey of civilization entitled,

106 W. D. Gallagher, *Facts and Conditions of Progress in the North-West* (Cincinnati, 1850), pp. 38-39, and *passim*.

107 E. L. Magoon, *Republican Christianity* (Boston, 1849), p. 288, and *passim*.

108 Magoon, " The Divine Use of Commerce," Hunt's *Merchants' Mag.*, XXVII (July, 1852), 35.

Westward Empire: or The Great Drama of Human Progress.
In this work Magoon gave full development to his thesis that
civilization is always moving west, and he also affirmed:

> Without an intelligent faith in the divine purpose to incite
> and control perpetual progress toward the perfection of man-
> kind, history is an insoluble enigma, a huge pile of detached
> fragments, and the great drama of humanity must forever re-
> main devoid of all proper results.[109]

The resources for the material expansion of the nation
seemed to be virtually limitless. However, the ways and means
of their development provoked controversies in which the idea
of progress was invoked on all sides in support of the various
arguments. Although the territory beyond the Mississippi had
only been touched upon in the years before the Civil War, there
was a widespread feeling that the West was to be the grand
theatre of future progress. For the country as a whole, despite
the periods of economic depression, the years from 1815 to 1860
were generally prosperous ones. In keeping with this prosperity
and with the growth of its natural resources, the population
tripled. To both the aliens and the native Americans these
abundant resources appeared to furnish a reason for believing
in the idea of progress. Although the immigrants received a
mixed reception in the United States, their numbers grew steadily during these decades. Also supported by the material progress of the nation, many of the Protestant clergy gave it their
enthusiastic blessing. At the same time, in answer to the barbarism of the frontier and to the popularity of Catholicism among
the immigrants, the Protestant churches supported the home
missionary movement as the way to future progress. Therefore,
with many diverse groups the material expansion and prosperity
of the country engendered an optimistic faith in progress.

109 Magoon, *Westward Empire* (New York, 1856), p. ix, and *passim*;
see also his "Westward Science in America," Hunt's *Merchants' Mag.*,
XXXV (Oct., 1856), 415-427.

CHAPTER IV

THE ADVANCING FAITH IN SCIENCE

THE material expansion of the nation was dramatically emphasized by the stream of scientific inventions which accompanied the industrial revolution in America during the decades from 1815 to 1860. Although both theoretical and applied science attracted attention in this period, the older interest of the eighteenth-century enlightenment in pure science was supplanted by the increasing domination during the nineteenth century of utilitarian science. To the generality of the American people it was the practical application of the powers of science that furnished the most obvious evidence of progress. Succeeding chapters will indicate some of the effects which this technological advance exerted on the concept of progress entertained by different groups in American life. However, it may be useful to examine first the notion of technological progress held by some of the early advocates of the cause of science and progress.

In the United States an illustration of this trend away from pure science was shown in the importance attributed to Francis Bacon and his inductive system. It was therefore appropriate that the "Account of Lord Bacon's Novum Organon Scientiarum . . .," written originally for the *British Library of Useful Knowledge* by Henry Brougham, the English utilitarian, should be published in the *American Library of Useful Knowledge* for 1831.[1] While Bacon's works were probably more reverenced than read in America, still the declarations of faith in technological improvement often began by paying homage to him as the father of all modern scientific progress. And although allusions to his inductive system pervade the literature of the idea of progress, Samuel Tyler, a Maryland lawyer, in *A Discourse of the Baconian Philosophy* (1844), provided a systematic ac-

1 *American Library of Useful Knowledge*, pub. by . . . the Boston Society for the Diffusion of Useful Knowledge (vol. I, Boston, 1831), pp. 207-266.

For Bacon's influence as an exponent of utilitarian science, see: R. F. James, *Ancients and Moderns* (St. Louis, 1936), *passim*.

count which best illustrates this debt to Bacon. Believing " that Bacon has done more to advance the progress of the human mind than any inspired man known to history," Tyler attributed the power of England and the advances already made by science to his inductive system, which, he declared,

> possesses within itself the principle of perpetual progress; for, it is not like the ancient philosophies, confined to speculative principles . . . but it is commensurate with the phenomena of the universe . . . It is therefore not like the ancient philosophies, a means of culture and progress for one people or epoch only . . . The nations which have been most under its influence have risen superior to all the rest of the human family, and have advanced progressively, and their speed is daily accelerated to a degree of intellectual development and moral superiority, and political power, which seem to indicate that it is destined to form the type of the civilization of a greater part, if not of all the human race.[2]

As Bacon was the intellectual father of science, so the discoveries of printing and of steam power were considered the sires of that long stream of inventions which was to give reality to the American faith in progress. In the words of the popular *Scientific American*:

> We may justly attribute the great social advancement made in the world since the art of printing was discovered, to the art of printing itself.[3]
>
> The art of printing stereotypes the discoveries of the present generation, and the next has but to wear the gems . . . It is thus that the world progresses in invention, communities are benefitted and civilization advances.[4]

2 Samuel Tyler, *A Discourse of the Baconian Philosophy* (1st pub. 1844; 3rd ed.; Wash. and Baltimore, 1877), pp. 92-93; see also: C. F. McCay, *Inaugural Address* (Columbia, S. C., 1855), p. 6, and *passim*.

3 *Sci. Am.*, IV (Nov. 18, 1848), 69.

4 *Ibid.*, VI (Aug. 30, 1851), 397; see also: S. W. Royston, *An Address on the Rise and Progress of Society* . . . (New Haven, 1844), pp. 8-9.

However, the scientific achievement which made possible the industrial revolution was the application of steam to manufacturing and transportation. " This simple, but great machine," the *Scientific American* again observed, as the American army swept through Mexico, " has revolutionized the age, and has done more to exalt humanity and benefit the human race, than all the victories of Caesar or the triumphs of Napoleon." [5] " The steam engine attended by four men, can accomplish as much as five hundred horses. Wonderful indeed has been the progress of useful science during the last fifty years!" [6] Daniel Webster, statesman of the rising industrial order, in 1847 at the occasion of the opening of a new railroad, spoke of the " era of steam," and declared:

> That is the invention which distinguishes this age . . .
> Let me say, fellow-citizens, that in the history of human inventions there is hardly one so well calculated as that of railroads to equalize the condition of men . . .
> This great improvement comes to your farther assistance. It will give you new facilities, connect you more readily with other portions of the State, and most assuredly, according to all experience, create new objects for the application of your enterprise and your labor. You do not yet begin to feel the benefits which it will confer on you.[7]

The printing press and the steam engine owed their origin to the genius of an earlier age. In Europe during the period from 1815 to 1860 the industrial revolution entered its main phase, and significant progress was made in both pure and applied science. With the application of steam power to transportation and manufacturing, railroads were built and the iron and

5 *Sci. Am.*, II (June 19, 1847), 309.

6 *Ibid.*, II (June 26, 1847), 317.

7 Daniel Webster, " Opening of the Northern Railroad to Grafton, N. H." (1847), *Writings and Speeches*, IV, 108-111; see also: Joseph Blunt, " Lecture on Coal, before the American Institute," *Speeches*, pp. 257, 273; J. L. Tellkampf, "American Atlantic Mail Steamers," Hunt's *Merchants' Mag.*, XV (July, 1846), 51.

textile industries greatly expanded. The English scientist, Michael Faraday, enlarging on the work of some of his distinguished predecessors, made possible the increased utilization of electricity in the commercial field. In agriculture the importance of chemistry was made apparent by the work of the German, Justus von Liebig. Underlying this progress in physical science was the idea of the conservation of energy with its corollaries of the indestructibility of matter and of energy. Of even greater importance to the theory of progress was the work in the natural sciences which culminated in the theory of evolution. Before Charles Darwin, Lamarck, Lyell and others made significant contributions to the doctrine of descent and to the problem of the antiquity of man.[8]

In America during this period great achievements were also recorded in practical science, the equal of such earlier triumphs of ingenuity as Fulton's steamboat and Whitney's cotton gin. Joseph Henry, the physicist and first secretary of the Smithsonian Institute, shared with Faraday the discovery of the principle of the dynamo, and also paved the way for Morse's completion of the telegraph. The transformation of agriculture was furthered by the McCormick reaper. Elias Howe and other Americans joined in making the sewing machine an efficient household necessity. The pain of surgery was relieved by the use of ether and chloroform as anaesthetics. Mass education and self-culture were spread by the improved rotary presses which made possible the cheap newspapers of the forties and fifties.

However, among the various inventions of the period attributable to American skill, the telegraph was the one most widely discussed as the harbinger of future progress. When Morse completed his first successful line, the *Report of the Commissioner of Patents,* in noting the significance of the event, stated:

Among the most brilliant discoveries of the age, the electromagnetic telegraph deserves a conspicuous place. Destined as

8 W. T. S. Sedgwick and H. W. Tyler (rev. by Tyler and R. P. Bigelow), *A Short History of Science* (New York, 1939), chs. 16, 17, and Appendix A, pp. 396, 402.

it is to change as well as hasten transmission of intelligence, and so essentially to affect the welfare of society, all that concerns its further developments will be hailed with joy.[9]

Morse's accomplishment was also hailed as a great step in progress by the leading Southern magazines of the day.[10] Impressed by his achievement, a writer in *DeBow's Review* for 1846 commented:

> To him who has watched the progress of discovery and invention in the different countries of Europe and America, scarcely anything now will appear to be impossible . . . We cease to limit the powers of the mind. We cease to draw the demarcation between the possible and the impossible . . . We limit not what man may achieve, nor determine what is beyond his reach. For us it is sufficient to contemplate what man has done.[11]

Morse, himself, in a letter to a friend written in 1855, predicted in optimistic fashion that one of the effects of the telegraph would be to " bind man to his fellowman in such bonds of amity as to put an end to war." [12]

When the principle of the telegraph was extended across the ocean in 1858 by Cyrus Field's Atlantic cable, Horace Greeley, aware of the significance of the event for newspaper circulations, declared in the prospectus of his *New York Weekly Tribune* that " The successful laying of the trans-Atlantic Telegraphic Cable marks a new era in the history of Human Progress." [13] One of the editors of the *Knickerbocker Magazine* ex-

9 *Report of the Commissioner of Patents . . . 1844,* 28 Cong., 2 Sess., Senate Doc. no. 75, p. 5.

10 See for example: *S. Q. Rev.,* XIII (April, 1848), 373; *S. Lit. Mess.,* XIV (June, 1848), 374-376.

11 " Morse's Electro-Magnetic Telegraph," *DeBow's Rev.,* I (Feb., 1846), 133.

12 Morse to Norvin Green (July, 1855), in Morse's *Letters and Journals,* II, 345.

13 *New York Weekly Tribune,* XVII (Sept. 18, 1858), 4.

pressed the opinion that the cable showed how the pen and press were to become mightier than blood or bullets.[14] In Virginia, George Fitzhugh, a conservative writer on sociological subjects, was intoxicated with enthusiasm by the news of the cable. With a fine disregard for his earlier pessimism in regard to the workings of capitalism, he asked if this achievement meant just more degradation for the masses and replied:

> No! (the thought flashes across my mind.) 'Till the other day these improvements and these inventions had that effect. But within a few years past the rich fruits of modern progress have descended to the masses . . .[15]

The printing press, the steam engine, and the telegraph were grandiose accomplishments, of much practical benefit and the inspiration of eloquent tributes. However, as Walt Whitman observed, " Even in the lesser conveniences of life what a wonderful progress has been made within a very few years." Impressed by the invention of matches, Whitman on the eve of the depression of 1857 urged his readers to

> Think of the numberless contrivances and inventions for our comfort and luxury which the last half dozen years have brought forth—of our baths and ice houses and ice coolers—of our fly traps and mosquito nets—of house bells and marble mantels and sliding tables—of patent ink-stands and baby jumpers—of serving machines and street-sweeping machines—in a word give but a passing glance at the fat volumes of Patent Office Reports and bless your star that fate has cast your lot in the year of our Lord 1857.[16]

14 J. O. Noyes, " The Atlantic Telegraph," *Knickerbocker*, LII (Oct., 1858), 396.

15 George Fitzhugh, " The Atlantic Telegraph, Ancient Art, and Modern Progress," *De Bow's Rev.*, XXV (Nov., 1858), 508; see also: C. F. Briggs and A. Maverick, *The Story of the Telegraph and a History of the Great Atlantic Cable* (New York, 1858), pp. 11-22.

16 Walt Whitman, " Porcelain Manufactories," *Brooklyn Daily Times* (Aug. 3, 1857), quoted in *I Sit and Look Out: Editorials from the Brooklyn Daily Times*, selected and ed. Emory Holloway and Vernolian Schwarz (New York, 1932), p. 133; see also: Newton Arvin, *Whitman* (New York, 1938), pp. 210-213.

This march of invention heralded the growing industrialization of the American economy, but in pre-Civil War America, agriculture was still the predominant industry, and therefore the progress of science was also considered in regard to the needs of the farmer.[17] As a writer in a popular agricultural journal observed in 1834, "When Science speeds the Plough, Wealth and Honour are awarded to the Ploughman."[18] This same idea was expressed by Thomas G. Fessenden, the famous editor of the *New England Farmer*. In the Prospectus to the first issue of his magazine, Fessenden noted the great improvements and discoveries being made in agriculture, and he declared that they were "of paramount importance, not only to the practical farmer, but to the whole community," because: "Every human being has an interest in that art which is the foundation of all other arts, and the basis of all civilization."[19] Henry Ellsworth, first Commissioner of Patents, and a lifelong agriculturist, also pioneered in calling attention to the effects which machinery would exert on the future of agriculture and on the general progress of society. In his *Report* for 1837 he noted that the developments in agricultural machinery made it "scarcely possible to conjecture to what extent the labor of the agriculturist may be diminished, and the products of the country increased, by these improvements."[20] In addresses made be-

17 For a penetrating analysis of the role of the idea of progress in American agricultural thought, see the article by P. H. Johnstone, "Old Ideals Versus New Ideas in Farm Life," *Farmers in a Changing World: The Yearbook of Agriculture 1940* ([Washington, 1940]), pp. 111-170.

18 *New Eng. Farmer*, XII (July 9, 1834), 422; see also: "The Science of Agriculture," *New York Weekly Tribune*, II (May 6, 1843), 5; and the articles in the *Am. Agriculturist*, III (Feb., 1844), 52-53; IV (Nov., 1845), 347.

19 T. G. Fessenden, "Prospectus," *New Eng. Farmer*, I (Aug. 3, 1822), 1; see also: Isaac Goodwin, "An Address...the Worcester Agricultural Society," *ibid.*, III (Dec. 10, 1824), 153-155.

20 *Report of the Commissioner of Patents...1837*, 25 Cong., 2 Sess., Senate Doc. no. 105, p. 4; see also the *Reports* for 1838, 1842, and 1843, in House Docs. nos. 80, 109, 177 (25 Cong., 3 Sess.; 27 Cong., 3 Sess.; 28 Cong., 1 Sess.), pp. 58; 6-8; 133.

fore agricultural societies, speakers advocated the application of science and invention to agriculture as a means of progress.[21] Toward the close of our period, in 1856, Samuel Shute, a clergyman and college professor, in delivering an address on *The Progress of the Race* to a Y. M. C. A. group in Pennsylvania, gave a typical expression of this faith in scientific agriculture. Praising the application of science to the improvement of everyday life as a characteristic of modern times, he declared:

> And so far as *labor-saving machines* are concerned, what with the mowers and reapers, the cornshellers and cradlers; the grain drillers and hay rakes; the beehives and butter churns—we could make a list in favor of modern agriculture, as long as the catalogue of the ships which went to Troy.[22]

The first attempt to discuss these achievements and prospects of science and invention in a systematic way was made by Jacob Bigelow, a professor of medicine at Harvard, who in 1829 published his *Elements of Technology*.[23] In the Introduction to his book Bigelow stressed the application of science to the arts of life as the especial characteristic of modern times and as the means of saving time, labor, and expense. Science, Bigelow felt, had made the weakest man equal to the strongest:

> We accomplish what the ancients only dreamt of in their fables; we ascend above the clouds, and penetrate into the abysses of the ocean . . .
> But it is not the contrast with antiquity alone, that enables us to appreciate the benefits which modern arts confer. In the

21 Henry Colman, "An Address..." *New Eng. Farmer*, XII (Jan. 29, 1834), 228; G. P. Marsh, *Address before the Agricultural Society of Rutland County* (Rutland, 1848), p. 24, and *passim*; G. R. Russell, *An Address before the Norfolk Agricultural Society...1851* (Boston, 1851), pp. 4, 23, and *passim*.

22 S. M. Shute, *The Progress of the Race* (Baltimore, 1856), p. 9.

23 For some early academic orations on the progress of science, see: Jacob Bigelow, *Inaugural Address* (Boston, 1817), pp. 12-13, and *passim*; Denison Olmsted, *An Oration on the Progressive State of the Present Age* (New Haven, 1827), *passim*; T. S. Grimké, *An Address on the Character and Objects of Science* (Charleston, 1827), *passim*.

present inventive age, even short periods of time bring with them momentous changes. Every generation takes up the march of improvement, where its predecessors had stopped, and every generation leaves to its successors an increased circle of advantages and acquisitions.[24]

Bigelow designed his book for the college classroom. Less practical in his Utopian conception of science, J. A. Etzler, a native of Germany, first published his book, *The Paradise Within the Reach of All Men, Without Labour, by Powers of Nature and Machinery* in the United States because its physical resources and republican form of government seemed more favorable to the reception of novel ideas. Etzler's plan was a proposition to apply to the use of man those hitherto undeveloped powers of nature derived from the wind, the tide, and the heat of the sun. While he felt that the past progress of the world had been slow and reformers often condemned to scorn, he was confident that the present age would prove more susceptible of progress and advance. In contrast with those who tied their Utopia to a primitive form of existence, Etzler offered a plan for transforming the world through scientific training and the use of machinery.[25] Etzler even tried to attract the attention of President Jackson and Congress to his scheme,[26] and in 1841 published a sequel, in which he elaborated in more detail his scientific paradise. In this latter work, as an added appeal for the adoption of his ideas, Etzler urged:

> Let my system be known to those poor struggling masses, who seek amelioration of their condition in some change of mere governmental or social forms and leaders—and what will become of their revolutionary ideas and desires?

24 Jacob Bigelow, *Elements of Technology* (Boston, 1829), pp. 4-5.

25 J. A. Etzler, *The Paradise Within the Reach of All Men* ... (London, 1836), pp. 1-4, 56-59, 121, 166 ff.; the Am. ed. was pub. in Pittsburgh in 1833; see also the review by Henry Thoreau, "Paradise (to be) Regained," *Dem. Rev.*, XIII (Nov., 1843), 460-462.

26 Etzler, *op. cit.*, pp. 207-215.

It is for you, you leaders, real or imaginary ones, of revolutions, to think of that now—and you will see a much more glorious field for your activity before you, than any change of governments and social forms.

It is peace, wealth, happiness, not at the expense of your fellow creatures, but by creative means applied to the, as yet, unused rich resources of nature, you have to look for, and which is here plainly before you.[27]

Etzler's books connected progress and technology in a grand Utopian program for the future. Less visionary in its predictions, and at the same time giving some indication of the prevalence of the concept, was the idea of scientific progress set forth in the periodical literature and in the published speeches of the decades before the Civil War. While a host of minor statesmen of varying political convictions, and from both the North and the South, made speeches exhibiting their faith in the progressive influence of practical science,[28] the outstanding address on the subject was the work of Joel R. Poinsett, a South Carolinian statesman and diplomat. Poinsett had been influential in the establishment at Washington of the National Institute for the Promotion of Science with the money left the United States by James Smithson,[29] and it was fitting, therefore, that he be selected to deliver a discourse on the occasion of the Institute's first anniversary. He considered the Institution especially valuable because it provided an illustration of the increasing con-

27 Etzler, *The New World: or, Mechanical System* (Phil., 1841), p. 67.

28 H. L. Pinckney, *The Spirit of the Age* (Raleigh, 1836), pp. 9-12; J. A. Dix, *Address...before the Alpha Phi Delta* (Albany, 1839), p. 7, and *passim*; Samuel Young, *Lecture on Civilization* (Saratoga Springs, 1841), pp. 8-11; B. F. Porter, *The Past and the Present* (Tuscaloosa, 1845), pp. 28-29; F. W. Lincoln, *An Address... 1845* (Boston, 1845), pp. 7-18; Levi Woodbury, "On the Promotion and Uses of Science" (1845), *Writings*, III, 24-51; and his "On the Promotion of Agriculture, Manufactures and Commerce" (1849), *ibid.*, III, 96-117; G. S. Boutwell, *Address delivered at Concord...* (Boston, 1850), pp. 26-28, and *passim*.

29 J. F. Rippy, *Joel R. Poinsett, Versatile American* (Durham, N. C., 1935), ch. 14.

nection of the sciences with the practical arts. He told his listeners that the progress of the world, during the past half-century, had been " due altogether to the application of science to useful purposes, and of the useful arts to the progress of science." And he rejoiced that " in this march of intellect, so far as it leads to practical results, our country has kept pace with the most enlightened nations of the world . . ." [30]

The faith in the progress of science, expressed by Poinsett and others, could also be found in the magazine literature of the Middle Period. Already in 1825, a writer, aware of the increasingly great progress in science, wondered whether the invention of labor-saving machinery might not eventually cause a surplus production and result in idleness. However, he admitted that this presented " rather a gloomy prospect," and he concluded hopefully:

> but " sufficient for the day is the evil thereof," and it would not be wise to make ourselves miserable, because, in the improvement of our own condition, it is possible that posterity, may have *too much* of the good things of life! Still, however, it is a point by no means settled, whether scientific power has not already reached an extent that would be prejudicial to the happiness of mankind, provided all that are capable of using it were to adopt it.[31]

Across the Atlantic, in England, this writer's misgivings seemed already answered by the poverty of the laboring masses to whom scientific progress apparently meant only further social degradation. Proponents of technology in America were therefore quick to blame England's difficulties on its unprogressive form of government or to explain its misfortunes as a temporary hiatus in the march of progress. In New England, where the factory system was developing during the early 1830's, the learned *North American Review* devoted articles to

30 J. R. Poinsett, *Discourse on the Objects . . . of the National Institution* (Washington, 1841), p. 8.

31 " Improvement," *Niles' Reg.*, XXVIII (April 23, 1825), 114.

the defence of machinery. If the progress from the new industrial tendencies seemed delayed, the writers counselled that the evils of poverty and unemployment were only temporary. Viewing machinery in its ultimate effects as " intimately connected with the great topic of human progress," one writer declared:

> What we claim for machinery is, that it is in modern times by far the most efficient physical cause of human improvement, that it does for civilization, what conquest and human labor formerly did and accomplishes incalculably more than they accomplished.[32]

The optimism of the *North American Review* was re-echoed by some of the more popular periodicals of the thirties. In an article on " The Prospects of the Age " for the *Knickerbocker Magazine,* a writer, in his enthusiastic belief that the *" great age of utility* has come," predicted that eventually machinery and science would help the masses, increasing both their comforts and their chances for leisure time.[33] To the same periodical, Doctor Samuel L. Metcalf, a former resident of the South, who visited England in 1831 and returned to live in New York City, contributed articles on scientific subjects. In a review of the progress made in geology, Metcalf noted the constant tendency of scientific knowledge to expand, and he asserted:

> We feel perfectly assured that the period is not very distant, when the general principles of science will be so arranged and simplified, that the present labor of years will be accomplished in as many months—that we shall be enabled to explore every corner of nature's wide domain, with a rail-road speed, and avail ourselves of a thousand rich treasures of nature and art now unknown to mankind. The present age is emphatically marked by boldness and originality.[34]

32 "Effects of Machinery," *North Am. Rev.*, XXXIV (Jan., 1832), 229, 224; see also: "Defence of Mechanical Philosophy," *ibid.*, XXXIII (July, 1831), 122-136; "Reform in England," *ibid.*, XXXIV (Jan., 1832), 53.

33 "The Prospects of the Age," *Knickerbocker*, VII (Jan., 1836), 49-53.

34 S. L. Metcalfe, "The Interest and Importance of Scientific Geology," *Knickerbocker*, III (April, 1834), 225.

Then in those widely-circulated periodicals of the 1830's especially devoted to the ladies, the titles: " The Arts," " Practical Science," " The March of Mind," and " Human Improvement " were placed over essays which discussed in optimistic fashion the practical advantages and future implications of scientific improvement.[35]

With the subsidence of the depression of 1837 into the more generally prosperous period of the late forties and early fifties, and with the industrialization of the American economy steadily increasing, the progress of science assumed an even greater practical importance. The successful issue of the Mexican and Oregon controversies, and the subsequent discovery of gold in California, provided new fields for business expansion. Reflecting these trends an extensive literature on the progress of science filled the American magazines of the period. In the *Harbinger,* organ of the Associationists, the twenty-six year old inventor, William Francis Channing, in 1846, startled by the great significance of the news that Michael Faraday, the English scientist, had discovered a reaction between light and electricity, asked:

> Are thinking men aware of the immense strides which human science is making toward the comprehension and control of nature? . . .
> Why are there no more laborers in this field which is so boundless, on the cultivation of which the hopes and progress of the race so much depend, and which presents such sublime subjects for human thought.[36]

Channing's query was answered by a host of writers. A few months before his article was published, the *Scientific American* had been founded as " the advocate of industry and journal of scientific, mechanical and other improvements." Written in a

35 *New York Mirror,* VIII (July 31, 1830), 31; *Godey's Lady's Book,* II (May, 1831), 230; *Portland Mag.,* I (March, 1835), 171-172; *Ladies' Repository,* I (Aug., 1841), 233-235.

36 W. F. Channing, " The Progress of Science," *Harbinger,* II (Feb. 21, 1846), 165-166.

patriotic and popular style, articles in the new magazine were devoted to showing how practical science was the characteristic of the age and the cause of American progress.[37] Contributing to its pages in 1847, Sarah G. Bagley, one of the Lowell mill girls, wrote:

> It requires no small amount of discernment to discover the impress of the progress of the age. It is emphatically the age of improvement. The arts and sciences have been more fully developed, and the great mass of society are feeling its influence.[38]

While it was admitted by one of the *Scientific American's* writers that "Very frequently we hear complaints of the evils resulting from the progress of improvement," [39] the emphasis of the articles was on the defence of machinery against all attacks. The possibility of overproduction was denied, and it was also argued that the progress of science was beneficial because it enable goods to be manufactured more cheaply. Although it was conceded that the distribution of wealth and goods was often faulty, the consensus of the contributions to the magazine was " that every new and useful machine, invented and improved, confers a general benefit upon all classes,—the poor as well as the rich." [40]

In 1850 the anniversary of the half-century was celebrated in a series of magazine articles reviewing the past progress of science and predicting an even greater scientific progress in the

37 See for example: "The Utility and Pleasures of Science," *Sci. Am.*, II (Aug. 21, 1847), 381; "Progress of Science and Mechanical Art," *ibid.*, III (Oct. 30, 1847), 45; "The Progress of Inventions and Inventors," *ibid.*, VIII (June 4, 1853), 301; "Scientific Progress," *ibid.*, n. s. I (Oct. 1, 1859), 225; "Progressive Science," *ibid.*, n. s. II (Jan. 2, 1860), 5.

38 S. G. Bagley, "The Progress of the Age," *ibid.*, II (Feb. 6, 1847), 157.

39 "Improvement," *ibid.*, II (July 17, 1847), 341.

40 "Machinery and Labor," *ibid.*, VI (March 29, 1851), 221; see also: "Results of Machinery," *ibid.*, IV (Feb. 24, 1849), 181.

future.[41] The general opinion was that, in the words of a writer in the *Southern Quarterly Review*:

> The wonderful progress of physical science is one of the most striking features of the present age . . .
> To write soberly, and without enthusiasm, of the present state of scientific developments, would require a degree of phlegmatism to which we would not willingly plead guilty.[42]

Throughout the fifties this faith in scientific progress was the theme of elaborate articles in the popular periodicals of the decade. In *Graham's Magazine* and in Hunt's *Merchants' Magazine* contributors praised technological progress as of real benefit to the masses.[43] The *North American Review,* in an article on " The Tendencies of Modern Science," noted that they were progressive under the beneficent control of Providence.[44] Not so religious or cautious in his view, a writer in the *Democratic Review* expressed the opinion that electricity and machinery would so transform life that fifty years hence: " Men and women will then have no harassing cares, or laborious duties to fulfill. Machinery will perform all work—automata will direct them. The only task of the human race, will be to make love, study and be happy." [45]

The optimistic reviews of a half-century's scientific progress, contained in these secular publications, were also found in some of the religious writings of the time. At the turn of the half-century, Christian clergymen delivered orations and wrote

41 See for example: W. F. Channing, " The Anniversary of a New Half Century," *Spirit of the Age,* I (Dec. 8, 1849), 357; " Editors' Table," *Godey's Lady's Book,* XLI (Dec., 1850), 380; Parke Godwin, " The Last Half-Century " (New York *Evening Post,* Jan. 1, 1851), in Godwin's *Out of the Past* (New York, 1870), 145-175.

42 *S. Q. Rev.,* XVII (April, 1850), 160.

43 *Graham's Mag.,* XL (June, 1852), 565-567; G. M. Weston, " Improved Conditions of Labor," Hunt's *Merchants' Mag.,* XXXIV (April, 1856), 403-415.

44 *North Am. Rev.,* LXXII (Jan., 1851), 84-85, 115.

45 " The Spirit of the Times; or, The Fast Age," *Dem. Rev.,* XXXIII (Sept., 1853), 261.

articles in which they recognized the advance of science as one of the characteristics of a progressive age and century.[46] *The Half Century; or, a history of changes that have taken place, and events that have transpired, chiefly in the United States, between 1800 and 1850* was compiled by Emerson Davis, a New England Congregational minister, and prefaced with an Introduction by Mark Hopkins, also a Congregational clergyman, and the famous President of Williams College. The book itself combined a statistical survey of material and cultural progress with an emphasis upon the superintending role of Christianity.[47] A similar volume was Robert Baird's *The Christian Retrospect and Register; a summary of the scientific, moral and religious progress of the first half of the XIXth century.* Baird, a Presbyterian clergyman, with a strong interest in public education and temperance, divided his work into the two parts of material and moral progress. In the chapter on the "Moral Aspects of Science" Baird rejoiced that the inventions of science were strengthening religion:

> What elements of power are here entrusted to us! These arts of printing that multiply the Word of God literally with every minute,—these accumulations of capital still active, still accumulating,—these means of communication over sea and land,—through the broad earth,—who does not hear the voice of God in all these?[48]

46 E. P. Humphrey, *An Address delivered before the Literary Societies of Centre College, Ky.* (Louisville, Ky., 1850) ; J. W. Andrews, *An Oration ...at Yale College...* (New Haven, 1850) ; N. S. Beman, *Characteristics of the Age* (Troy, N. Y., 1851) ; George Junkin, *Progress of the Age* (Phil., 1851), *passim.*

"The Past Fifty Years," *Puritan Recorder*, XXXV (Jan. 3, 1850), 2; "A Half Century's Progress," *Church Rev.*, IV (April, 1851), 60-91; "The Signs of the Times," *Meth. Q. Rev.*, XXXV (July, 1853), 426-446.

For a much different view, skeptical of the half-century's progress, see: Horace Bushnell, "The Age of Homespun," in *Litchfield County Centennial Celebration...* (Hartford, 1851), pp. 105-130.

47 Emerson Davis, *The Half Century* (Boston, 1851), *passim.*

48 Robert Baird, *The Christian Retrospect and Register* (New York, 1851), p. 188; also the Introd., Section XIV, and ch. 28; see also Baird's, "Our Age—Its Progress, Prospects, and Demands," *Bib. Repos.*, 3rd ser., V (Jan., 1848), 79-96.

The acceptance of scientific progress by some of the leading Protestant clergy of the period was often a defensive movement against those irreligious tendencies which they felt were implicit in science unleavened by religion.[49] Prominent clergymen, in their capacity as college presidents, delivered learned addresses on the theme that true progress resulted only from a fusion of of the forces of both science and religion. Francis Wayland, the Baptist President of Brown, in a discourse in 1835 on *The Dependence of Science upon Religion* advanced the thesis that religion exercised a valuable restraining influence on its impulsive force.[50] Edward Hitchcock, a Congregational minister and onetime President of Amherst, in his numerous works on geology took pains to show that the progress of science and of religion was not antagonistic.[51] In his address on *Science and Religion*, in 1856 Mark Hopkins, the President of Williams, developed the idea that the progress of science was a part of a greater plan being carried forward by God.[52]

Prominent in the list of irreligious tendencies so alarming to the Christian ministry was the science of geology. Beginning with the notorious controversy of 1833 in which Thomas Cooper, the famous English emigré and the President of South Carolina College, had protested against Benjamin Silliman's attempts to reconcile geology with the Biblical story of the

49 See, for example, two addresses at Yale College by prominent New School Presbyterian clergymen: Albert Barnes, *An Oration on the Progress and Tendency of Science* (Phil., 1840), *passim*; William Adams, *Christianity the End and Unity of All Sciences and Pursuits* (New York, 1847), *passim*.
See also: "The Progress of Science and Its Connection with the Scripture," *Q. Rev. Meth. Epis. Church South*, XI (Jan., 1857), 64 ff.

50 Francis Wayland, *The Dependence of Science Upon Religion* (Providence, 1835), *passim*.

51 Edward Hitchcock: "The Connection between Geology and Natural Religion," *Bib. Repos.*, V (Jan., 1835), 113-138; *The Highest Use of Learning* (Amherst, 1845), pp. 4-5; *The Religion of Geology and Its Connected Sciences* (1st pub. 1851; Boston, 1859), Lecture 13, and *passim*. ..

52 Mark Hopkins, *Science and Religion* (Albany, 1856), pp. 22-23, and *passim*.

creation,[53] this science received the criticism directed at the theory of evolution in a later period of American history. In the conflict between geology and religion the idea of progress was a useful conciliating influence to which some of the well known geologists of the period lent their support. Charles Lyell's *Principles of Geology,* first published in England in the early 1830's and later in the United States, included a chapter on the " Theory of the progressive development of organic life at successive geological periods." [54] In the third volume of this well-known work, Lyell summarized Lamarck's arguments in favor of the transmutation of the species, but he then concluded with a declaration of his faith in Providential guidance.[55] Arnold Guyot, the Swiss geologist, soon after his emigration to the United States in 1848, published his book *Earth and Man,* in which he predicted a great future progress for America through science guided by the Christian religion.[56] In the words of a contemporary review of Guyot's work, " To those nations only who have received this light [of Christianity], has been granted this progress in the march of improvement." [57] Without a peer as an American geologist, James Dwight Dana was also during the 1850's foremost in the defense of geology against the charge of irreligion. Geology, Dana felt, illustrated a grand series of progressive epochs, of which man was the culmination and God

53 Benjamin Silliman, "Consistency of Geology with Sacred History," a Supplement in his Am. ed. of Robert Bakewell's, *An Introduction to Geology* (2nd Am. ed.; New Haven, 1833), pp. 389-466; Thomas Cooper, *On the Connection between Geology and the Pentateuch* ... (Boston, 1833), *passim*; see also: Maurice Kelley, *Additional Chapters on Thomas Cooper* (Orono, Maine, 1930), pp. 20-24, and W. M. Smallwood in collab. with M. S. C. Smallwood, *Natural History and the American Mind* (New York, 1941), ch. 8.

54 Charles Lyell, *Principles of Geology* (Boston, 1842), I, 226-260.

55 *Ibid.,* III, 406, and *passim.*

56 Arnold Guyot, *Earth and Man* (first pub. 1849; Boston, 1857), pp. 319-326.

57 *S. Q. Rev.,* XIX (April, 1851), 440; see also the review in the "Editor's Table," *Harper's New Monthly Mag.,* XVIII (Dec., 1858), 119-124.

the author.[58] In answer to the attacks on geology, he protested, " Science should not be feared. Her progress is upward as well as onward, to clearer and clearer visions of infinite beneficence." [59]

This controversy between religion and geology was clearly brought out in the extended debate between Dana and Tayler Lewis, a conservative Professor of Greek at Union College, Schenectady. Against Lewis, who, in his argument for the Biblical theory of creation, substituted a cyclical law of rise and decline for the concept of progress,[60] Dana replied in three long articles in the *Bibliotheca Sacra*. Dana interpreted Lewis' " six days of creation " as six long periods, " the progression of physical changes and of living beings, being on this principle, in harmony with the Bible record." [61] Instead of Lewis' pessimistic cyclical theory, Dana divided the age of man into three historical periods: " of mere material existence and physical progress, of life and organic progress," and lastly of " spiritual progress; whose germs are even now expanding in the soul of man; but whose flowers and fruit will appear, only in time to come." [62] From a study and reading of the Bible, Dana declared that he had found evidence of a law of progress not only for the earth but also " a parallel progress in living beings, from the time of their first appearance; the earlier tribes of inferior grade; then others, ranging to a higher level in species; and so on, gaining in superiority, through the ages, according to an exact system. And we have learned, besides, that all this progress, both of lands and life, reached its culminant point in

58 J. D. Dana, *Address before the American Association for the Advancement of Science, August, 1855* (Cambridge, Mass., 1855), pp. 4, 36.

59 Dana, " Science and Scientific Schools," *Am. Journal of Educ.*, II (Sept., 1856), 364, and *passim*.

60 Tayler Lewis, *The Six Days of Creation* (Schenectady and London, 1855), pp. 233-240.

61 Dana, " Science and the Bible," *Bibliotheca Sacra*, XIII (Jan., 1856), 94-98, 112.

62 *Ibid.*, pp. 127-128.

man." [63] Although he believed in progress, it was not, he felt, indefinite or perpetual, and therefore he reached almost the same conclusion as Lewis, but without the latter's pessimism.

> Our argument [Dana wrote], based on nature's teachings, has given us reason to believe that the universe had a beginning, and will have an end; that it has its limits in space; that its progress has been a regular progress, like that of germ-development in its system and epochs, and with only such decays as were necessarily involved in its progress and the one final decay; that, from the beginning to the end, it corresponds to but one grand cycle of progress, like one progressing individuality among living species; that with man it reached the Day of Rest or Divine Repose, its meridian of life or finished growth, when the education of mind began.[64]

The concept of scientific progress developed in the magazine literature of the period, in the addresses by the statesmen and clergymen of the country, and in the attempts at systematic treatises made by Bigelow and Etzler, received perhaps its fullest exposition in the *Reports* of the Commissioners of Patents. The emphasis in these *Reports* was placed on the value of the various scientific inventions to the mass of the people. In this regard an examiner, in making his report to the Commissioner in 1845, declared:

> In reviewing the patents for the year, it has been my object to call your attention to such, and such only, as indicated progress—to those which possessed important usefulness in themselves, or that peculiar and striking novelty which is calculated to render them a centre, around which inventions will clustre.[65]

One of these early Patent Office *Reports* was commented upon in 1844 by an orator who maintained that there was no limit to

63 *Ibid.*, XIV (July, 1857), 465-466.

64 *Ibid.*, p. 496.

65 *Report of the Commissioner of Patents 1845*, 29 Cong., 1 Sess., House Doc. no. 140, p. 82; see also: *Report . . . 1844*, 28 Cong., 2 Sess., Senate Doc. no. 75, p. 507.

improvement. Paying his respects to Bacon for freeing science from philosophy and "planting it firmly upon the rocks of *common sense*," the orator noted that Bentham had enlarged on Bacon with the happy result that

> The age of *philosophy* has passed, and left few memorials of its existence. That of *glory* has vanished, and nothing but a painful tradition of human suffering remains. That of utility has commenced, and it requires little warmth of imagination to anticipate for it a reign lasting as time, and radiant with the wonders of unveiled nature.[66]

The Patent Office Commissioners themselves especially stressed the practical benefits of scientific progress. Edmund Burke, the Commissioner under Polk, defended the right of the inventor to patent his discoveries because they " contribute much to the convenience and welfare of Man." [67] Listing the significant inventions in the history of science from the printing press to the telegraph " as striking instances of the effect of the labors of the inventor upon society and civilization," Burke stated:

> Even the most humble discovery contributes its due proportion to relieve the human family of its burdens, and administer to its comforts, and to accelerate and aggrandize its unceasing and triumphant progress in the improvement of its condition, and the expansion and perfection of its lofty nature and destiny.[68]

When the United States sent an exhibit to the World's Exposition at London in 1851, despite the lack of an appropriation

66 Willis Hall, *An Address delivered August 14, 1844 before the Society of Phi Beta Kappa in Yale College* (New Haven, 1844), pp. 30, 16-18; see also: "American Patents and Inventions," *U. S. Cath. Mag.*, V (Nov., 1846), 581.

67 *Report of the Com. of Patents 1846*, 29 Cong., 2 Sess., House Doc., no. 52, p. 2.

68 *Ibid.*, p. 5; see also the *Report of the Com. of Patents 1855*, 34 Cong., 1 Sess., House Doc. no. 12, pp. 8-11.

from the government, the *Report of the Commissioner of Patents* referred to the praise won by American inventions as demonstrating " the progressiveness of the human mind when in the enjoyment of liberty." [69] J. Holt, the last Commissioner before the Civil War, noted in 1857 that " the inventions of the past year have been decidedly utilitarian . . ." Then he concluded :

> while there is thus in the past so much to excite our pride, there is in the future yet more to excite our hopes. If that future is to be measured by the strides of that past, rapid as has been our advancement, it is but reasonable to infer that we have scarcely crossed the threshold of the temple of human knowledge . . .[70]

From 1849 to 1852 the Commissioner of Patents was Thomas Ewbank, an Englishman who came to the United States in 1819 at the age of twenty-seven, because he felt that an individual's capabilities were too limited in a monarchy and would prove more useful in a democratic society. For sixteen years Ewbank was a successful manufacturer, but in 1836 he retired to devote his time to study, travel, and writing. Criticized in Congress for filling his *Reports* with elaborate essays on the more general aspects of science,[71] Ewbank nevertheless doubled the force of examiners and laid the foundations of the present patent system. Moreover in these much criticized essays of his *Reports* Ewbank made the most significant contemporary contribution to an understanding of the social implications of technological progress. Ewbank's first *Report* attributed human progress to the advances made in science and art. Taking issue

69 Edward Riddle, " Report on the World's Exposition," in *Report of the Com. of Patents 1851,* 32 Cong., 1 Sess., House Doc., no. 102, p. 485; see also: D. A. Wells (ed.), *Annual of Scientific Discovery ... for 1852* (Boston, 1852), p. 1; Horace Greeley, *Art and Industry ... at the Crystal Palace New York ...* (New York, 1853), Introd., and ch. 30.

70 *Report of the Com. of Patents 1857,* 35 Cong., 1 Sess., House Doc. no. 32, pp. 3, 5.

71 *Cong. Globe,* 31 Cong., 1 Sess., House of Rep. (March 7 and 12, 1850), pp. 473 ff., 503 ff.; Senate (May 6, 1850), pp. 916 ff.

with the customary protest that moral improvement was being neglected for material progress, he wrote:

> Not till mechanical as well as ethical science is fully explored and universally applied can man attain his destiny, and evil be swept from the earth . . .
>
> Even as arts multiply and flourish, the chief labor of working out the great problems of existence continues to devolve upon inventors. Without them the prospects and hopes of the present had neither been seen nor felt. It is they who, by discovering new physical truths, are establishing the grandest of moral ones—*Perpetual Progress*—illimitable advancement in social, civil, and intellectual enjoyments . . .
>
> Though not suspected, the power of inventors over human affairs, is already supreme; machinery even now governs the world, though the world does not acknowledge it.[72]

In 1854, a few years after his removal as Commissioner of Patents, Ewbank published *The World a Workshop; or, The Physical Relationship of Man to The Earth*. In this little book, he expressed his belief that the knowledge of truth was progressive and that the world was designed by its Creator to be developed by people actively working according to the precepts of science.[73] Not finding such universal confidence in others, Ewbank devoted himself to showing that the world was a vast, inexhaustible workshop or factory with its material amenable to man and designed for his constant use.[74] If the world was indeed a factory, fire, coal, and machinery were all necessary elements of progress. "Fire," Ewbank noted, "gives us what Eden had not. If a flaming sword drove one man out, the knowledge of flame has put within the reach of all men blessings unknown there." [75] Considering coal, " a first element of prog-

---

72 *Report of the Com. of Patents 1849, Part I,* 31 Cong., 1 Sess., House Doc. no. 20, pp. 488-491.

73 Thomas Ewbank, *The World a Workshop* (New York, 1855), Preface, pp. v-x.

74 Ibid., pp. 20, 27.

75 *Ibid.*, p. 53.

ress for all time," Ewbank felt that, " it is preposterous to suppose the supplies of coal can ever be exhausted or even become scarce. The idea is almost blasphemous." [76] He defended machinery as necessary for the full subjection of nature and also because " The extent to which human toil has in this way been relieved, is one of the best things accomplished in the present century." [77] Ewbank regretted " that as Lord of the earth, man as yet has no adequate conception of his high destiny," but he was confident that the world was beginning to listen to the truth of his maxim: *" Faith in human power."* [78] As enemies of his ideas of material and moral progress, he condemned those who overemphasized the spiritual things of life and those who, from excessive gentility, scorned honest labor.[79] Ewbank then joined science and religion, labor and thought, in a synthesis full of faith and hope in future progress:

> The industry of an age or of a people is as the vegetable and animal products they grow and minerals they raise, while their position on the scale of progress is marked by the elaboration they give to those substances, and the uses they make of them . . .
>
> The popular absurdity that labor was imposed as a punishment receives no sanction from the Scriptures—not a particle. The original and all-comprehending injunction, " replenish the earth and subdue it," was given before " the fall." In it, the true relationship of man to the earth, and the business of his life, are compressed in half-a-dozen words. On agriculture and the arts his powers, mental and physical, were to be concentrated. No intimation of limits to his progress in them is conveyed. They were the germs from which his prosperity was to arise, and from their ever-growing developments the ripest fruits were to be gathered.[80]

76 *Ibid.*, p. 73.

77 *Ibid.*, p. 144.

78 *Ibid.*, p. 163.

79 *Ibid.*, p. 171.

80 *Ibid.*, pp. 182, 183-184.

In 1860 Ewbank published two books which symbolized the end of one and the beginning of another era in the history of the idea of American technological progess. With the Civil War and the triumph of industrialism in the offing, his *Inorganic Forces Ordained To Supersede Human Slavery* was devoted to the thesis that scientific progress would make Negro slavery obsolete. Ewbank wrote:

> The value of the revelation—that all forces are resolvable into organic elements and obtainable in unlimited quantities —who can estimate! To it is to be ascribed the start which civilization has taken in the present century and to it primarily will be due all future progress . . . But for this wonderful and most beneficent provision negroes would be captured and sold in greater numbers than ever. There would be no end to their enthralment.
>
> Not only does the ultimate extinction of human slavery depend on it, but the complete subjugation of the earth and the application of all its resources to human happiness.[81]

In the other of these two books published in 1860, Ewbank, evidently influenced by the theories which culminated in Darwin's *Origin of the Species* (1859), declared that "there is a law of growth for the species as definite as for the individual," and he also connected the progress of man to the earth's geological stratification.[82] From a survey of the elements of modern progress, Ewbank drew the optimistic conclusion:

> The tendency of modern civilization is full of promise. In arts and sciences the present leading races leave behind all the most energetic that have hitherto figured on the earth. In the midst of such movements who would not exclaim: "Better fifty years in Europe than a cycle in Cathay?" . . .
>
> A millennium is not a fallacy but a certain result of progress. If we believe in this there is no ignoring that And why should not our orb be as much a theatre of felicity as any other in

81 Ewbank, *Inorganic Forces Ordained to Supersede Human Slavery* (New York, 1860), p. 24, and *passim*.

82 Ewbank, *The Position of our Species* (New York [1860 ?]), pp. 4, 21.

the heavens? Can the purpose of its creation be otherwise fully accomplished? We believe not.[83]

The extensive interest in the possibilities for progress resulting from the technological development in the era from Jackson to Lincoln was in part the result of the fact that, as two prominent historians of American civilization have said of this period " It was science, not paper declarations relating to the idea of progress, that at last made patent the practical methods by which democracy could raise the standard of living for the great masses of the people." [84] Of course, the progress of science was also appropriated to their own advantage by the rising class of industrial capitalists in America. Put to such use, the progress of science was feared by certain labor and reform groups who argued that a new social system was necessary if they were to benefit from the great technological advances. In the speeches and writings of the representatives of the new business class, however, the idea of progress was invoked to show that the hardships of the factory system were only temporary evils to be displaced eventually by an era of production and plenty in which the mass of people might more largely share. The conflict between social reform and social stability, in the midst of a growing industrial society, will therefore be the theme of the next two chapters.

83 *Ibid.*, pp. 29, 32.
84 C. A. and M. R. Beard, *The Rise of American Civilization*, I, 737.

CHAPTER V

PROGRAMS FOR A NEW SOCIETY

In the United States during the Middle Period the advance of science inspired a widespread faith in the idea of progress itself, but in the midst of this general enthusiasm the optimism of certain segments of the American people was adversely influenced by the evils increasing along with the march of science. Especially affected by scientific progress were important groups of the laboring classes—skilled craftsmen displaced by machinery, or mechanics forced to accept the privations of factory labor. Aware of the condition of labor in England since the industrial revolution, and fearful lest America become the heir of England's misfortunes, labor spokesmen in New England, New York, and other industrial centers called for progress by social and economic reforms. Sympathetic with the demands of the early labor movement and critical of the materialistic standards of the rising business class, many American intellectuals and humanitarians also sought to realize their lofty visions of future progress in the reform movements of the day. From abroad the Utopian socialisms of Owen and of Fourier came to claim their American followers. At home the Unitarian and transcendental philosophies, extending a challenge to the faith of the age in material progress, also provided a renewed emphasis on the moral and individual nature of progress. Among these reform groups the machine itself was not condemned so much as was its selfish misuse by man, and this discontent with industrialism was resolved, therefore, by the hope of a better social system in which technological progress might work its magic unalloyed.

During the 1820's these discontented groups were offered a panacea for the evils of industrialism in the Utopian program for future progress proposed by the famous English manufacturer and reformer, Robert Owen. By his frequent sojourns and experimental community in America, Owen became almost as much a part of the New World as of the Old. Following his first visit, in 1824, the views of Owen and his American sympathizers were widely circulated among radical reformers in this country. Owen shared the eighteenth-century faith in the natural goodness and perfectibility of man, if he were uncorrupted by the evils of his environment. He was convinced that by a proper education and training of youth, by granting equality of opportunity to all, and by a union of all individuals in a social system, a new and happy society could be created to supplant the evils of the existing, individualistic, industrial society. He felt that man was designed to be progressive and that the means of progress were largely under man's control. America, Owen hoped, would be the nucleus from which his social system would spread throughout the world.[1]

Owen's son, Robert Dale Owen, in a series of articles on " Wealth and Misery," published in the *New Harmony Gazette* for 1826, presented in concise form his concept of existing evil and of future progress. Although science as yet had seemed only to increase the inequality and the misery of man, Robert Dale Owen advanced the idea that in the future it would so stimulate production that wealth would be made available to all, and he even maintained:

> The world, in its progressive movement towards knowledge and happiness, is rapidly approaching a point when commercial competition must cease. Nations are becoming too wealthy and prosperous to be commercial. A system of distribution which requires *scarcity* to support it, becomes worse than useless at a time of plenty. Wealth is already beginning to be like water, too easy of production to remain an article of commerce.[2]

1 Robert Owen, *Two Discourses on a New System of Society* (Pittsburgh, 1825), *passim*; *A New View of Society* (1st pub. 1813-1816; 1st Am. ed. from 3rd London ed., New York, 1825), pp. 16-22; " Oration, Containing a Declaration of Mental Independence," *New Harmony Gazette*, I (July 12, 1826), 329-332; "Address...at a Public Meeting of the Inhabitants of New Harmony," *ibid.*, III (April 23, 1828), 204-205.

2 Robert Dale Owen, *Wealth and Misery* (Extracted from the *New Harmony Gazette, 1826*; New York, 1830), p. 10; see also: R. W. Leopold, *Robert Dale Owen* (Cambridge, 1940), *passim*.

Then in 1830, appending a note to these earlier articles, he declared:

> I see that the immense modern powers of production *might be* a blessing, and that they *are* a curse. I see that machinery, instead of aiding the laborer, is brought into the market against him; and that it thus reduces his wages and injures his situation.[3]

Robert Dale Owen was accused by a correspondent in the *Working Man's Advocate* of being an enemy of technological progress.[4] However, he agreed with his critic that the fault lay not in machinery but in its perversion under the contemporary commercial system.[5] The Owens were joined by other advocates of the cause of labor in their denunciation of the inequality of the existing economic system.[6] By the Fall of 1828, however, Owen's colony at New Harmony was proving a short-lived cure, and his followers in their hope of progress turned therefore to education and politics.

Most zealous in the cause of free enquiry and universal education was Frances Wright, the Scotswoman who shocked American society in the late 1820's by delivering a number of public addresses. In the first of her *Course of Popular Lectures*,

3 R. D. Owen, *Wealth and Misery*, p. 14.

4 W. J., "An Enquiry into the Influence of Labor Saving Machinery on the Condition of the Laboring Classes," *Working Man's Advoc.*, I (Feb. 6, 1830), 1.

5 R. D. Owen, "Labor Saving Machinery," *ibid.*, I (Feb. 13, 1830), 1; see also: R. W., "To Robert Dale Owen," *ibid.*, I (April 10, May 22, 1830), 2; "Labor Saving Machinery by An Unlettered Mechanic," *ibid.*, II (Sept. 8, 1830), 2.

6 See for example: L. Byllesby, *Observations on the Sources and Effects of Unequal Wealth* (New York, 1826), chs. 1-3; S., "Gray Light, No. II," *New Harmony Gazette*, I (Dec. 28, 1825), 108-109; "Distress of Productive Industry," *ibid.*, II (Sept. 5, 1827), 382; "Prospectus," *Working Man's Advoc.*, I (Jan., 1830), 3; [Paul Brown], *The Radical; and Advocate of Equality* (Albany, 1835), pp. 44-47; John Commerford, "Address delivered before the General Trades' Union of New York," *Working Man's Advoc.*, VII (Sept. 19, 1835), 1.

she noted that man was distinguished from the animals by the principle of improvement, and declared:

> to accelerate the progress of our race, two means present themselves; a just system of education, and a fearless spirit of enquiry; and that while the former would remove all difficulties from the path of future generations, the latter would place far in advance even the present.[7]

In the United States, at the beginning of the Jacksonian period of reform, Frances Wright and her associates had good cause to hope for the progress of education. She herself rejoiced that American institutions were characterized by change and progress, and she called for the adoption of a national system of republican education as the key to real improvement.[8] At times Frances Wright despaired of civilization, but on the whole, around 1830, she had faith that, in America, at least, man's capacity for progress, developed by a correct system of education, would create a new and better society.[9]

Associated for a time with Frances Wright and Robert Dale Owen in the New York City labor movement of the 1830's was Thomas Skidmore, a strong advocate of an equal division of property and of public education. Skidmore believed that the unequal rights to property prevented the progress which the printing press, the right of suffrage, and public education were beginning to make possible. He looked with favor upon a large and increasing population, opposed free trade, and believed scientific inventions of great advantage to man. Although he regarded science and knowledge as capable of indefinite ex-

7 Frances Wright, *Course of Popular Lectures* (3rd ed.; New York, 1830), p. 37; see also: W. R. Waterman, *Frances Wright* (New York, 1924), chs. 6-8.

8 Wright, *op. cit.*, pp. 42-44, 171-175, 199-202.

9 For the variations in her opinion, see: "Civilization," *Free Enquirer*, 2nd ser., I (April 29, 1829), 209; "Address on the State of the Public Mind...," *ibid.*, 2nd ser., II (July 24, 1830), 305.

pansion, Skidmore, however, felt their immense potential good
could best be developed by public education.[10]

In New England, Seth Luther and Frederick Robinson, two
labor sympathizers, denounced the patriotic boasting which
disguised the degradation of American labor, and called for
education to realize America's early ideals of freedom and equality.[11] Robinson, speaking in 1834 before the Trades Union of
Boston and vicinity, declared that the condition of a people can
never be stationary:

> Hence we are doomed to never ceasing exertion for the en-
> joyment of our rights, and the improvement of our condition,
> until we work out the reform of society, and by the complete
> enjoyment of the blessings of equality, the common good of
> all the people shall constitute the interest of all . . .
>
> The cause of the people, I trust and believe, is now prog-
> ressing. And it only needs for us to carry the first, the great
> reform, which we have proposed, the equal, mental and phys-
> ical education of all, at the expense of all, and our emancipa-
> tion from the power of aristocracy will be effectual and eter-
> nal.[12]

An especially ardent advocate of the rights of labor was
Orestes A. Brownson during the early years of his life. Before
his conversion to Catholicism in 1844, Brownson had been
identified with a variety of radical New England causes. Associated with the transcendentalists and the Brook Farm experiment, he had also been for a short while a follower of Robert
Owen and Frances Wright. Disillusioned with his experiences
in the Workingmen's Party of the early thirties, Brownson

10 Thomas Skidmore, *The Rights of Man to Property* (New York, 1829),
pp. 10-15, 125-127, 265, 277, 381-384; see also: Stephen Simpson, *The
Working Man's Manual* (Phil., 1831), p. 235, and *passim.*

For a different view, see: "Agrarian and Education Systems," *Southern
Rev.,* VI (Aug., 1830), 17, 31.

11 Seth Luther, *An Address to the Working Men of New England* (3rd
ed.; Phil., 1836), p. 16, and *passim;* Frederick Robinson, *An Oration delivered before the Trades Union of Boston* (Boston, 1834), pp. 8-9.

12 Robinson, *op. cit.,* pp. 4, 22.

turned to religious and moral reform as the way to social progress.[13] From time to time a Presbyterian, a Universalist, and a
Unitarian, Brownson in 1836 organized his own " Society for
Christian Union and Progress " as the church for the laboring
classes of Boston. He felt that the infidelity of the day was popular because it accepted the progressive spirit of the age, while
the conventional churches and clergy opposed social progress.
Believing that individual progress had to be accompanied by
social progress, he included the latter among the three articles
of his own church. In his *New Views of Christianity, Society
and the Church,* published in 1836 and dedicated " to the members and friends of the Society for Christian Union and Progress," he developed the idea that God intended man for progress. Hitherto advancing by instinct, he declared that " the time
has now come for humanity to understand itself, to accept the
law imposed upon it for its own good, to foresee its end and
march with intention steadily towards it. Its future religion is
the religion of progress." [14]

Brownson was strongly opposed to the inequalities of American society, which he felt were the result of the wealth and
privileges of the favored minority, and he therefore gave his
support temporarily to the Democratic party of Andrew Jackson. In his *Boston Quarterly Review* for 1839 he admitted that
the Democratic party was " an imperfect embodment of the
great idea of progress," but he also advised that : " That party
embraces the general principles of liberty, of progress, which
include within them, as the oak is included in the acorn, all

13 On Brownson's varied career, see: A. M. Schlesinger, Jr., *Orestes A.
Brownson—A Pilgrim's Progress* (Boston, 1939), *passim*; H. S. Mims,
"Early American Democratic Theory and Orestes Brownson," *Science and
Society*, III (1939), 166-198.

14 O. A. Brownson, *New Views of Christianity, Society, and the Church*
(Boston, 1836), p. 113, ch. 10, and *passim*; see also: Brownson's " Education
of the People," *Chr. Ex.*, XX (May, 1836), 153-169; *A Discourse on the
Wants of the Times* (Boston, 1836), *passim*; " Letter from O. A. Brownson,"
West. Mess., III (April, 1837), 601-604; " Progress Our Law. A Discourse,"
Boston Q. Rev., III (Oct., 1840), 397-409.

possible reforms." [15] Then in the Summer of 1840, in a famous
article on " The Laboring Classes," Brownson attacked the
Church and hereditary property in such an extreme fashion as
to injure the Democratic prospects in the forthcoming election.[16] In this essay he declared that everywhere labor was
oppressed and poor, and he pictured the fundamental social
problem as a war of economic classes, with operative arrayed
against employer and labor against wealth. The first stages in
man's progress had been due to the clergy and the church, but
now he felt that true progress would result only from a thorough change in the very system of society itself. In his plan for
reform and progress, Brownson called for the rescue of Christianity from the priests, the repeal of all monopolistic laws by
the government, and the substitution of such laws as might be
necessary to maintain equality for the laboring class.[17]

Discouraged by the Whig victory in the election, Brownson
turned in his hope of progress from a confidence in the virtue
and intelligence of the people to a limited faith in authoritarian
government and an increasing reliance on the Church. He continued to denounce the oppression of labor under an industrial
order, and he defended himself against the charge of becoming
a reactionary. Without abandoning the concept of progress, but
opposed to a radical change in society, he announced in 1843
" that the only true way of carrying the race forward is through
its existing institutions." [18]

15 Brownson, "Democracy and Reform," *Boston Q. Rev.*, II (Oct., 1839),
486, 514; see also his *Oration before the Democracy of Worcester* (Boston,
1840), pp. 33-35, and *passim*.

16 Schlesinger, *op. cit.*, pp. 89 ff.

17 Brownson, "The Laboring Classes," *Boston Q. Rev.*, III (July, 1840),
372-393; for Brownson's defence of his article and his general position, see:
ibid., III (Oct., 1840), 460-472; for an unfavorable review invoking the
idea of progress against Brownson, see: "Brownson on the Laboring
Classes," *West. Mess.*, VIII (Nov., 1840), 316-330.
For an interesting anticipation of Brownson's argument, see: T. Fisk,
"Capital against Labor," *Working Man's Advoc.*, VI (July 25, 1835), 1.

18 Brownson, "Democracy and Liberty," *Dem. Rev.*, XII (April, 1843),
386.

The idea of progress in the hope it portended for social reform had been essential to the philosophy of the early labor movement and to Owen's Utopian socialism. During the 1840's Robert Owen continued to urge America to adopt his schemes,[19] while his son, Robert Dale Owen, was elected to Congress and came to feel that education and " the safety-valve of the public lands " might afford the means of progress temporarily in America.[20] However, in the decade of the forties it was the principles of the French Utopian socialist, Charles Fourier, which attracted the attention of those who derived their faith in progress from their hope of a new social system.[21]

Fourier's plan of association was based psychologically on the free and full development of human nature. Economically it proposed to render labor and industry attractive by dividing society into communal groups or phalansteries. The Fourierist system was believed by its disciples to be a plan of scientific socialism, the adoption of which would achieve the millennium. It was first popularized in America by Albert Brisbane, an Amer-

For the growing conservatism of Brownson's concept of progress in these years, see his articles: " The Policy to be Pursued Hereafter," *Boston Q. Rev.*, IV (Jan., 1841), 68-84; " Social Evils, and Their Remedy," *ibid.*, IV (July, 1841), 269; "The Present State of Society," *Dem. Rev.*, XIII (July, 1843), 17-38; " Popular Government," *ibid.*, XII (May, 1843), 529. For a defence of Brownson's essential progressiveness, see: W. H. Channing, " The Democratic Review and O. A. Brownson," *Present*, I (Nov. 15, 1843), 72.

19 See, for example: Owen's, *The Book of the New Moral World* ... (1st Am. ed.; New York, 1845), *passim*; " Robert Owen on the Mode to Change Immediately in Practice, Beneficially for All, the Present Inferior Circumstances throughout Society, for Superior," *Quarterly Journal and Rev.*, I (Oct., 1846), 321-325.

20 R. D. Owen, *Cong. Globe*, 29 Cong., 1 Sess., House of Rep. (April 22, 1846), pp. 713-714; " One of the Problems of the·Age," *Dem. Rev.*, XIV (Feb., 1844), 167.

21 For some comments, in which Fourierism was considered the harbinger of a new era, see: Charles Lane, " Social Tendencies," *Dial*, IV (July, 1843), 65-86; L. M. Child, " Progress and Hope," *Present*, I (Jan. 15, 1844), 230-234; " Progress," (from the *Social Reformer*), *Working Man's Advoc.*, n. s., I (June 29, 1844), 2; Margaret Fuller Ossoli, Letter to W. H. Channing from Rome (May 7, 1847), in her *Memoirs*, III, 132.

ican, who as a youth had studied abroad under Hegel, Cousin, and Guizot. He had been disappointed with their ideas, however, and also with the socialism of Saint Simon, before he became a disciple of Fourier. He returned home in 1834, began lecturing on Fourierism, and in 1839 formed a Fourierist society. Then a year later he published his *Social Destiny of Man* based on Fourier's writings. This book attracted the attention of Horace Greeley, who in 1842 permitted Brisbane to use the *Tribune's* columns to expound the principles of association.[22]

Fourierism, as developed by Brisbane, called for progress by a complete social reform instead of by the slow political reforms of the day. Although the United States was recognized as a nation characterized by the spirit of improvement, it was felt that the theory of progress was not so well known here as in Europe. Fourierism was also believed to be an entirely new scheme of regeneration owing nothing to the irregular progress of the past.[23] However, it did divide the history of the world into four periods, from the savage to the civilized, in the last of which " man acomplishes the task of his social infancy,—the development of the elements of Industry, Art and Science, which and necessary to the founding of Asociation . . ." [24] Although it was admitted that the existing stage of civilization was a step in human progress, it was felt that an uncritical admiration of its achievements only concealed its evidences of misery and incipient decline.[25] For example, in the United States there was an unwaranted confidence that republican institutions could prevent this decay and that social progress could be attained gradually. Therefore, Brisbane's book emphasized the view that Fourier was the genius capable of furthering the human instinct for progress:

22 See Brisbane's own account: *Albert Brisbane, A Mental Biography* with a character study by his wife Redelia Brisbane (Boston, 1893), ch. 9; see also: Horace Greeley, *Recollections of a Busy Life* (New York, 1868), chs. 19 and 20.

23 Albert Brisbane, *Social Destiny of Man* (Phil., 1840), pp. 92, 95, 199-200.

24 *Ibid.*, pp. 277.

25 *Ibid.*, pp. 285, 331.

Nature—not trusting the fulfillment of her plans to human science or to the efforts of individuals—has implanted in man an instinct of social progress, which, it is true, will lead him through a series of transformations, to the attainment of his Destiny; but she has also reserved for his intelligence the noble prerogative of hastening this progress, and of anticipating results, which, if left to the gradual movement of society, would require centuries to effect. Social progress therefore, may be effected by instinct or by genius . . .

The first progress of the human race is to develop industry and the arts and sciences; the second is to combine them and found Association.[26]

Brisbane in the Fall of 1843 continued his work for the cause with the founding of a Fourierist magazine, *The Phalanx*. In the Prospectus of this journal it was announced that " THE PHALANX will discuss political, social, and religious questions on the broadest grounds of universality and impartiality, and with reference to their practical bearing upon Social Progress and the Happiness of Mankind." [27] Many of the articles were devoted to a denunciation of the evils of machinery, as operated under the American system of political instead of social reform, and the view was maintained that

The power of Production is unlimited, and the world may be filled with riches . . . and all may possess and enjoy them abundantly, if *Labor is but rightly organized*. Is not the question worthy of the highest consideration?" [28]

Horace Greeley did not accept Brisbane's insistence on Fourierism as the only true exposition of progress,[29] but he was himself an enthusiastic advocate of association during the 1840's. As early as 1841, an article in Greeley's *New Yorker* con-

26 *Ibid.*, pp. 331-332.

27 " Prospectus," *Phalanx*, I (Oct. 5, Nov. 4, 1843), Title Page.

28 " Exposition of Views and Principles," *ibid.*, I (Oct. 5, 1843), 7.

29 Horace Greeley to " Friend Dana " (Oct. 10, 1842), in the Horace Greeley Miscellaneous Papers (New York Public Library).

trasted the futility of attempting social reforms through lectures and lyceums, with the hope offered by the principles of association. It was believed that one hundred families united together in a socialistic community " might enjoy in plenty the means of physical comfort and intellectual progress, and at the same time accumulate wealth with far greater rapidity and certainty than under the present discordant system." [30] Then in 1846 and 1847, Greeley in his *Tribune* devoted a lengthy series of articles to defending association against the attacks of the *Courier and Enquirer*.[31] Although these years marked the close of extensive Fourierist influence in America, Greeley continued to include the idea of association and socialism in his concept of progress.[32] In a lecture on the significance of the Crystal Palace in 1851, Greeley urged labor to overcome the evils of machinery by association and cooperation:

> Labor working *against* Machinery is inevitably doomed ... Labor working *for* Machinery, in which it has no interest, can obtain in the average but a scanty, precarious and diminishing subsistence; while to Labor working *with* Machinery, which it owns and directs, there are ample recompense, steady employment, and the prospect of gradual improvement.[33]

Another important advocate of Fourierism was Parke Godwin, an editor of the *Evening Post* during much of this period. In 1843 he began his own paper, *The Pathfinder*, dedicated to the task of finding the right path to the goal of " FREEDOM

30 " Social Reform," *New Yorker*, X (Jan. 16, 1841), 281.

31 Greeley, *Association Discussed* (pamphlet containing the *Tribune* and *Courier and Enquirer* articles; New York, 1847), *passim*.

32 Greeley, " Life—the Ideal and the Actual," *Nineteenth Century*, II (1848), 17-23; " Tendencies of Modern Civilization," *Holden's Dollar Mag.*, III (Jan., 1849), 36-39; " Which is Democracy?" *New York Weekly Tribune*, X (Sept. 28, 1850), 3; " Humanity," in *Hints Toward Reforms* ... (New York, 1850), p. 396; see also: Lindsay Swift, *Brook Farm* (New York and London, 1900), p. 276.

33 Greeley, *The Crystal Palace and Its Lessons. A Lecture* (Private Copy, N. Y. P. L.; New York, 1851), p. 26.

and PROGRESS!" [34] Godwin mourned the slow advance of the
world, but, as his short-lived journal drew to its close, he noted
the hope offered the aims of his publication by Fourierism.
Fourier's program, he believed, was not Utopian, but a definite
and precise social science. Therefore he was not hesitant in pro-
claiming:

> We lay no claim to indulgence on the ground of incipient
> science, but boldly claim the power and the will to solve every
> problem of social progress which can possibly arise; and we
> further pledge ourselves that in all cases of progressive social
> organization, the principles of true science guarantee and im-
> prove the interests of all honest classes without exception.[35]

The following year Godwin published *A Popular View of The
Doctrines of Charles Fourier,* to whom, he wrote, "we give our
warmest gratitude for having, under God, taught us the true
method of *Societary* Progress, including both social and individual advancement." [36]

In 1844 Godwin also published another book, which was
based on the ideas of Victor Considerant, the French Fourierist, and in which democracy was discussed as an instrument of
world regeneration. Godwin regretted that democratic principles
no longer existed in fact, and he denounced the laissez faire attitude which was dividing society into classes and crushing labor.
He protested:

> Human beings are not mere commodities, whose price aug-
> ments and diminishes with the supply in the market. Society
> owes them a guaranty of life and work. They possess a right
> to labor, which is the most sacred of all rights. Labor is their
> property; the highest form and source of all property. They
> have intellectual and moral faculties which must be developed.
> God has placed them on earth to advance.[37]

34 "Raising the Standard," *Pathfinder,* I (Feb. 25, 1843), 1.

35 "The Social Pathfinder," *ibid.,* I (May 13, 1843), 179.

36 Parke Godwin, *A Popular View of the Doctrines of Charles Fourier*
(New York, 1844), p. 28.

37 Godwin, *Democracy, Constructive and Pacific* (New York, 1844),

Although Godwin believed " our modern world of industry is a veritable HELL," he admitted that in America, " there has been progress; but it has not been by means of, so much as in spite of, our politics." [38] As a remedy he called for the adjustment of social relations and the organization of industry on the basis of a union of the interests of Capital, Labor, and Talent, along the lines of Fourierism. Confident of the eventual triumph of Fourier's schemes, Godwin asked: " Is it not that the world is travailing in the birth throes of a mighty and better Future." [39] Godwin's interest in socialism continued for some years, but in 1846 with Fourierism declining in America, he admitted in a letter to Charles A. Dana:

> Society is not prepared, except perhaps here and there, for so grand a *leap* into Association proper. Besides, its progress, is a growth and not a jump . . . We have failed because we have desired to go too fast and too far at once . . . the duty of Associationists is to take up Society, where it is, and carry it on gradually to its ulterior destiny.[40]

An important accession to the ranks of the Associationists came in 1844 when the transcendental community at Brook Farm became a Fourierist phalanstery. In the " Introductory Statement " to the new constitution adopted at Brook Farm after the change, it was emphasized that Association was a universal and not a partial reform of society. Not destructive or revolutionary, the work of the community was rather considered " a necessary step in the progress which no one can be blind enough to think has yet reached its limit . . ." Hopeful of assistance from the outside world, the authors of the " Introductory Statement " were confident that their object would be finally attained: " that human life shall yet be developed, not in discord and misery, but in harmony and joy, and

38 *Ibid.*, pp. 21-25.

39 *Ibid.*, p. 43.

40 Godwin to Dana (June 12, 1846), in Bryant-Godwin Papers (New York Public Library).

that the perfected earth shall at last bear on her bosom a race of men worthy of the name." [41]

Many of the early apostles of Fourierism, like Brisbane and Greeley, were frequent visitors to Brook Farm, but especially instrumental in the conversion of the community was William Henry Channing,[42] nephew of William Ellery Channing, and also a Unitarian minister. The younger Channing in his early writings had stressed unity and brotherhood as the way to progress.[43] Then in the Fall of 1843, he founded his magazine, *The Present,* proposing to show the grounds for a reconciliation among reform groups and calling " for the Union and Growth of Religion, Science, and Society." In the "Introduction " to his journal Channing wrote:

> Therefore, in every sphere, however small, let each declare, that Love is the Law of Liberty, that Faith is for ever a Free Inquirer, that Doubt of enlarging Good is virtual Atheism, and Fear of Progress the unpardonable Sin. So let us attest the truth, that the Heavenly Father recreates his universe and regenerates his children, by causing their perennial Growth.[44]

Feeling the need for a social reorganization if this unity were to be achieved, Channing declared: " The error of the modern doctrine of liberty, has been its tone of selfish independence; its idol has been individualism; its sin, lawlessness; its tendencies, to anarchy." [45] As his magazine came to the close of its short

41 George Ripley, Minot Pratt and C. A. Dana, "Introductory Statement" (Brook Farm, Mass., Jan. 1844), quoted in O. B. Frothingham, *George Ripley* (Boston and New York, 1882), pp. 172-173; and in John T. Codman, *Brook Farm* (Boston, 1894), pp. 42-43.

For the enthusiastic comments of one of the members of Brook Farm, see: Marianne Dwight Orvis, *Letters from Brook Farm, 1844-1847,* ed. Amy L. Reed (Poughkeepsie, 1928), pp. 16, 26, 33, 65-66, 113, 178.

42 J. H. Noyes, *History of American Socialisms* (Phil., 1870), p. 117; Swift, *Brook Farm,* p. 217.

43 W. H. Channing: "Progressiveness in Character," *West. Mess.,* VI (Feb., 1839), 270-272; "Liberty," *ibid.,* VII (Sept., 1839), 308-314.

44 Channing, "Introduction," *Present,* I (Sept., 1843), 5.

45 Channing, "Call of the Present.—No. 1 Social Reorganization," *ibid.,* (Oct. 15, 1843), 43.

life in the Spring of 1844, Channing in an article, entitled
" Heaven upon Earth," called for progress through cooperation
and association.[46] The vogue of Fourierism declined, but Channing, unshaken in his faith in progress, related his hopes for
the future to the Christian Socialist movement, founding the
Religious Union of Associationists [47] and a new magazine, *The
Spirit of the Age.*

From 1845 to 1849 the chief repository for the writings of
the American Fourierists, and for many other believers in
progress by reform and innovation, was *The Harbinger, Devoted to Social and Political Progress.* Successor to Brisbane's
Fourierist organ, *The Phalanx, The Harbinger* was published
at Brook Farm with George Ripley, the chief founder and leader of the community, as its editor. Ripley, who had formerly
been a Unitarian minister, in his numerous articles for *The
Harbinger* expressed a firm faith in progress through an application of the principles of association and Christianity.[48] In the
" Introductory Note " or first editorial, he quoted William
Ellery Channing's strictures on civilization and then, addressing
those who believed in progress, he declared:

> With a deep reverence for the Past, we shall strive so to use
> its transmitted treasures, as to lay in the Present, the founda-
> tion of a better Future. Our motto is, the elevation of the
> whole human race, in mind, morals, and manners, and the
> means, which in our view are alone adapted to the accomplish-
> ment of this end, are not violent outbreaks and revolutionary
> agitations, but orderly and progressive reform.[49]

46 Channing, " Heaven Upon Earth," *ibid.*, I (April 1, 1844), 425.

47 For his views at this stage of his life, see: Channing, *The Christian
Church and Social Reform* (Boston, 1848), *passim.*

48 George Ripley, " Tendencies of Modern Civilization," *Harbinger*, I
(June 28, 1845), 33-35; " Signs of Progress," *ibid.*, I (June 28, 1845), 47-48;
" Society as Tested by Experience," *ibid.*, II (April 11, 1846), 283-284;
" Relation of Associationists to Civilization," *ibid.*, VI (Dec. 4, 1847),
36-37.

49 " Introductory Note," *ibid.*, I (June 14, 1845), 8-9.

Ripley was aware of the ugly "tendencies of modern civilization"—its poverty, physical and moral wretchedness, intellectual degradation, and revolting crime, but he saw "signs of progress." The evils of existing society, he believed, were a necessary preliminary stage which would be succeeded by association, the system which he felt was uniquely adapted to promote progress. To the friends of *The Harbinger*, on the occasion of the magazine's second anniversary, Ripley renewed his pledge of social progress:

> We wish to devote " The Harbinger " with more entire consecration than ever to the promotion of this great work. We would make it the organ of social reform, on the broadest scale, the true herald of a future which is to rise upon a world in glory and exceeding joy; and to this end, would continue to express our faith in the reality of a divine order of society, to illustrate the principles of Associative Unity on which it is founded, and to direct the aspirations for truth and good, unattained in the present state, to the objects by which they can be gratified.[50]

Owenism and Fourierism inspired a vast literature in which the idea of progress was considered in terms of a thorough social reform, but in the 1840's and 50s' the concept of progress was also related to other panaceas. In contrast to Utopian socialism, Josiah Warren, the founder of philosophical anarchism in the United States, and a former member of Owen's community at New Harmony, advocated a scheme of economic and per-

50 Ripley, " To the Friends of the Harbinger," *ibid.*, III (June 13, 1846), 12. See also the less optimistic articles by C. A. Dana: " Labor for Wages," *ibid.*, II (April 25, 1846), 318-319; " New Social System," *ibid.*, II (May 9, 1846), 349-350; " Progress of Society," *ibid.*, II (May 16, 1846), 364; " The Other Side of the Picture," *ibid.*, III (Aug. 8, 1846), 142-143.

And by H. H. Van Amringe, " Machinery and Pauperism," *ibid.*, II (May 23, 1846), 375; " The United States," *ibid.*, II (May 30, 1846), 388; " God's Method in Reforms," *Nineteenth Century*, II (1848), 601-616.

For a later work, connecting the idea of progress with Fourierism, published after the vogue of association had declined, see: G. H. Calvert, *Introduction to Social Science* (New York, 1856), *passim*.

sonal freedom which he believed was capable " of elevating the condition and character of our race to the fulfilment of the highest aspirations and purest hopes of the most devoted friends of humanity." [51] A disciple of Warren's, Stephen Pearl Andrews, called by Noyes " the American rival of Comte," [52] believed that the generic principle of all the progressive movements of the age—of Protestantism, of democracy, and of socialism—rested on the sovereignty of the individual, and he declared: " I assert that the law of genuine progress in human affairs is identical with the tendency to individualize." [53] Looking forward to a future state in which no government at all would be needed, Andrews praised the aristocratic parlor gathering, in which the individuality of each one is granted and the intercourse of all is free, as the highest type of society yet achieved. Confident that this Utopia of the parlor could be transferred to all society, he asked:

> Is it conceivable that in all the future progress of humanity, with all the innumerable elements of development which the present age is unfolding, society generally, and in all its relations, will not attain as high a grade of perfection as certain portions of society, in certain special relations, have already attained? [54]

Andrews was especially impatient with those who considered progress inevitable. Instead he urged that it be sought intelligently, according to the principles of a science of society based on his and Warren's ideas of individualism.[55]

51 Josiah Warren, *Equitable Commerce* (New Harmony, 1846), p. 72, and *passim*.

52 J. H. Noyes, *History of American Socialisms*, p. 94.

53 S. P. Andrews, *The True Constitution of Government* ... (New York, 1852), pp. 16-18, 25.

54 *Ibid.*, p. 45.

55 Andrews, *Cost the Limit of Price* (New York, 1852), pp. 20-21, and *passim*; see also: E. M. Schuster, *Native American Anarchism: A Study of Left Wing Individualism* (Northampton, Mass., 1932), pp. 91-112.

Another associate of Warren, and the chief apostle of Comte in America before the Civil War, was Henry Edger,[56] an Englishman, who came to the United States in 1851, full of hope that it was the land of social progress.[57] Edger presented positivism as the true science of progress superior to the other partial reforms of the day. Critical of both the radical and the retrograde parties, he declared:

> the Positive Philosophy has already laid the foundations whereon its adherents may proceed henceforth to construct that Future, which, while realizing all sane aspirations in regard to social progress, will more profoundly consolidate social order than its actual special defenders can dream of, or dare hope for . . .
>
> This gradual substitution of positive in place of fictitious conceptions, in a word of science in place of theology, as the basis of the common opinion, constitutes in fact the fundamental natural law of human progress.[58]

Anarchism and Utopian socialism were the two extreme philosophies of those who denied the possibility of future progress under the laissez faire, capitalistic society existing in America. While their ideologies attracted the favorable notice of many persons prominent in American life and thought, the country as a whole accepted no such radical programs of progress. Whatever the realities of the American scene in the decades before

56 A biography of Edger is soon to be published by R. E. Schneider of The College of the City of New York.

57 Henry Edger, Letter to the London *Leader* (Feb. 5, 1854), in R. L. Hawkins, *Positivism in the United States, 1853-1861* (Cambridge, 1938), pp. 125-126; also ch. 3.

58 Edger, *The Positivist Calendar* (Modern Times, Long Island, 1856), pp. 11, 13, and *passim*; see also Harriet Martineau's translation and condensation of Comte's *Positive Philosophy* (3rd ed.; New York, 1856), Preface and Introd.

The early influence in America of the positive philosophy was not great although one writer did predict that: "Perhaps no work of modern times is destined to exert a deeper and more lasting influence upon human thought and human progress..." O. S. Munsell, "Comte's Positive Philosophy," *Q. Rev. of the Meth. Epis. Church South*, XI (July, 1857), 321.

the Civil War, faith in the free individual living in a free society formed the keynote of the popular philosophy of progress.
However, like the Utopian socialists, aware of the dangers inherent in such a society, certain leaders of the Unitarian and
transcendental movements, without desiring to curb the free
individual, sought to refine and ennoble his way of life. Although the various religious sects on the whole gave a conservative interpretation to the idea of progress, in New England a
large group of clergymen, sympathetic with Unitariansm and
transcendentalism, looked forward to an individual regeneration and also to a better social system in their concept of progress.

William Ellery Channing, organizer of the Unitarian
Church, and a great influence on many of the transcendentalists,
had a staunch faith in the idea of progress. Born in Rhode
Island in 1780, and for almost forty years until his death in
1842 the minister of the Federal Street Church in Boston,
Channing represented the turning point between the philosophy
of the enlightenment and transcendentalism.[59] Graduating from
Harvard in 1798 he went as a private tutor to Virginia, where
he learned to hate slavery, and where his New England Federal-
ism became transformed through its contact with Jeffersonian
liberalism. As a youth Channing had been aided in formulating
his concept of social progress by reading Adam Ferguson's
Civil Society,[60] and in his early sermons in Boston he showed
his concern over the social and moral condition of man in his
progress toward perfectibility.[61] Believing that man was capable
of and destined for progress, Channing felt that Calvinism and
Catholicism were doomed by the progressive spirit of the age.[62]

59 H. W. Schneider, "The Intellectual Background of William Ellery
Channing," *Church History*, VII (March, 1938), 3-23.

60 W. E. Channing, *Memoir*, I, 64.

61 See extracts of sermons delivered from 1810 to 1820 in: Channing,
Memoir, I, 315-316; II, 40-47, 67-69.

62 Channing, "The Moral Argument against Calvinism" (1820), *Works*
(14th ed.; Boston, 1855), I, 240; "On Catholicism" (1836), *ibid.*, II,
269-271.

Freedom of thought and will were necessary for progress, and progress in turn was the great goal of liberty.[63] In discussing the suffering for this freedom undergone by the abolitionists he wrote to James G. Birney in 1836:

> The progress of society depends on nothing more, than on the exposure of time-sanctioned abuses, which cannot be touched without offending multitudes . . . The world is to be carried forward by truth, which at first offends, which wins its way by degrees, which the many hate and would rejoice to crush.[64]

The last years of Channing's life were marked by the turbulence of Jacksonian reform and by the increasing devotion of the nation to material progress. In an earlier chapter Channing's optimistic attitude in regard to the effects of the depression of 1837 was noted. This viewpoint also prevailed in his opinion concerning some of the other aspects of the times. In a letter to the Rev. Henry Channing in 1839, William Ellery declared that despite the failure of civil and religious liberty to fulfill all their original expectations, his faith in the future was unshaken.[65] Believing that God's designs unfolded slowly, and strong in his faith in human nature, Channing was not dismayed by conservative opposition to progress. To Harriet Martineau, the English writer, he affirmed his belief that " the law of progress teaches us that the seeds of something better are to be looked for in the past." [66] Channing hoped that the materialism of the age with its scientific achievements might eventually be transformed into spiritual and cultural standards, more considerate of the welfare of the masses. Feeling that the

63 Channing, "Remarks on the Character and Writings of Fenelon" (1829), ibid., I, 172-173; "Remarks on National Literature" (1830), ibid., I, 247.

64 Channing, "The Abolitionists. A Letter to James G. Birney" (from The Philanthropist, Dec. 20, 1836), ibid., II, 161.

65 Channing to the Rev. Henry Channing (July 28, 1839), Memoir, III, 308.

66 Channing to Miss Harriet Martineau (Oct. 24, 1840), ibid., III, 309.

reaction from the principles of the French Revolution had been natural, he was also sanguine of the eventual triumph of its ideals.[67] In 1841, the year before his death, Channing in his lecture on " The Present Age " reaffirmed his essential optimism. At that time he declared:

> I see the danger of the present state of society, perhaps as clearly as anyone. But still I rejoice to have been born in this age. It is still true that human nature was made for growth, expansion; this is its proper life, and this must not be checked because it has perils ...
>
> History and philosophy plainly show to me in human nature the foundation and promise of a better era, and Christianity concurs with these.[68]

Channing's call to the ministry to take up the cause of social progress was re-echoed by a whole host in Unitarian circles. James Freeman Clarke, George W. Burnap, and other Unitarian clergymen, in their sermons and addresses delivered during the forties and early fifties, maintained that it was an age of progress in which Christianity should exercise a liberalizing influence.[69] Contributors to Unitarian periodicals contrasted the progressiveness of the Unitarian belief in man's free will and his responsible agency with the conservatism of the Calvinist

67 Channing to Harmanus Bleecker (Feb. 7, 1842), *ibid.*, III, 132-133.

68 Channing, " The Present Age " (1841), *Works*, VI, 168, 179; see also: "Dr. Channing's Letter," *Herald of the New Moral World*, I (Sept. 16, 1841), 129-131.

69 George Ripley, *The Claims of the Age on the Work of the Evangelist* (Boston, 1840), pp. 4-5, 10-11; J. F. Clarke, *The Well-Instructed Scribe; or, Reform and Conservatism* (Boston, 1841), pp. 3-5, and *passim*; E. B. Hall, "Relation of the Christian Ministry to Reform," *Chr. Ex.*, XLI (Sept., 1846), 157-173; Samuel Barrett, "Relation of Liberal Christianity to our Age and Country," *ibid.*, XLIII (Sept., 1847), 187-199; G. W. Burnap, *Discourses on the Rectitude of Human Nature* (Boston, 1850), pp. v, 1-22; W. P. Lunt, *The Union of the Human Race* (Boston, 1850), p. 9; Orville Dewey, *The Laws of Human Progress* (New York, 1852), *passim*.

For an earlier discussion, see: Warren Burton, *Cheering Views of Man and Providence* (Boston, 1832), chs. 2, 21.

and Catholic theologies.[70] Writing in 1844 " On the Signs and Prospects of the Age," Orville Dewey, a popular Unitarian clergyman and author, expressed the optimistic spirit, characteristic of so many in the Unitarian Church who discussed progress, in his statement that:

> The very thought, the very hope of progress, is the most certain omen of progress. And that thought is deeply seated in the heart of the world; it is most familiar to the mind of the age; and the age, the world will never let it go. No reform now is deemed impossible; no enterprise for human betterment, impracticable. Every thing may be made better; the veriest conservative admits that. All the mental activity of the world converges to that point ... To all discouragements, to all alarms, to all predictions of evil, we say, WE BELIEVE IN GOD !" [71]

Heir to William Ellery Channing's prestige and influence, Theodore Parker, the noted theologian and reformer, during the 1850's expressed an equally strong faith in the idea of progress. Parker believed that God gave man the capacity to regulate his own progress,[72] and that " From the beginning of human history there has been a progressive development of all the higher faculties of man ..." [73] In a sermon preached at

70 S. Osgood, " Progress of Theology," *West. Mess.*, V (July, 1838), 231-234; " The Unitarian Reform," *ibid.*, VI (Nov., 1838), 1-10; " Free Responsible Agency," *Chr. Ex.*, XXXV (Nov., 1843), 198-209; F. H. Hedge, " The Churches and the Church," *ibid.*, XLI (Sept., 1846), 193-204; E. S. Gannett, " The Nature and Importance of Our Theology," *ibid.*, XLVII (July, 1849), 119; O. B. Frothingham, " Man and Nature, in Their Religious Relations," *ibid.*, LIV (May, 1853), 461; G. W. Burnap, " The Errors and Superstitions of the Church of Rome," *ibid.*, LV (July, 1853), 62.

71 Orville Dewey, " On the Signs and Prospects of the Age," *ibid.*, XXXVI (Jan., 1844), 22.

72 Theodore Parker, *Lessons from the World of Matter* (Boston, 1865), p. 299.

73 Parker, *Sermons of Theism, Atheism, and the Popular Theology* (Boston, 1856), p. 75.

the Pennsylvania yearly meeting of Progressive Friends in 1858, he declared:

> In the human race nothing is ever still; the stream of humanity rolls continually forward, change following change; nation, succeeds to nation, theology to theology, thought to thought. Taken as a whole, this change is a Progress, an ascent from the lower and ruder to the higher and more comprehensive . . .
>
> The Progress of Mankind is continuous and onward, as much subject to a natural law of development as our growth from babyhood to adult life.[74]

The great material and scientific progress of the past, Parker felt, indicated future religious progress [75] and also that all human institutions, " like the machines of the World of Art, are amenable to perpetual improvement, subject to continual revision in the progressive development of mankind." [76] Among the obstacles to progress, in Parker's opinion, were the ecclesiastical institutions, established and stubbornly adhered to by all religious sects. And in a well known address delivered before a teacher's institute in New York State in 1849, he commented:

> In Morals, as in Science, the Church is on the anti-liberal side, afraid of progress, against movement, loving " yet a little sleep, a little slumber; " conservative and chilling, like ice, not creative, nor ever quickening, as water. It doffs to use and wont; has small confidence in Human Nature, much in a few facts of Human History[77]

74 Parker, " Four Sermons Preached at the Pennsylvania Yearly Meeting of Progressive Friends," *Proceedings of ... Progressive Friends* (New York, 1858), p. 50.

75 Parker, *Lessons from the World of Matter*, p. 312.

76 Parker, "A Discourse of the Relations between the Ecclesiastical Institutions and the Religious Consciousness of the American People," *Proceedings of ... Progressive Friends* (New York, 1855), p. 62.

77 Parker, *The Public Education of the People* (Boston, 1850), p. 33; see also his "A Discourse of the Relations ...," *op. cit.*, pp. 82-83; and his " Four Sermons ...," *op. cit.*, p. 77.

In 1859 Parker, forced to leave his church by the illness soon to claim his life, wrote to his old congregation an autobiographical letter, in which he also summed up his faith in the progress and perfectibility of man:

> From the infinite perfection of God there follows unavoidably the relative perfection of all that He creates. So, the nature of man, tending to a progressive development of all his manifold powers, must be the best possible nature, most fit for the perfect accomplishment of the perfect purpose, and the attainment of the perfect end, which God designs for the race and the individual.[78]

The unity of life in the individual, the teachings of geology and of history, all helped to convince Parker, not only that mankind's past had been progressive, but also that " this progressive development does not end with us; we have seen only the beginning; the future triumphs of the race must be vastly greater than all accomplished yet." [79]

The Unitarian Church was confined principally to the Atlantic coast, but the influence of its ministers like Parker extended beyond their own sect and region. Many of the Unitarian clergy also were able to exert an important intellectual force in the nation from their connection with transcendentalism, which in the forties succeeded Unitarianism as the popular reform philosophy of the day. Uniting the liberalism of the early Unitarian theology with the thought of French and the German philosophers like Cousin and Kant, transcendentalism, by placing its emphasis on moral and individual progress, gave hope to those who were distressed by the materialism of the rising industrial order.[80]

[78] " The Letter from Santa Cruz, called ' Theodore Parker's Experience as a Minister ' " (Letter to the Members of the Twenty-Eighth Congregational Society of Boston...April 19, 1859), in John Weiss, *Life and Correspondence of Theodore Parker* (New York, 1864), II, 471.

[79] *Ibid.*, II, 472; see also: H. S. Commager, *Theodore Parker* (Boston, 1936), pp. 194-196.

[80] For some contemporary indications of the influence of Cousin and Kant on transcendentalism and on the idea of progress, see: George Ripley

The unusual promise of the transcendental philosophy was explained in the writings of its devoted disciples. In an article in *The Dial,* transcendentalist magazine, J. A. Saxton, a farmer, author, and lecturer, contrasted the conservatism of Locke's philosophy of materialism with the hope of progress offered by transcendentalism. Scientific and material progress, he felt, was only a manifestation of the prerequisite, intuitive, moral progress which transcendentalism explained. Believing that man's " destinies are guided by an intuition of something higher, than sense can give him any conception of," Saxton wrote that the history of humanity " has been, and will ever be a history of progress, constant, perpetual . . ."

> As with individuals, so with nations, every step of progress makes each succeeding one easier. Every improvement in the social institutions of a nation prepares the way for another, that is to follow it, brings it nearer, and gives assurance that it shall be accomplished with less expense of human happiness.[81]

(ed.), *Philosophical Miscellanies* (Specimens of Foreign Standard Literature, vols. 1-2; Boston, 1838), I, 29; " Transcendental Theology," *Chr. Ex.,* XXX (May, 1841), 189-223; James Murdock, *Sketches of Modern Philosophy* (Hartford, 1842), chs. 14-15; " Spirit and Tendencies of the New School of Philosophy," *Dem. Rev.,* XV (July, 1844), 17-32; Weiss, *Life . . . of Theodore Parker,* I, 160-162.

See also: W. L. Leighton, *French Philosophers and New England Transcendentalism* (Charlottesville, 1908), *passim*; H. C. Goddard, *Studies in New England Transcendentalism* (New York, 1908), pp. 136-144, and *passim*; Woodbridge Riley, *American Thought from Puritanism to Pragmatism* (2nd ed.; New York, 1923), chs. 6, 8, 11; H. M. Jones, *America and French Culture, 1750-1848* (Chapel Hill, 1927), ch. 13; J. H. Muirhead, " How Hegel Came to America," *Philosophical Review,* XXXVII (May, 1928), 226-229; William Girard, *Du Transcendantalisme Considéré Essentiellement dans Sa Definition et Ses Origines Françaises* (Berkeley, 1916), pp. 351-498.

81 J. .A. Saxton, " Prophecy-—Transcendentalism—Progress," *Dial,* II (July, 1844), 104, 107; for a similar emphasis on inward progress, see the Letter to A. Brooke by Charles Lane and Bronson Alcott (*Herald of Freedom,* Sept. 8, 1843), quoted by C. E. Sears, *Bronson Alcott's Fruitlands* (Boston and New York, 1915), p. 52; for a critical view of this

Margaret Fuller, editor of *The Dial,* high priestess of transcendentalism, and one of the most unusual women of her time,
in her correspondence of 1840 explained her hopes for the new
philosophy. Of the opinion that the United States was a land
chiefly characterized by material progress, she sympathized
with those radicals who maintained that education and political
freedom did not by themselves counteract the growing power of
the commercial aristocracy. Although she believed that society
was made for the individual man, she also was forced to admit:

> Utopia it is impossible to build up. At least my hopes for
> our race on this planet are more limited than those of most
> of my friends. I accept the limitations of human nature, and
> believe a wise acknowledgment of them one of the best condi-
> tions of progress. Yet every noble scheme, every poetic mani-
> festation, prophesies to man his eventual destiny. And were
> not man ever more sanguine than facts at the moment justify,
> he would remain torpid, or be sunk in sensuality. It is on this
> ground that I sympathize with what is called the " Transcen-
> dental party," and that I feel their aim to be the true one.[82]

Ralph Waldo Emerson, foremost philosopher of the transcendental movement, and for a short time a Unitarian minister, in
his writings illustrates the many facets of the American concept
of progress.[83] Born in Boston and educated at Harvard, Emerson was enjoying success as a young minister when he decided
in 1832 to break with the Second Unitarian Church of Boston
over the ceremony of the celebration of the Lord's Supper. He
then embarked on a trip to Europe, in the course of which he
had an eventful meeting with Thomas Carlyle, the English disciple of the German idealist school. Also alive to the philosophy

philosophy, see: " Transcendentalism," *S. Q. Rev.,* II (Oct., 1842), 458-
460, 471.

See also: Merle Curti, " The Great Mr. Locke America's Philosopher,
1783-1861," *Huntington Lib. Bull.,* no. 11 (April, 1937), 122 ff.

82 Margaret Fuller Ossoli, in *Memoirs* (1852), I, 205-206.

83 For an excellent, detailed discussion, see: Mildred Silver, " Emerson
and the Idea of Progress," *Am. Lit.,* XII (March, 1940), 1-19.

of Coleridge and Goethe, Emerson returned home to the United States, where the setting was favorable for him to begin his life's work as a lecturer. In the youthful entries in his *Journals* Emerson had combined a patriotic enthusiasm for American progress with his feeling that the progress of the species was a progress in the individual alone.[84] Then in 1836 Emerson produced the celebrated little treatise on *Nature* in which he set the tone for much of his later work. Criticizing the age as too retrospective, he proclaimed that exhaustion could not be true of man or nature. He also believed that there was an infinite scope to the activity of man under the Spirit, and he wrote: " It is esential to a true theory of nature and of man, that it should contain somewhat progressive." [85] Applying these thoughts to the American scene, Emerson, a year later, in his noteworthy Phi Beta Kappa address, *The American Scholar,* called for the creation of an American literature commensurate with " the auspicious signs of the coming days, as they glimmer already through poetry and art, through philosophy and science, through church and state." [86]

In the minds of Emerson and the transcendentalists, the progress of society depended primarily upon the improvement of its individual members. With the publication of his important first series of *Essays* in 1841, Emerson examined in detail this relationship of the individual to society. In the famous piece on " Self-Reliance " he took issue with the comfortable American assurance in the inevitable progress of society. Calling society a wave, he maintained that the progress in the arts of civilization had been accompanied by a deterioration in the individual man. "All men plume themselves on the improvement of society, and no man improves," he declared.

84 R. W. Emerson, *Journals,* I, 74, 103, 201-203, 219-220, 299-300; II, 400; IV, 85, 137-138, 158, 306, 473; V, 24, 230.

85 Emerson, " Nature " (1836), *Complete Works* (Cent. ed.; Boston and New York, 1903-1906), I, 61, 3.

86 Emerson, " The American Scholar " (1837), *ibid.,* I, 110; see also: " Literary Ethics," (1838), *ibid.,* I, 158 ff., 164.

Society never advances. It recedes as fast on one side as it gains on the other. It undergoes continual changes; it is barbarous, it is civilized, it is christianized, it is rich, it is scientific; but this change is not amelioration. For every thing that is given something is taken. Society acquires new arts and loses old instincts.[87]

Scornful of the false deference paid to property and to government, Emerson urged that a greater self-reliance would revolutionize men and institutions, and he wrote: " Nothing can bring you peace but yourself. Nothing can bring you peace but the triumph of principles." [88] Declaring in another essay that " The infallible index of true progress is found in the tone the man takes," [89] Emerson, against the concept of material progress, placed the idea of the over-soul with its transcendental implications of truth and beauty.[90] He labelled the life of man " a self-evolving circle," maintaining the view that " this incessant movement and progression which all things partake could never become sensible to us but by contrast to some principle of fixture or stability in the soul. : Whilst the eternal generation of circles proceeds, the eternal generator abides." [91] The individual, however, was not bound to the standards of a bygone generation. Limitation was the only sin, and Emerson believed that men should face the future with real enthusiasm:

There are no fixtures in nature . . .

There is not a piece of science but its flank may be turned tomorrow; there is not any literary reputation, not the so-called eternal names of fame, that may not be revised and con-

87 Emerson, " Self-Reliance " (1841), *ibid.*, II, 84, and *passim*; see also: " Politics " (1844), *ibid.*, III, 216.

88 Emerson, " Self-Reliance," *ibid.*, II, 90; see also: " Heroism " (1841), *ibid.*, I, 262.

89 Emerson, " The Over-Soul " (1841), *ibid.*, II, 286.

90 Emerson, " Compensation " (1841), *ibid.*, II, 122; " The Transcendentalist " (1842), *ibid.*, I, 359.

91 Emerson, " Circles " (1841), *ibid.*, II, 304, 318.

demned. The very hopes of man, the thoughts of his heart, the religion of nations, the manners and morals of mankind are all at the mercy of a new generation.[92]

During the early 1840's Emerson became increasingly affected by the reform movements of the period. Unable to maintain his customary aloof attitude, in his popular addresses he praised reform as the means of future progress. In his " Lecture on the Times," in 1841, he noted that there were always two parties in history, the party of the Past and the party of the Future. Of the two Emerson preferred the second group, " the speculators." The age, he believed, was one of revolution, and he declared:

> At the manifest risk of repeating what every other Age has thought of itself, we might say we think the Genius of this Age more philosophical than any other has been, righter in its aims, truer, with less fear, less fable, less mixture of any sort.[93]

Later, in 1844, in speaking on the topic " The Young American," Emerson called attention to the youth and resources of the country, to the new social movements heralded by the Etzlers and Fouriers, and he announced:

> Gentlemen, the development of our American internal resources, the extension to the utmost of the commercial system, and the appearance of new moral causes which are to modify the State, are giving an aspect of greatness to the Future, which the imagination fears to open. One thing is plain for all men of common sense and common conscience, *that here,* here in America, is the home of man.[94]

With the reform energy of the country blunted by the Mexican War and increasingly absorbed by the struggle over slav-

92 *Ibid.,* II, 302, 308-309.

93 Emerson, " Lecture on the Times " (1841), *ibid.,* I, 287; see also: " Man the Reformer " (1841), *ibid.,* I, 248-251.

94 Emerson, " The Young American " (1841), *ibid.,* I, 391, and *passim.*

ery, to men like Emerson the evil seemed to be outweighing the good in American life. In his own New England the land speculators and the rising industrial class were in the saddle. Emerson, who had once in his enthusiasm over the railroads exclaimed: " Machinery and Transcendentalism agree well, . . ." [95] in 1847 observed of the Lowell capitalists:

> They are an ardent race, and are fully possessed with that hatred of labor, which is the principle of progress in the human race, as any other people. They must and will have the enjoyment without the sweat. So they buy slaves, where the women will permit it; where they will not, they make the wind, the tide, the waterfall, the steam, the cloud, the lightning do the work, by every art and device their cunningest brain can achieve.[96]

A decade later, in 1857, lecturing on " Works and Days," Emerson asked: " What have these arts done for the character, for the worth of mankind? Are men better?" And he replied: " 'Tis too plain that with the material power the moral progress has not kept pace. It appears that we have not made a judicious investment. Works and days were offered us, and we took works." [97]

Emerson did not consistently overrule either the actuality or the possibility of the progress of civilization. Against the idea that this progress was automatic and inevitable, he counselled individual and moral regeneration as the effective agent in social progress. Optimistic over the undeveloped powers of humanity and of nature, he also feared the perversion of these powers by the rising American business class. A pessimism over the domination of American life by the forces of material progress there-

95 Emerson, *Journals* (1843), VI, 397.

96 *Ibid.*, VII (1847), 300; see also: " The Method of Nature " (1841), *Complete Works*, I, 191-193.

97 Emerson, " Works and Days " (1857), *ibid.*, VII, 166; but see: *Journals* (1856), IX, 27-28, 42.

fore clouded the natural optimism and idealism of his nature, to which the idea of progress so strongly appealed.

Emerson's friend and transcendental partner, Henry Thoreau, carrying individualism to the conclusion of philosophical anarchism, did not even share Emerson's varying enthusiasm for the times. After his graduation from Harvard in 1837, Thoreau spent the greater part of his life in his birthplace, Concord, Massachusetts. Here he pursued an idyllic life, intermittently teaching school or doing odd jobs, cultivating his friendship with Emerson and the other transcendentalists, tramping in the woods, or sojourning at Walden Pond. In one of his early published writings he reviewed Etzler's Utopian book, *Paradise to be Regained,* for the *Democratic Review* of 1843. Skeptical of the efficacy of Etzler's schemes, Thoreau complained that the book " feeds our faith rather than contents our understanding." Even more critical of Etzler's goal of achieving mere physical comfort and pleasure, Thoreau emphasized the importance of the individual in any schemes for future progress.[98]

" Near the end of March, 1845," Thoreau " went down to the woods by Walden Pond." Here he built his home and lived by his own efforts for almost a year. He did not advocate that others follow his example, and he considered himself neither a hermit nor the founder of a new Utopia. He wished simply to see if it were possible for an individual to get at the heart of life, unfettered by the complications of his environment. It was an attempt to find out the real purpose for the business of living, not an effort to exchange permanently a civilized for a primitive existence. In *Walden,* the record of his experiment, which he finally published in 1854, Thoreau delivered a classic protest against the evils of modern progress. He denounced the whole cult of efficiency and of material accumulation for its disregard of the improvement of the individual man. Civilization

98 H. D. Thoreau, " Paradise (to be) Regained," *Dem. Rev.,* XIII (Nov., 1843), 460, 462; also in Thoreau's *Writings* (Boston and New York, 1906), IV, 280-305.

had become more complicated, while its inhabitants were only "more experienced and wiser" savages.[99] Thoreau admitted that civilization might become a blessing, but he argued that the stream of scientific inventions were accomplishing just the opposite result. To Thoreau his experiment was a personal success, a change of scenery which gave him a new perspective of life. However, his message, exposing the illusion of a hundred modern improvements, was drowned out by the growing industrialization of American life.[100]

The objections to the society of his time which Thoreau expressed in *Walden* also influenced his attitude toward the growing power of government. Following the war between the United States and Mexico, Thoreau in his essay on *Civil Disobedience* accepted the motto, " That government is best which governs least . . ." The progress of America, he believed, had been achieved by forces other than its government. Admitting that, " The progress from an absolute to a limited monarchy, from a limited monarchy to a democracy, is a progress toward a true respect for the individual," he asked: " Is a democracy, such as we know it, the last improvement possible in government? Is it not possible to take a step further towards recognizing and organizing the rights of man?" [101] Early in the fifties, Thoreau, in writing to a friend, complained that increased material wealth only made life more complicated, and he announced:

The whole enterprise of this nation, which is not an upward, but a westward one, toward Oregon, California, Japan, etc., is totally devoid of interest to me, whether performed on foot or by a Pacific railroad. It is not illustrated by a thought; it is not warmed by a sentiment; there is nothing in it which one should lay down his life for, nor even his gloves,

99 Thoreau, *Walden* (1854), *ibid.*, II, 44.

100 *Ibid.*, II, 57 and *passim*; see also his " Journal " (Aug. 6, 1858 and Dec. 26, 1860), *ibid.*, XVII, 78-79; XX, 295.

101 Thoreau, " Civil Disobedience " (1849), *Writings*, IV, 386, 356-357.

—hardly which one should take up a newspaper for. It is perfectly heathenish,—a filibustering *toward* heaven by the great western route. No; they may go their way to their manifest destiny, which I trust is not mine.[102]

These radical and transcendental visions of a new society were developed in the extensive prose writings of many reformers and social critics. However, the spirit of their philosophy of progress received one of its finest brief expressions in a poem of James Russell Lowell, who made his mark as a reformer with his trenchant criticism of the motives of the Mexican War in his *Bigelow Papers*. In this poem, " A Glance Behind the Curtain " (1843), Lowell affirmed his belief that the progressive destiny shaping man's course could be strengthened by human effort:

> New times demand new measures and new men;
> The world advances, and in time outgrows
> The laws that in our fathers' day were best ;
> And, doubtless, after us, some purer scheme
> Will be shaped out by wiser men than we,
> Made wiser by the steady growth of truth.
> We cannot hale Utopia on by force;
> But better, almost be at work in sin,
> Than in a brute inaction browse and sleep.[103]

Lowell's call to action came at a time when Thoreau and Emerson, like the Fourierists and early labor spokesmen, were finding themselves in opposition to many of the trends of American life. To the transcendentalists the debasement of the individual was the primary fault to be corrected; to the Utopian socialists it was the false system of society. Labor groups resented their oppression by the rising industrial class. Intellectuals were dismayed by the materialistic philosophy of the new business class. Differing in their analyses these various critics

102 Thoreau to H. Blake (Feb. 27, 1853), *ibid.*, VI, 210.

103 J. R. Lowell, "A Glance Behind the Curtain" (1843), *Complete Writings* (Boston and New York, 1904), IX, 144.

of American society were, however, united in their belief that reform was needed for true progress, and in their confidence that their plans would be adopted. Not complacent believers in the prospect of a gradual, automatic improvement, they were nevertheless steadfast in their faith that the future could be bettered. Keeping alive the struggle for liberal reform, these dissidents maintained the idealistic aspect of the idea of progress and protested against its absorption by the forces of manifest destiny and material progress. Moreover, for all reform groups, the dynamic philosophy and optimistic psychology, engendered by such an idea as that of progress, was a necessary element for the growth of their programs of social improvement.

CHAPTER VI

THE DEFENCE OF SOCIAL STABILITY

IN contrast with the groups which interpreted progress in the light of a social reform were those whose distrust of the times found expression in a pessimistic or a conservative interpretation of the idea of progress. Foremost among these conservatives were the church spokesmen who counselled that social progress be surrounded and restrained by the stabilizing influence of religion. Intellectuals, steeped in the traditions of the classics and history, cynical of the possibility of reform, and distrustful of an age of innovation, also became the advocates of social stability or the voices of despair. Representatives of the propertied interests of the country, uncertain of the implications of the idea of progress, did their best to emphasize its gradual and conservative aspects. Therefore the idea of progress, vague enough to be interpreted in the light of their own interests and beliefs, seldom had to be denied completely by the advocates of social stability.

In the religious writings of the period Christianity was invoked as the decisive element in the progress of civilization. Christian clergymen, in addressing college audiences, expressed their regret that the possibilities of religion were neglected, and they predicted great future progress and a perfect state of society only if the promise of Christianity was realized.[1] Among the orthodox ministers true progress was believed impossible unless the efforts of man were inspired by the Grace of God. Contributors to the popular religious periodicals of the day therefore advocated an unquestioned reliance on the progressive purposes of a divine Providence. In the words of the *Presbyter-*

1 See for example: Lyman Beecher, *The Memory of Our Fathers* (Boston, 1828); Jonathan Blanchard, *A Perfect State of Society* (Oberlin, 1839); W. D. Snodgrass, *An Address ... Washington College* (New York, 1845); Leonard Bacon, *Christianity in History* (New Haven, 1848); W. H. Green, *The Destiny of Man* (Phil., 1853); Nathan Lord, *The Improvement of the Present State of Things* (Hanover, 1853).

ian Quarterly Review of 1853 : " Our strongest reason for faith in the doctrine of Progress, after all, is that it is the great rule of Providence, which predetermined and is controlling all the evolutions of time." [2]

The question of whether the Christian theology itself was progressive also aroused considerable agitation among the religious sects. In 1845 George Bush, a leading Presbyterian clergyman, about to leave his church and join the Swedenborgian Church of New Jerusalem, published his widely-noted controversial book, *Anastasis,* in which he argued the thesis " that the knowledge of Revelation, like that of Nature, is destined to be continually on the advance." [3] Bush believed that the same law of " gradual development " pertained to both nature and religious truth, and he therefore announced " that biblical science, like all other sciences, is *progressive* . . ." [4] Taking a middle position on this question of the progress of theology, William Adams, a leading New School Presbyterian, decided that, although the laws of religion did not change, there was progress : " In the rectification of our own opinions and speculations concerning Christianity ; and in the growth of our own faculties, to discern more and more of its innumerable relations and unfolding glories." [5] Adams then concluded :

> Progress !—'tis the law of our nature. Nor let any man who studies the scriptures for himself, and searches into the har-

2 "Laws of Progress," *Presby. Q. Rev.,* II (Dec., 1853), 421 ; see also: L. P. Hickok, " The Idea of Humanity in Its Progress to Its Consummation," *Bib. Repos.,* 3rd ser., III (Oct., 1847), 731-748; " Progress," *Ladies' Repos.,* VI (Jan., 1846), 27-28; " Christianity : Our Help and Hope," *Freewill Baptist Q.,* II (Oct., 1854), 361-383 ; " Christianity the World's Great Need," *ibid.,* VII (Jan., 1859), 1-32; W. G. W. Lewis, " True Progression," *Ladies' Repos.,* XX (April, 1860), 231-237.

3 George Bush, *Anastasis* (New York and London, 1845), p. 13; for a different view, see: [John W. Yeomans], " Bush on the Resurrection," *Bib. Rep.,* XVII (Jan., 1845), 140-143; see also: " Progress in Doctrinal Theology and Biblical Interpretations," *Freewill Baptist Q.,* V (Jan., 1857), 21-30.

4 Bush, *Anastasis,* pp. 15, 17.

5 William Adams, " The Law of Progress in Its Application to Christianity," *Bib. Repos.,* 3rd ser., III (April, 1847), 200.

monies and relations of truth with an eager mind, ever
imagine that the time will come when there will be a limit
to his advancement ... [6]

The idea that Christianity was progressive in its theology
was accepted by many writers, both secular and clerical, who
urged the church to broaden its narrow viewpoint and undertake the role of leadership in a progressive society. In an article
typical of others containing this view, Horace Greeley, the reform editor, deplored the failure of the moral to keep pace with
the material progress of the age. Believing that God desired
progress and that the Gospel was " ever living, ever new," he
declared, " because it is so do we insist that its truths shall be
freshly applied to the overthrow of every detected evil, the
furtherance of every known good." [7] The proponents of Christian reform also denounced the opposition to the idea of progress offered by certain theologians and especially by the Miller-
ites with their theory of the imminent millennium. In attacking
the otherworldliness of these groups, an editorial in Adin Ballou's *Practical Christian* expressed the idea that

> if this thought of human progress be a dream, it were well
> for us to dream on forever, for it is a thought that gives
> infinite worth and beauty to existence, and inspires a hope
> and courage which will themselves do much towards realiz-
> ing the glorious ideal. Without the prospect, human life would
> be comparatively a worthless boon, and the Creator might
> well repent himself for the bestowment of it. [8]

6 *Ibid.*, p. 213.

7 Horace Greeley, " The Age We Live In," *Nineteenth Century*, I (1848),
50-54; see also: " The Progress and the Defects of Christian Civilization,"
Freewill Baptist Q., I (Jan., 1853), 10-30; W. J. Sasnett, *Progress: Considered with Particular Reference to the Methodist Episcopal Church.
South* (Nashville, 1855), pp. 7-12, 312-319, and *passim*; D. H. Barlow, " The
Present as It Is, and the Future to Be," *Graham's Mag.*, XXXIX (Nov.,
1851) 257-260.

An extended argument for social Christianity and progress was made by
the political economist [Stephen Colwell], *Politics for American Christians*
(Phil., 1852), *passim*.

8 " Signs of Progress," *Practical Christian*, XII (June 21, 1852), 14;
see also: Adin Ballou, *Practical Christian Socialism: A Conversational*

Sympathetic with the program of progress by reform, the Unitarian leaders like Channing and Parker, in their writings, already discussed in the previous chapter, had advocated the cause of liberal Christianity. However, the Unitarian clergy were exceptional in their stand for social progress. In the other Christian churches the emphasis was rather placed on some form of social stability. Toward the close of the forties many of the orthodox church leaders became particularly alarmed at the irreligious tendencies of some of the reform movements of the period. In a characteristic statement of their fears, a writer in the *New Englander,* the organ of the liberal Congregationalists, warned that reform and progress were being corrupted by an excess of radicalism and by a spirit of infidelity. Believing " that the end of popular progress is not the improvement of man's external social and political condition " but rather " the improvement of the individual man," he concluded: " Popular progress must be guided by Christianity to prevent its issuing in anarchy." [9]

In an attempt to allay these fears of radicalism Henry Ward Beecher, the great revivalist preacher from the West, just entering upon his remarkable career as minister of the Plymouth Congregational Church in Brooklyn, took up the question of reform and Christianity in his Thanksgiving Day sermon in 1847. Beecher rejoiced " *in the upward and progressive tendency of the great elements of good,*" and he noted that truth having been discovered already by Christianity, progress might be expected not from any new discoveries but by the " practical *applications* of the long known and simplest truths of the Bible." [10] Unafraid of " the excesses of reformers " and of " the irreligious tendencies of many of the schemes of Progress," he

Exposition of the True System of Human Society (Hopedale and New York, 1854), pp. 31, 127-128, 175-189, and *passim.*

9 " The Dependence of Popular Progress Upon Christianity," *New Englander,* V (July, 1847), 437, 445, and *passim.*

10 H. W. Beecher, *A Discourse delivered at the Plymouth Church* (New York, 1848), pp. 12, 19.

counselled: " We are so calmly certain that the religion of Christ contains the germ of all right reformation, that we await, with sure prescience, the disaster of all reforms which spurn or neglect it." [11] He was not alarmed by the popularity of the associations of the Fourierists and other reformers, for he felt that

> Our faith in any great and constant Progress rests chiefly upon one Association, THE CHURCH, when she shall become the exponent of the benevolence of the Gospel, and the representative of the spirit of Christ. The truth which she has so long preached to the dull ear is beginning to be heard. Nor should the Church be the one to suspect or oppose that progress which has sprung from her own preaching. The great truths of religion and humanity are abroad in the world. Let him who wishes shame and disaster oppose them.[12]

A subject of particular concern in conservative religious circles at the time of the revolutionary movements of 1848 was the effect of socialism on the progress of civilization and on the future of the church. In those years immediately following the revolutions, many clergymen and writers contributed to conservative religious reviews articles concerned with the hope of progress offered by the Gospel in a world which, they feared, was beset by revolution, socialism, and infidelity.[13] In 1854

11 *Ibid.*, p. 20.

12 *Ibid.*, p. 20; see also the report of Beecher's Lecture, "The Conservative and the Progressive," in the *New York Weekly Tribune*, XII (Jan. 29, 1853), 2.

13 A. Coquerel, quoted in the "Editors' Table," *Godey's Lady's Book*, XXXVII (Aug. 1848), 114; B. B. Edwards, "The Advancement of Society in Knowledge and Virtue," *Bibliotheca Sacra*, V (May, 1848), 358-375; Charles White, "The Conservative Element in Christianity," *ibid.*, IX (July, 1852), 540-562; Samuel Harris, "The Demands of Infidelity Satisfied by Christianity," *ibid.*, XIII (April, 1856), 272-314; "Progress of Society," *Puritan Recorder*, XXXIV (June 21, 1849), 98; "The Present State of the World, " *ibid.*, XXXV (Dec. 5, 1850), 194; "Socialism in the United States," *Chr. Rev.*, XV (Oct., 1850), 520-543; "Socialism," *Church Review*, II (Jan., 1850), 491-504; "Modern Theories of Social Progress," *ibid.*, V (April, 1852), 9-25; S. P. E., "The Element of Stability in Modern Society," *Holden's Dollar Mag.*, VI (Dec. 1850), 734-736; "The Logic of Religion," *Bib. Rep.*, XXVII (July, 1855), 421-422.

William R. Williams, a man of scholarly interests destined to complete over fifty years service as pastor of the Amity Baptist Church in New York, published a little volume entitled *Religious Progress,* in which he warned that all civil and social change must be preceded by an individual and moral improvement. In an age of scientific discovery and of political agitation, Williams argued for a return to the Gospel and for the substitution of God's law of human brotherhood for man's resort to revolution.[14] He declared: " There will be social progress, then; but it will be sober, and considerate, and self-restrained; not demanding the impossible, and not fretting at and fighting against the inevitable." [15] In another attempt to clarify the attitude of the conservative clergy toward the reform movements of the day, Lyman H. Atwater, a Congregational minister in Connecticut, and later a professor of philosophy at Princeton, wrote in 1852 that the conflict was not over progress but over " different kinds and methods of progress." Against agrarianism and radicalism, he maintained, in a passage characteristic of many similar ministerial expressions, " that stability, at least a good degree of it, is essential to all true progress." [16]

The concept of the church acting as a conservative check on the idea of progress received extensive support from some of the Catholic spokesmen. Bishop Hughes of New York believed that man was naturally evil and that the degree of progress already attained by society had been due to Christianity. " Wherever Christianity has not gone there has been no progress," he declared, for:

> The world preaches progress, but it recognizes no fixed starting point—no definite aim. Its ideas of progress are con-

14 W. R. Williams, *Religious Progress* (Boston and New York, 1854), Lecture I; see also his earlier academic address, *The Conservative Principle in our Literature* (New York, 1844), p. 22, and *passim.*

15 Williams, *Religious Progress*, pp. 26-27.

16 L. H. Atwater, " The True Progress of Society," *Bib. Rep.*, XXIV (Jan., 1852), 19, 21; see also: S. C. Bartlett, *The Duty and Limitations of Civil Obedience* (Manchester, N. H., 1853), pp. 4-6.

fused; it has not any standard or regulator of moral right and wrong in its political code; its principles are the passions and caprices of the day.[17]

An important Catholic lay philosopher, and the author who perhaps devoted the most attention to the idea of progress of all American religious writers before the Civil War was Orestes A. Brownson, the radical reformer who became a convert to Catholicism in 1844. During the years immediately preceding his conversion, Brownson's articles in the *Boston Quarterly Review* revealed his dissatisfaction with the kind of progress advocated by reformers and his increasing reliance on the Christian church in his hopes for the future advancement of humanity.[18] Then in the beginning of 1844 he founded a new journal, confessing in his first editorial " the same unquenchable desire for individual and social progress . . . but only progress under and through existing institutions." [19] Disillusioned with his appeals to the laboring classes, Brownson turned to " the more favored classes themselves " and to moral and religious influences, announcing that : " Here is my hope for the world. There is a higher power than that of man; a mightier reformer than human agency." [20]

During the following decade Brownson devoted many articles to denouncing Protestantism and those radical tendencies of the day, gathered under the banners of Fourierism, transcendentalism, comeouterism, Young America, and revolution itself.[21] Side by side with his bitter criticism of the philosophy of

17 John Hughes, " The Church and the World " (1850), *Complete Works* (New York, 1866), II, 73; see also his " Influence of Christianity upon Civilization " (1843), *ibid.*, I, 351-370; " Christianity, the Only Source of Moral, Social, and Political Regeneration " (1847), *ibid.*, I, 558-573.

18 *Boston Q. Rev.*, I (April, 1838), 192-199; *ibid.*, I (July, 1838), 377-384; *ibid.*, V (Jan., 1842), 60-84; *ibid.*, V (April, 1842), 154.

19 " Introduction," *Brownson's Q. Rev.*, I (Jan., 1844), 4, 19.

20 *Ibid.*, I (Jan., 1844), 24-26.

21 *Ibid.*, I (April, 1844), 188-189; *ibid.*, I (July, 1844) 367-385; *ibid.*, II (July, 1845), 293-294; *ibid.*, 2nd ser., II (Oct., 1848), 477; *ibid.*, 3rd ser., II (Jan., April, July, and Oct., 1854), 1, 137, 273, 409 ff., *passim*.

these movements, he placed his own concept of religious progress. Although Brownson admitted that the Catholic Church in America opposed the "movement party," he maintained:

> The Church does not oppose progress, but she may, we own, oppose your *doctrine* of progress ... Progress there may be, but not without a power foreign to the subject of progress. The error of the movement party is not in demanding progress, but in demanding it of man alone, and where it is suicidal to demand it. The condition of progress is fixed, permanent, and immovable religious and political institutions. The movement party overlook this fact, and demand progress in institutions themselves.[22]

Brownson especially criticized the Protestants for what he believed was their faith in natural and material progress,[23] but he was careful to assert that Catholicism did not completely deny American material progress.[24] Hopeful that a spiritual regeneration might accompany this material prosperity, Brownson in 1859 wrote:

> The age attaches, no doubt, too much importance to what is called the progress of society or the progress of civilization, which, to the man whose eye is fixed on God and eternity, can appear of not great value. But we must take our age as we find it, and accept as far as we lawfully can, respect even its prejudices where they are not sinful, in the hope of winning its regard for that higher progress proposed by the church, and possible only in her communion.[25]

The Catholic Church in its stand against innovation seemed to be the most steadfast representative of social stability in a world of change. Expressing this view, a contributor to a popu-

22 *Ibid.*, III (Jan., 1846), 124.

23 *Ibid.*, 2nd ser., II (April, 1848), 152-153, 159; *ibid.*, New York ser., II (April, 1857), 198-200.

24 *Ibid.*, 2nd ser., V (Oct., 1851), 452-461; *ibid.*, 3rd ser., III (Oct., 1855), 522-523; *ibid.*, New York ser., I (Oct., 1856), 423-426.

25 *Ibid.*, New York ser., IV (April, 1859), 280.

lar Southern periodical wrote on the eve of the Civil War that Catholicism " does not ride the hobby of progress in full speed, endangering the life of the adventurous rider, but it jogs along on its heavy pack-horse, at a slow pace, measuring the distance to be travelled over, and surveying the obstacles to be overcome." [26] An emphasis upon a moral reform of the individual formed a major part of the concept of progress maintained in all religious circles. However, the possibility of progress through human effort alone was denied because it was felt that true progress had to be divinely inspired and guided by the church. Therefore in the orthodox Christian churches, where social reform was often feared as a threat to religious advancement, the idea of progress was interpreted as an essentially conservative influence on society.

Tayler Lewis, who, like Orestes A. Brownson, wrote on religious subjects, was a staunch classicist and a Protestant. Lewis had been admitted to the bar, but he preferred teaching, becoming a professor of Greek in 1838 at the University of the City of New York and in 1850 transferring to Union College, Schenectady. His main interest, however, was the study of religion, and in this connection he defended conservatism as the way of progress. In a discourse on *The Revolutionary Spirit* in 1848, Lewis admitted that there was a type of conservatism which looked on government and religion as instruments to defend property and keep the masses in order. However, he declared that true conservatism opposed revolution and favored the preservation of existing institutions because

> it regards time, and the gradual but certain improvement of the race, through the advance of science, philosophy, and religion, as the great means of progress, whatever may be the forms through which they operate,—causing monarchies and republics to share alike in their progressive meliorating influences . . . [27]

26 Americus Featherman, " Catholicism," *De Bow's Rev.*, XXIX (Nov., 1860), 584.

27 Tayler Lewis, *The Revolutionary Spirit* (New York, 1848), p. 6, and *passim*; see also his *Faith the Life of Science* (Albany, 1838), *passim.*

A year later, in 1849, Lewis denounced the idea of progress as " downright impiety," objecting that it left no place for evil and the offices of religion. He believed that the only true progress was moral and individual and that " the word, by being made to mean every thing, comes to *signify* nothing." [28] A professor of Greek, Lewis was very critical of modern, utilitarian education with its disregard of the authority of the state and the church, in favor of every man becoming the " former of his own intellectual character," and he asked :

> under what circumstances, and at what periods, may we expect more of a mediocre sameness, than when the age is every where boasting of this very tendency to individualism? Or when may we look for less of true originality than at a time when every child is taught to repeat this inane self-laudation, and all distinction of individual thought is lost, because no man has room for anything else than a barren idea of progress, a contempt for the past, and a blinding reverence for an unknown future? The appeal is made to history and experience; let them answer.[29]

In 1851 Lewis became one of the chief authors of the " Editor's Table " of the recently established *Harper's New Monthly Magazine*.[30] Although the contributions were unsigned, the ones devoted to discussing progress, during the three years Lewis wrote for *Harper's,* are identical with his attitude toward the subject. While the material progress of the age was conceded, doubt was expressed that the mass of men were any wiser or happier. Note was taken of the increase in crime and of the political corruption accompanying the growth of American cities. The confidence of the people in their liberal institutions

28 Lewis, *Nature, Progress, Ideas* (Schenectady, 1850), pp. 32, 35.

29 Lewis, " Three Absurdities of Certain Modern Theories of Education," *Bib. Rep.*, XXIII (April, 1851), 290-291.

30 S. A. Allibone, *A Critical Dictionary of English Literature, and British and American Authors . . .* (Phil., 1882), II, 1093; F. L. Mott, *A History of American Magazines, 1850-1865* (Cambridge, 1938), p. 389.

and the philosophy of the various "isms" were both questioned.[31] In reply to the excuse that " it is an 'age of progress;' it is a 'transition period;' and these features of the times that look so ugly to the jaundiced idea of croaking conservatism, are but its necessary and temporary attendants," the Editor's Table responded: "Alas! it is this very style of defense that most darkens the prospects of the future." [32]

The skepticism of Lewis' editorials for *Harper's* was also found in some of the other popular periodicals of the forties and fifties. In contrast to the optimistic faith in improvement expressed in so much of the magazine literature of the period, these conservative writers objected to the popular coupling of the reform spirit with the idea of progress. Contributors to the *Knickerbocker Magazine,* a popular New York literary journal, were particularly zealous in developing the conservative aspects of the idea of progress. Replying to some criticism of the commercial spirit by Harriet Martineau, writing in a British review, a contributor to the *Knickerbocker* for 1839 accused her of desiring a Utopia of equality. In the belief that " man was not created for such a condition of existence," Miss Martineau's American critic argued that commerce was an important agent in civilization and that progress was accomplished through individual effort and not by visions of Utopias.[33] Of the opinion " that the road of human progress is paved with the toils and trodden-down aspirations of generation after generation," another writer in the *Knickerbocker* in 1840 concluded " that the chimerical attempts at 'human improvement' which are contended for by the opiniatory cut-throats of the age, are almost invariably unproductive or impracticable, because the state of society at the time will not admit of such lopsided prog-

31 " Editor's Table," *Harper's New Monthly Mag.,* III (Nov., 1851), 846-847; V (Nov., 1852), 839-842; VI (Dec., 1852), 125-128; VII (Sept., 1853), 552-556.

32 *Ibid.,* VIII (Feb., 1854), 411.

33 " The American Merchant," *Knickerbocker Mag.,* XIV (July, 1839), 3, *passim.*

ress . . ." [34] For the same journal in 1848 an author admitted some merit in the system of Fourierism, but he denounced the extravagant methods pursued by the advocates of reform, and against "the progressive spirit" he opposed the conservative, "to serve as a check and a balance on the former." [35] In a satirical *Knickerbocker* article Thomas W. Lane affirmed in 1852 "that we consider Bloomerism as the most dangerous of modern 'isms,'" but then, denying any undue conservatism, he wrote:

> we are the friends of progress, and when it comes in our way are not averse to giving a friendly kick to the great ball of onward improvement; our opposition is to the speed at which we are about to be driven.[36]

Those popular magazines of the period especially devoted to the ladies added to their pleas for progress by an attention to female education, their call for a deeper regard for the conservative and moral characteristics of true progress. In *The Ladies' Repository,* published in Cincinnati by the agents of the Methodist Book Concern, and edited by a succession of Methodist clergymen, the conservative implications of the idea of progress were discussed at length. Benjamin F. Tefft, the editor of the *Repository* from 1846 to 1852, and also a college educator, believed that progress was the result of individual and moral improvement under the guiding influence of Christianity. Viewing inequality as inevitable, Tefft denounced the schemes of the Utopian socialists and praised democracy because it gave free reign to the individual.[37] Other contributors to the magazine's pages stressed the gradual nature of true progress and the necessity of a reliance on religion. This viewpoint was well expressed

34 "Emigration," *ibid.*, XVI (Dec., 1840), 471-472.

35 "False Doctrines of the Day," *ibid.*, XXXII (August, 1848), 152.

36 T. W. Lane, "Bloomerism: An Essay," *ibid.*, XL (Sept., 1852), 240.

37 B. F. Tefft: "Progress of the Individual," *Ladies' Repos.*, VIII (May, 1848), 153-155; "Progress of Society," *ibid.*, VIII (June, 1848), 185-189; "The Philosophy of Society," *ibid.*, XII (March, April, May, 1852), 81 ff., 121 ff., 161 ff.

by a characteristic article in the issue of April, 1858, in which the writer declared:

> Progress is a word promising much, but deceiving many. Real progress is steady but not hurried. It is an advance in the straight, plain way, and not a veering to this side and that, or a following any crooked by-path for a change, with the delusive hope of stumbling on some great treasure. On the road of true progress the traveller can look backward and see how far he had ·advanced, and forward and see whither his steps lead.[38]

In two of the leading political reviews in the country it was also argued that progress was not a radical concept. For the Whigs the *American (Whig) Review* affirmed in 1845 that its party, " in all things essentially conservative," was also " the real party of progress and improvement." [39] The *Review* itself claimed to be " the organ, for the nation, of a *just conservative* PROGRESS." [40] Other contributors to its pages in 1845 denounced the materialism and the radical democracy which they felt was corrupting any hope of true moral and individual progress.[41] The following year one of the journal's authors saw American institutions characterized by " the two great antitheses—the conservative and the progressive principles." Since in the United States " the progressive is undoubtedly the strongest tendency," he believed that " the reflecting friends of true freedom and progress are constantly called upon to lend their aid to the weaker side." [42] The *Democratic Review,* the unofficial organ of the other party, had been founded in 1837

---

38 Henry Matson, " Progressives," *ibid.*, XVIII (April, 1858), 223-224; see also: B. M. Genung, " Revolutions of Time," *ibid.*, VII (August, 1847), 245-246; Z. E. D., " Reformers and Reforms," *ibid.*, XI (August, 1851), 287-288.

39 " Introductory," *Am. (Whig) Rev.*, I (Jan., 1845), 1.

40 " Our Position Introductory," *ibid.*, II (July, 1845), 1.

41 Maryland, " Our Country," *ibid.*, I (March, 1845), 275-279; " The Progress and Disorganization," *ibid.*, II (July, 1845), 90-99.

42 " Civilization: American and European," *ibid.*, IV (July, 1846), 27.

and for some years advocated a vigorous reform program. However its policies underwent many changes, and in 1856 the editor, Spencer W. Cone, devoted a long article to the topic "Progress vs. Isms." Very critical of the idea of progress, as advocated by radical and socialistic writers, Cone regretted that the people were confusing change with the true progress represented by Christianity and moral betterment. He charged that "Nothing in the world has so much retarded the progress of men as ISMS," and he concluded: "A true progressive spirit is that which takes the world as it is for a basis, and proposes a possible modification and improvement." [43]

The conservatism and the pessimism which crept into some of the periodical and religious literature also figured in the writings of some of the best American novelists of the period. Romanticists like James Fenimore Cooper and William Gilmore Simms, looking backward to the early days of the Republic, considered the material progress of the thirties and forties a progress in degradation. Writers like Nathaniel Hawthorne and Herman Melville, troubled by the disparity between the glorious ideals and the naked materialism of so much of American life, came to satirize and reject the idea of progress.

Probably the most popular novelist in the period before the Civil War was James Fenimore Cooper, a Democrat in politics, but an aristocrat in his personal life.[44] Cooper at the beginning of the Jacksonian period delighted in the material progress of the nation. In his *Notions of the Americans Picked Up By A Travelling Bachelor* (1828) Cooper, impersonating an Englishman, gave an extremely optimistic characterization of the United States. With its intelligent populace, free institutions, and great natural resources, he believed America enjoyed the essentials of true progress and civilization. Although America

43 S. W. Cone, " Progress vs. Isms," *Dem. Rev.*, XXXVIII (Sept., 1856), 113-114, and *passim*.

44 For a good account of Cooper which considers his concept of progress, see: J. F. Ross, *The Social Criticism of Fenimore Cooper* (Berkeley, 1933), chs. 2-5.

had no worthwhile paintings, it had more and better ploughs than the whole of Europe, so that Cooper declared: "In this single fact may be traced the history of the character of the people, and the germ of their future greatness." [45] And he further observed:

> The construction of canals, on a practical scale, the mining for coal, the exportation of cotton goods, and numberless other improvements, which argue an advancing state of society, have all sprung into existence within the last dozen years. It is knowledge of these facts, with a clear and sagacious understanding of their immense results, coupled with exciting moral causes, that render the American sanguine, aspiring, and confident in his anticipations. He sees that his nation lives centuries in an age, and he feels no disposition to consider himself a child, because other people, in their dotage, choose to remember the hour of his birth.[46]

Settled in Europe in the early 1830's, Cooper ignored the warnings of some of his friends and continued to consider America a land of destiny,[47] but upon his return home in 1833 he too rejected the new times in America heralded by the Jacksonian upheaval. Addressing the hero of his novel *Homeward Bound,* published in 1838, Cooper wrote: "You have been dreaming abroad, . . . while your country has retrograded, in all that is respectable and good, a century in a dozen years." [48] In *Home as Found,* a sequel to the above work published in the same year, Cooper denounced the provincialism, love of change, and glorification of mediocrity which, he felt, characterized American progress. No longer enamored with the frontier, speculative sort of life that had temporarily collapsed with the depression of 1837, Cooper offered as a model village:

45 J. F. Cooper, *Notions of the Americans* (Phil., 1828), II, 115.

46 *Ibid.,* II, 331-332.

47 *Correspondence of James Fenimore Cooper,* I, 268, 274.

48 Cooper, "Homeward Bound" (1838), *Works* (Mohawk ed.; New York and London, [1896-1897]), p. 223.

not one of those places that shoot up in a day, under the unnatural efforts of speculation, or which, favored by peculiar advantages in the way of trade, becomes a precocious city while the stumps still stand in its streets; but a sober country town, that has advanced steadily *pari passu* with the surrounding country, and offers a fair specimen of the more regular advancement of the whole nation in its progress towards civilization.[49]

Cooper now sought an aristocratic type of civilization designed for gentlemen of property. America, he considered to be somewhere in the middle of the scale of progress. Alarmed by the tendency toward mob rule and by the tyranny of public opinion, he turned in his hopes for the future to religion.[50]

Cooper was by inheritance a large landholder in central New York. Bitterly opposed to the anti-rent movement in that state during the early forties, he published in 1845 and 1846 a trilogy based on this question. In one of these volumes he announced his belief that progress " is a spirit that assumes the respectable character of a love of liberty; and under that mask . . . gives play to malice, envy, covetousness, rapacity, and all the lowest passions of our nature . . ." [51] When the hero of these novels was captured by the anti-renters, Cooper made the further observation that

We live in an age of what is called progress, and fancy that man is steadily advancing on the great path of his destiny to something that we are apt to imagine is to form perfection. Certainly I shall not presume to say what is or what is not, the divine intention as to the future destination of our species on earth; but years and experience must have taught me, or I should have lived in vain, how little there is among our boasted improvements that is really new; and if we do

49 Cooper, " Home as Found " (1838), *ibid.*, p. 126, and Preface, pp. iii-v.

50 Cooper, *The American Democrat* (first pub., 1838; New York, 1931), pp. 183-184, and *passim*; see also Cooper's Letter to Anson Gleason (Dec. 16, 1848), in his *Correspondence*, II, 600-601.

51 Cooper, " The Chainbearer " (1845), *Works*, p. 46.

possess anything in the way of principles that bear on them the impress of inviolability, they are those that have become the most venerable, by having stood the severest test of time.[52]

Cooper also satirized the doctrine of progress by giving in one of the novels the speech of an anti-renter, who declared:

> I respect and venerate a squatter's possession; for it's held under the sacred principle of usefulness. It says, ' Go and make the wilderness blossom as the rose,' and means, ' progress ' . . .
>
> Fellow-citizens, a great movement is in progress! ' Go ahead!' is the cry, and the march is onward; our thoughts already fly about on the wings of the lightening, and our bodies move but little slower, on the vapor of steam—soon our principles will rush ahead of all, and let in the radiance of a glorious day of universal reform and loveliness and virtue and charity, when the odious sound of rent will never be heard, when every man will sit down under his own apple, or cherry tree, if not under his own fig tree.[53]

In 1850, the year before his death, Cooper still out of joint with the times, published a novel designed to draw attention to " some of the social evils that beset us . . ." [54] He denounced the disposition to confuse change with true progress, and he saw no hope in either extreme reform or extreme conservatism. " Neither course is in the least suited to the actual wants of society, and each is pernicious in its way." [55] Noting that the telegraph sped truth and falsehood alike, Cooper expressed his conviction that in an age of progress individuality was lost and law was disregarded.[56]

---

52 *Ibid.*, p. 319.

53 Cooper, " The Redskins " (1846), *Works*, pp. 254-256; for a sermon preached against the anti-renters at this time which invoked the idea of progress, see: H. F. Harrington, *The Responsibleness of American Citizenship* (Albany, 1845), p. 9, and *passim*.

54 Cooper, " The Ways of the Hour " (1850), *Works*, Preface, p. iii.

55 *Ibid.*, p. 69.

56 *Ibid.*, pp. 283-284, 309, 432.

In some ways the Southern counterpart of Cooper, William Gilmore Simms, one of the leading writers of his section, in 1841 likened the age to an uncontrolled omnibus.[57] A year later, in an oration at the University of Alabama, Simms announced that America, in all the finer elements of civilization, had declined since its separation from England. Critical of the continual westward movement of the American people, he maintained:

> A wandering people is more or less a barbarous one . . . Every remove, of whatever kind, is injurious to social progress; and every remove into the wilderness, lessens the hold which refinement and society have hitherto held upon the individual man.[58]

Simms also strongly denounced the American love of gain and passion for material progress which, he declared, " seems to be the whole amount of our national idea of progress." [59] Against such a criteria of progress, Simms urged the claims of intellectual and cultural standards.[60] An advocate of an independent American literature, he was also imbued with the interests of his own section, identifying the Mexican War and Negro slavery with the progress of civilization.[61] Out of tune with much

57 W. G. Simms, " The Philosophy of the Omnibus," *Godey's Lady's Book*, XXIII (Sept., 1841), 107.

58 Simms, *The Social Principle* (Tuscaloosa, 1843), p. 36.

59 *Ibid.*, p. 46.

60 On this question of material versus intellectual and cultural progress, see the orations in the South by: J. C. Bruce, *An Address ... University of North Carolina ...* (Raleigh, 1841), *passim*; A. B. Meek, "Americanism in Literature" (1844), in *Romantic Passages in Southwestern History* (3rd ed.; Mobile and New York, 1857), pp. 107-143; and his " Jack Cadeism and the Fine Arts " (1841), *ibid.*, pp. 145-190; for Simms' review of Meek's "Americanism in Lit.," see the former's, *View and Reviews in American Literature, History and Fiction* (New York, 1845), pp. 1-19.
See also for a Northern view: "Introductory to the Year 1849," *Am. (Whig) Rev.*, IX (Jan., 1849), 4.

61 For Simms' connection of the concept of progress with these questions, see especially: " The Morals of Slavery " (1837), in the *Pro-Slavery Argu-*

of the progress of the age, Simms found cause to rejoice only in its more conservative institutions and tendencies.

The equal of Simms and Cooper in their pessimistic attitude toward the idea of progress, Nathaniel Hawthorne and Herman Melville were, however, more dissenters than conservatives. Hawthorne, a shy and retiring New Englander, was the friend of Emerson and many of the transcendentalists, but he did not always share their sympathy with the idea of progress. In 1841 he sojourned for a time at the transcendental community of Brook Farm, and then, a decade later, he recorded his disillusionment with this socialistic experiment in the pages of the *Blithedale Romance*. The original enthusiasm [62] with which he and the others had started out in their quest for Utopia had gradually been extinguished by a fatal defect in their whole scheme.[63] To the mind of Hawthorne the struggle for progress and reform was rendered impossible by the very nature of man and the universe. Man was not perfectible,[64] and his hopeful schemes, when translated into some form of organization, only served to accentuate the futility of his efforts. The reformer, in his steadfastness of purpose, neglected the important moral values of life and the soul of the individual.[65] In the conclusion of the novel the once happy community of Blithedale was deserted by even its most loyal friends. Zenobia, its leading spirit, was " weary of this place, and sick to death of playing at philanthropy and progress." [66] For his own verdict Hawthorne wrote:

ment (Charleston, 1852), pp. 260-264, 274-275; "Progress in America," *Dem. Rev.*, XVIII (Feb., 1846), 91-94; *Self-Development* (Milledgeville, 1847), pp. 20-25, and *passim*.

62 Nathaniel Hawthorne, "The Blithedale Romance" (1852), *Complete Writings* (Old Manse ed.; Boston and New York, 1903), VIII, 9-10, 22-24, 72-73, 84-87.

63 *Ibid.*, VIII, 52, 91, 106, 118-119, 123.

64 *Ibid.*, VIII, 141, 206.

65 *Ibid.*, VIII, 189-190, 285, 320.

66 *Ibid.*, VIII, 324.

As regards human progress (in spite of my irresistible yearnings over the Blithedale reminiscences), let them believe in it who can, and aid in it who choose. If I could earnestly do either, it might be all the better for my comfort.[67]

In some of his short stories Hawthorne also satirized the faith of his age in the idea of progress. In these stories his characters struggled in a web of circumstances as inexorable as the inevitability attributed to the idea of progress by some of Hawthorne's contemporaries. *The Birthmark* illustrated the futility of seeking and the impossibility of attaining the goal of human perfection. All the achievements of science and the refinements of genius were insufficient before the stark fact of the necessary imperfection of life.[68] *The Celestial Railroad* was devoted to much the same theme with the added warning that man's Utopia might not be the happy land of his imagination and aspiration.[69] The procession of life, itself, Hawthorne, in another tale, likened to a funeral march to an unknown goal, in the course of which men were arbitrarily and unfairly divided into rigid classes.[70] Very skeptical of all the efforts of the reformers to improve life or offer a better future, he showed how they touched only externals and neglected the necessity of an inward moral regeneration. In his story *Earth's Holocaust,* Hawthorne wrote in regard to the superficial efforts of the reformers:

How sad a truth, if true it were, that man's age-long endeavor for perfection had served only to render him the mockery of the evil principle, from the fatal circumstance of an error at the very root of the matter! The heart, the heart, —there was the little yet boundless sphere wherein existed

67 *Ibid.*, VIII, 352.

68 The Birthmark " (1843), *ibid.*, IV, 48-77.

69 " The Celestial Railroad " (1843), *ibid.*, IV, 259-288.

70 " The Procession of Life " (1843), *ibid.*, IV, 289-311.

the original wrong of which the crime and misery of this outward world were merely types.[71]

Herman Melville, even more pessimistic than his friend Hawthorne, also wrote works in which he bitterly denounced the accepted standards and ideals of his time. Leaving an unhappy youth behind him, Melville went to sea in 1837 at the age of seventeen. After an interval of school teaching, he again set sail in 1841. By the time of his return home in 1844, he had experienced both the hardships of the life of a sailor and the delights of a long sojourn among the natives of the South Sea Islands. Publishing his observations and reflections in a series of novels, Melville became famous for extolling the virtues of the primitive societies which he had visited. In *Mardi* (1849), one of the more philosophical but less popular of these works, Melville satirized the complacent confidence of his fellow American citizens. He declared that the progress of the United States was the result of the youth of the nation, and he asserted that the people, despite all their boasts of political freedom, enjoyed no real equality. Although he noted that " each age thinks its own eternal," he on the contrary counselled that the wise should regard death " as the inflexible friend, who, even against our own wills, from life's evils triumphantly relieves us." [72]

The materialistic progress of the United States, toward which Melville and Hawthorne maintained an attitude of philosophical pessimism, was the main reason for the faith in the idea of progress shown by some of the representatives of the propertied classes. Typical of these conservative spokesmen was the scholarly Edward Everett of Massachusetts, who as a clergyman,

---

71 Hawthorne, " Earth's Holocaust " (1844), *ibid.*, V, 227-228.

On Howthorne's rejection of the idea of progress, see also: F. O. Matthiessen, *American Renaissance* (New York and London, 1941), p. 652.

In some of his hack writings Hawthorne expressed a different attitude toward progress. See, for example, his " Life of Franklin Pierce," *Writings*, XVII, 190-191.

72 Herman Melville, *Mardi and a Voyage Thither* (1849), *Works* (Constable ed.; London, 1922-1924), III, 36; IV, 236-242.

teacher, editor, and statesman interpreted the idea of progress as a weapon of social stability. In his early addresses on patriotic subjects, Everett contrasted the ancient, effete customs of Europe with the vast resources and youthful institutions of America. In a speech on " The History of Liberty," delivered on the Fourth of July, 1828, he affirmed that the American people were intrusted with the experiment of determining " how far life, and liberty, and property are safe, and the progress of social improvement is secure, under the influence of laws made by those who are to obey them . . ." [73]

A Whig Congressman from 1825 to 1835, Everett during this period made numerous addresses on the subjects of science, education, and labor. With the workingmen of New England enrolled under the standards of Jacksonian political reform, he emphasized scientific improvements and useful knowledge as the agents of progress and civilization. In his lectures before lyceum groups and mechanics' institutes, Everett spread the gospel of self-culture. Although the progress already made in science had been vast, he declared that " there can be no pause; for art and science are, in themselves, progressive and infinite." [74] Given a degree of education, he affirmed that very individual mind was " capable of making large progress in useful knowledge . . ." [75] And in a speech on the subject "Advantage of Knowledge to Workingmen," he depicted the idea of progress as a guarantee that the intellectual heritage of civilization was " all *to be shared out anew;* and it is for each man to say, what part he will gain in the glorious patrimony." [76]

However, in Everett's mind the education of the workingmen was only the substitute, and not the prelude, for social reform.

73 Edward Everett, " The History of Liberty " (1828), *Orations and Speeches*, I, 151.

74 Everett, " On the Importance of Scientific Knowledge to Practical Men " (1830), *ibid.*, I, 275.

75 *Ibid.*, I, 281.

76 Everett, "Advantage of Knowledge to Workingmen " (1831), *ibid.*, I, 327.

Natural wants satisfied, he believed that "artificial wants, or civilized wants, show themselves," and therefore in his "Lecture on the Workingmen's Party" he declared: "In other words, the innate desire of improving our condition keeps us all in a state of want." [77] On the Fourth of July at Lowell, in 1830, Everett termed the alliance between capital and labor, already exhibited in the cotton mills, a *"holy alliance"* and a step in accord with the laws of human progress.[78] The following year, in an "Address delivered before the American Institute of the City of New York," he announced that the Constitution of the United States had been passed to protect the rising manufacturing interests, and he also maintained that the prosperity of the United States was promoted by "free institutions of government,—laws affording security to property,—and the diffusion of education and useful knowledge." [79] As Everett rose in the political world during the forties and fifties he continued to affirm his belief in progress through social stability, relating his conservative convictions to the issues of the times.

The conservative treatment of the idea of progress, found in Edward Everett's public addresses, was also contained in the small volume of essays published in 1853 by a young New England literary figure, Charles Eliot Norton. The son of the conservative Biblical scholar, Andrews Norton, Charles Eliot Norton spent the years immediately succeeding his graduation from Harvard, in 1846, in the mercantile business interspersed with some extensive foreign travel. Then becoming financially independent upon the death of his father in 1853, Norton embarked upon a literary career in the course of which he earned respect as an editor, author, and teacher. In his book *Considerations on Some Recent Social Theories,* completed in his twenty-sixth year, Norton especially attacked the theory of socialism and its exemplification in the Fourierist movement. Entertaining a pessimistic opinion of the wisdom and intelligence

---

77 Everett, "Lecture on the Workingmen's Party" (1830), *ibid.,* I, 284.

78 Everett, "Fourth of July at Lowell" (1830), *ibid.,* II, 64.

79 Everett, "American Manufactures" (1831), *ibid.,* II, 75, 86-88; see also his "Accumulation, Property, Capital, Credit" (1838), *ibid.,* II, 288-312.

of the generality of the people, he declared: " Their progress must be stimulated and guided by the few who have been blessed with the opportunities, and the rare genius, fitting them to lead." [80] He rejected the principles of Equality, Communism, and the Solidarity of Peoples in favor of those of Love, Truth, and pure Liberty, and he announced his conviction that " It is the will of God—a will we may not understand nor question— that progress should be very gradual; not visible from year to year, and only with difficulty to be seen from century to century." [81] However, Norton also admitted that a certain degree of effort was needed if the past progress of the world were to continue and if the cause of the people was to be improved. He complained only against those social theorists who proposed to improve society by disregarding the rights of property and of the individual, and he declared, in concluding his conservative essay: " The progress which is permanent is made step by step, and not stride by stride." [82]

A conservative who exercised his influence partly from the professor's chair was Francis Lieber, who wrote the first systematic works on political science in this country. A liberal in many of his political views and a staunch nationalist, Lieber, in identifying the idea of progress with the preservation and accumulation of private property, however, expressed the conservative attitude that progress was possible only through existing established institutions.[83] A refugee from Germany, he came to the United States in 1827 after a disillusioning period of volunteer service in the Greek revolt. He expected to find no paradise or Utopia in America, but he felt that it was a new country more free and susceptible to novel ideas than any nation in Europe. On the eve of his departure, he wrote to his

80 [C. E. Norton], *Considerations on Some Recent Social Theories* (Boston, 1853), pp. 19-20.

81 *Ibid.*, p. 20.

82 *Ibid.*, pp. 139, 51-56, 75-77.

83 See the article by Merle Curti, " Francis Lieber and Nationalism," *Hunt. Lib. Q.*, IV (April, 1941), 270-276, 283-284.

family: " I shall feel that I am in a land of progress, where civilization is building her home, while in Europe we can scarcely tell whether there is a progression or retrogression." [84] Settled in the New World, Lieber wrote the inevitable travel book in which he commented on the great material progress and spirit of enterprise existing in America.[85] Then in 1835 he was made a professor of history at South Carolina College, succeeding Thomas Cooper, and, during the next twenty years of his tenure there, he wrote the works in which he developed his conservative, nationalistic concept of progress.

Lieber believed that civilization was the natural state of man, and that progress depended on the development of man's individuality, and upon the accumulation and preservation of property.[86] In his *Essays on Property and Labour,* published in 1841, he wrote that associations holding property in common soon decline and fail because:

> Man must ever return to his nature, and he promotes general progress and civilization only in so far as he conscientiously develops that nature which for wise ends his Maker has given him. Man is conscious that what he is, he is individually.[87]

Connecting man's destiny to a large population and a correspondingly increased production, Lieber saw a further necessity for the accumulation of property in his conviction that "the progress of civilization itself demands greater and greater accumulation." [88]

Lieber however did not long retain all his youthful enthusiasm for America. Early in 1843, as the country emerged from

84 Francis Lieber, *Life and Letters,* ed. T. S. Perry (Boston, 1882), p. 70.

85 Lieber, *Letters to a Gentleman in Germany* (Phil., 1834), pp. 49, 286-288.

86 Lieber, *Manual of Political Ethics* (Boston, 1838-1839), I, 124-125, 140, 147.

87 Lieber, *Essays on Property and Labour* (New York, 1841), pp. 180-181.

88 *Ibid.,* pp. 41, 42; see also the "Introduction" by the Rev. Alonzo Potter, pp. iii-xx.

a long depression, Lieber, disappointed at his failure to secure a professorship at Columbia University in New York, wrote a letter to a sympathetic trustee upbraiding the times in which more money was spent for luxuries than for professors. He then asked:

> When shall these times end! Wonderful, great times. Progress of Democracy! I doubt not, it is all true, all as rose-colored as Bancroft can wish for, only some people can't see it. What with repudiation, and disregard of all contracts and robbery, and rebellions in which the rebel has not the heart to strike, nor the government to hang, and unsteady aimless legislation, folly and impurity, our times often appear to me like the river Mississippi—mighty but muddy. Yet, there is no use in sighing. One cannot help being one's own contemporary, and none but the puddings we have can fill our belly.[89]

Lieber saw the key to civilization in the rise and fall of nations, but he rejoiced that in modern times, under the unity afforded by Christianity, many nations seemed to be advancing together.[90] Once started on the path of progress and civilization, he felt that God entrusted man with his own destiny,[91] which in

> Our age, marked by restless activity in almost all departments of knowledge, and by struggles and aspirations before unknown, is stamped by no characteristic more deeply than by a desire to establish or extend freedom among the political societies of mankind.[92]

Lieber also believed that the two important intellectual elements in all human progress were derived from historical development

89 Lieber, Letter to Samuel B. Ruggles (Feb. 7, 1843), in Francis Lieber Mss. (Library of Congress).

90 Lieber, "The Origin and Development of the First Constituents of Civilization" (1845), in *Reminiscences, Addresses, and Essays* (Miscellaneous Writings, vol. 1; Phil., 1881), pp. 213-214.

91 *Ibid.*, p. 223.

92 Lieber, *On Civil Liberty and Self-government* (Phil., 1853), I, 25.

and from abstract reasoning. While both were necessary, he considered the United States too much inclined to the abstract.[93] Therefore, in 1858, in his inaugural address on assuming a professorship at Columbia, he praised the historic reality represented by the development of the state, while he rejoiced that the abstract visions of model states and Utopias were popular only in an age,

> when society was not clearly conceived to be a continuity; when far less attention was paid to the idea of progress, which is a succession of advancing steps, and to the historic genesis of institutions; and when the truth was not broadly acknowledged that civilization, whether political or not, cannot divest itself of its accumulative and progressive character.[94]

The institution of the state, Lieber believed, protected the concept of liberty as both a right and a duty. This protection, he felt, was essential to modern civilization, and he declared: "As men and society advance, the greatest of institutions—the state —increases in intensity of action . . ." [95]

The idea of progress was central to the programs for social reform, but it also lent itself to adoption by conservative elements opposed to innovation. The conservatives affirmed a belief in progress as strong as that of the social reformers, but they claimed adherence to a different kind of progress. However as Joel Tyler Headley, the former clergyman, popular author, and future New York political figure, observed in 1846 regarding the idea of progress, it is " believed or disbelieved according to the tastes and occupations of men, rather than from the arguments they themselves use." [96] Against those con-

---

93 *Ibid.*, I, 281-283.

94 Lieber, " History and Political Science Necessary Studies in Free Countries " (1858), *Reminiscences*, pp. 359-360.

95 *Ibid.*, p. 357; see also his " The Ancient and the Modern Teacher of Politics " (1859), *ibid.*, pp. 369-387.

96 J. T. Headley, *The One Progressive Principle* (New York, 1846), pp. 3-4.

servatives with no taste for progress or reform, the claim, reminiscent of Bentham, was made that all progress and reform was once radical innovation. In a typical passage a writer in a reform journal in 1846 warned:

> Persons who complain of ultraism should remember that it is the harbinger of every thing better in the Future. All the great truths that are now so generally cherished were once ultraisms, as much scorned as they are now adored. When inquirers cease to be ultra all hope of earthly progress will die away.[97]

Writing three years later Edward Kellogg, a radical retired businessman, reminded the opponents of progress that all change was an innovation so that "Those who talk against innovation are often the greatest innovators."[98] A proponent of a greater equality of wealth and of the rights of labor, Kellogg declared: "The antiquity of laws and customs is not a proof of their excellence."[99] In similar vein, speaking before a college audience in 1850, Charles B. Sedgwick, a young lawyer and future Republican Congressman, derided the conservatism of the professional classes, who "harp upon the maxim that, 'all change is not improvement,' till they make it read that *no change* is improvement."[100]

On the whole the established classes, through representatives as divergent in their views as Cooper, Lewis, Lieber, and Everett, considered true progress to embrace a slow, gradual, and conservative advance without danger to the status quo. Against radical reformers eager for a social change, the conservatives argued that, since a certain degree of progress was inevitable, it should not be jeopardized by rash, revolutionary attempts to speed its course. In religious circles, the belief in conservative

---

97 "Ultraism," *Quarterly Journal and Rev.*, I (April, 1846), 191.

98 Edward Kellogg, *Labor and Other Capital* (New York, 1849), p. xxvi.

99 *Ibid.*, p. xxxiv.

100 C. B. Sedgwick, *An Oration ... Sigma Phi Fraternity ...* (New York, 1850), p. 25.

progress was expressed in the emphasis on divine authority and upon the necessity of a moral regeneration through the agency of the church. Among literary figures, both the conservatives and the pessimists were out of patience with what they feared was the failure of cultural to keep pace with material progress. In their reaction to a growing industrial society, conservatives and radical reformers, in both clerical and secular groups, therefore interpreted the idea of progress in the light of their own interests and aspirations.

CHAPTER VII

EDUCATION: THE UNIVERSAL UTOPIA

ALMOST universally accepted as a means of progress, yet subject to much controversy over its application, was the educational program evolving in the United States during the period from 1815 to 1860. In these decades a free public education was eventually made available for everyone except in the South. Further up the educational ladder and not yet seriously challenged by the high school or state university, the privately endowed academies and colleges increased their enrollments, broadened their curricula, and continued to arbitrate the destinies of higher education in America. Education during this period also became increasingly secularized. In the common schools the influence of the old religious societies declined with the advent of centralized state control. In the colleges the clergymen-presidents and trustees came to be in part supported by the funds of the rising order of merchant and manufacturing philanthropists.

No better example of the practical effect of the idea of progress could be found than in this tremendous growth of American education. In a democratic, progressive nation an educated populace was considered to be of vital importance. To meet the needs of a democratic government and to vindicate the establishment of universal manhood suffrage, an intelligent electorate was deemed necessary. In a speech before the House of Representatives in 1846 Robert Dale Owen, an American Congressman and the son of the famous English socialist, gave expression to this idea of the function of education in a progressive democracy. Owen, who was influential in the public school movement in Indiana, believed:

They who govern should be wise. They who govern should be educated. They who decide mighty questions should be enlightened. Then, as we value wise government, as we would have the destinies of our kind shaped by an enlightened tribunal, let the schools of the people, and the teachers who preside in these schools, and the system that prevails in these schools, be our peculiar care.[1]

Necessary to political democracy, education was also useful in an industrial society—arousing the hopes of the poor and allaying the fears of the rich. In this regard, a contributor to the popular *Godey's Lady's Book* observed in 1837 that,

> By diffusing the blessed light of knowledge, we shall not only rescue from bondage the oppressed, but we shall also avert a danger, than which a greater could not menace the earth with desolation—the danger of a revolution which shall annihilate every form of authority, and leave the mob, ignorant and deluded, to the utter licentiousness of their own fiery passions.[2]

Horace Mann, the great advocate and administrator of common schools, in his " Annual Report of 1848 " as Secretary of the Massachusetts Board of Education discussed " Intellectual education as a means of removing poverty, and securing abundance." [3] Seeing the American theory of equality of opportunity menaced by the extremes in wealth and poverty of a rising industrialism, Mann advocated education " as the great equalizer of the conditions of men,—the balance wheel of the social machinery . . . It does better than to disarm the poor of their hostility towards the rich; it prevents being poor." [4] In similar

1 R. D. Owen, *Cong. Globe*, 29 Cong., 1 Sess., House of Rep. (April 23, 1846), p. 714.

See also for similar sentiments by others: " Obligations of Literary Men," *Q. Journal and Rev.*, I (April, 1846), 111-121; C. B. Haddock, *The Patriot Scholar* (New Haven, 1848), pp. 10-11, 23-24; J. C. Bruce, " Popular Knowledge the Necessity of Popular Government," *S. Lit. Mess.*, XIX (May, 1853), 292-302.

2 J. A. B., " The Wants of the Age," *Godey's Lady's Book*, XIV (April, 1837), 164-165.

3 Horace Mann, "Annual Report of 1848," in *Life and Works* (Boston, 1891), IV, 245-268.

4 *Ibid.*, IV, 251.

fashion a contributor to Hunt's *Merchants' Magazine,* writing in 1853 on the subject of " Property and National Wealth," declared that " Intelligent laborers . . . can add much more to the capital employed in a business than those who are ignorant." [5]

An early instrument of democratic culture and learning was the American lyceum. First organized in Massachusetts in 1826, the lyceum during the 1830's became a nation-wide device for adult education and for stimulating the demand for common schooling.[6] In England the public lecture and the mechanics' institute had been used for some years to provide an education for the laboring classes. Henry Brougham, a persistent proponent of education, and a founder of the " Society for the Diffusion of Useful Knowledge," in 1825 published his *Practical Observations on Popular Education,* advocating cheap publications, book clubs or reading societies, and especially lectures, to provide some education for the working classes. Widely read in England, this work was in the following year reprinted by the *Massachusetts Journal,* and " offered to the attention of the American public, in the hope, that a determination will be formed to import to our society the benefit of the admirable scheme for social improvement of which it treats." [7]

In America during the early 1830's, statesmen of varying political convictions addressed these mechanics' institutes, advocating self-improvement as the means of social and national progress.[8] A leader of the lyceum movement and one of its most

5 J. H. Stearns, "Property and National Wealth," Hunt's *Merchants' Mag.,* XXVIII (Feb., 1853), 200.

6 C. B. Hayes, *The American Lyceum: Its History and Contribution to Education* (United States Dept. of Interior Office of Educ., Bull. no. 12; Washington, 1932), pp. xi-xii, 25-53; P. W. Stoddard, "The Place of the Lyceum in American Life" (Master's thesis Faculty of Educ. Columbia Univ.; Ms. in Teachers College Library). See also the article by S. L. Jackson, "Some Ancestors of the 'Extension Course,'" *New Eng. Q.,* XIV (Sept., 1941), 505-518.

7 Henry Brougham, *Practical Observations on Popular Education,* from the 20th London ed. (Boston, 1826), p. 3.

8 See the addresses by Joseph Story, Daniel Webster, and Edward Everett in the *American Library of Useful Knowledge* (vol. I, Boston, 1831) ; see

indefatigable lecturers, Edward Everett, a scholar, patriot, and conservative statesman, discussed the progressive implications of the diffusion of knowledge before learned audiences at Yale and Amherst [9] and also before the mechanics' institutes. In a speech delivered about 1830 before several institutions for scientific improvement, he declared that the capacity for progress of the human mind often withered because of the lack of a proper stimulus: "It is for want of the little that human means must add to the wonderful capacity for improvement born in man, that by far the greatest part of the intellect innate in our race perishes undeveloped and unknown." [10] "Mind, acting through useful arts, is the vital principle of modern civilized society," Everett noted in 1837, and he concluded that progress in the arts and sciences

> is a creation of the mind of man—an essence of infinite capacity for improvement. And it is of the nature of every intelligence, endowed with *such* a capacity, however, mature in respect to the past, to be at all times, in respect to the future, in a state of hopeful infancy. However vast the space measured behind, the space before is immeasurable; and though the mind may estimate the progress it has made, the boldest stretch of its powers is inadequate to measure the progress of which it is capable. [11]

also: Levi Woodbury, "Importance of Science in the Arts" (1831), *Writings*, III, 9-23; John Sergeant, *An Address...the Apprentices' Library Company of Philadelphia*... (Phil., [1832?]) ; G. C. Verplanck, *A Lecture ...before the Mechanics' Institute of the City of New York* (New York, 1833).

9 Edward Everett: "Education of Mankind" (Yale, 1833), *Orations and Speeches*, I, 404-441; "Education Favorable to Liberty, Knowledge and Morals" (Amherst, 1835), *ibid.*, I, 599-633.

10 Everett, "On the Importance of Scientific Knowledge to Practical Men" (1830), *ibid.*, I, 281-282; see also his "Advantage of Knowledge to Workingmen" (1831), *ibid.*, I, 307-328.

11 Everett, "The Importance of the Mechanic Arts" (1837), *ibid.*, II, 248, 254.

See also: The American Society for the Diffusion of Useful Knowledge, *Prospectus* (New York, 1837), p. 4, and *passim*.

In New England, where industrialism was confronted with labor discontent and Jacksonian reforms, this notion of self-culture was a useful panacea to present to the workingman. Daniel Webster, like Everett the spokesman of the conservative classes in his section, began his " Lecture before the Society for the Diffusion of Useful Knowledge " in 1836 with the customary observation that " One of the most striking characteristics of the present age is the extraordinary progress which it has witnessed of popular knowledge." Webster felt that a state of material prosperity and wealth, accumulated by laborers and by what he preferred to call " labor-doing machines," was a necessary prerequisite for this spread of knowledge. Since there was no monopolistic control of the fruits of science and machinery in America, he claimed that these advantages were therefore open to all.[12]

The mechanics themselves were not unreceptive to the idea of self-culture. Timothy Claxton, an English mechanic who had founded lecture institutes in London and, during his sojourn in America, also in Boston, urged the working class to devote their leisure time to self-improvement.[13] And in an article, " Literature and Science in Conjunction With The Mechanic Arts; or Considerations By A Mechanic, Offered As Incentives To Study, Especially To His Brother Artisans," contributed to the *Western Monthly Magazine* for 1834, the author stated:

> It is impossible to predict the future capabilities of scientific improvements, or to say to what extent they may yet be carried, especially when mechanics generally, shall become scientific inquirers, which we trust will soon be the case.[14]

Hopeful, in the expectation of an elevation in the status of labor and of a lessening class consciousness, the writer concluded that

12 Daniel Webster, "Lecture before the Society for the Diffusion of Useful Knowledge " (1836), in *Writings and Speeches*, XIII, 63, and *passim*.

13 Timothy Claxton, *Memoir of a Mechanic* (Boston, 1839), pp. 160-162, and *passim*.

14 *West Monthly Mag.*, II (Jan., 1834), 8-9.

the progress of labor would be better promoted by reading and self-education than by uniting in political parties.[15]

The doctrine of self-culture also contained a moral overtone which was popular in those religious circles which were distressed by the materialism of the age. In 1830 *Self-Education; or the Means and Art of Moral Progress* by Joseph Gérando was published in America in a translation from the French by Elizabeth Palmer Peabody. Gérando's work attracted some attention, and it was favorably reviewed at this time in the *Christian Examiner* by George Ripley.[16] Also important were the works of the popular Scottish scientific writer Thomas Dick. In his book *On the Improvement of Society by the Diffusion of Knowledge,* published in 1833 for Harper's widely-circulated Family Library, Dick developed his belief that the diffusion of knowledge, accompanied by a moral renovation, would overcome the natural depravity of man. He maintained: " The more learning a people have, the more virtuous, powerful and happy will they become; and to ignorance alone must the contrary effects be imputed." [17] In the review of this work for the Unitarian *Christian Examiner,* the writer, agreeing with Dick's emphasis on the importance of intellectual advancement, went on to declare:

> The present is not an exact transcript of any past age. We believe that human improvement is indefinite, that no almighty fiat has set limits to its progress. If the great intellects of our race are devoted, heart and soul, to the investigation of the truths of morals and religion, each succession of inquirers taking advantage of the lights struck out by their predecessors, we believe that no bounds can be fixed to their advancement.[18]

15 *Ibid.,* II (Feb., 1834), 87-88.

16 J. M. Gérando, *Self Education* (tr. from the French by E. P. Peabody; Boston, 1830), pp. 80-87, 434-435, 445-456; for the favorable review by George Ripley, see: *Chr. Ex.,* IX (Sept., 1830), 70-107.

17 Thomas Dick, *On the Improvement of Society* (New York, 1833), pp. 26-27.

18 *Chr. Ex.,* XV (Jan., 1834), 359; for a different view, see the article in the *Q. Chr. Spec.,* VI (Dec., 1834), 632-654.

A later volume by Dick, published in " The Christian Library " for 1836, defended the universal diffusion of knowledge against the charge that it was a rather Utopian scheme. Noting that education received government promotion only in Prussia and in the United States, Dick blamed indifference, not impracticability, for the failure of society to promote progress by spreading useful knowledge.[19]

The moral and ideal aspect of self-culture was well expressed by William Ellery Channing in his address on the subject. Channing, the noted Unitarian minister and liberal, assumed " that a man has within him capacities of growth, which deserve and will reward intense, unrelaxing toil," [20] and he urged:

> Be true to your own highest convictions. Intimations from our own souls of something more perfect than others teach, if faithfully followed, give us a consciousness of spiritual force and progress, never experienced by the vulgar of high life or low life, who march, as they are drilled, to the step of their times.[21]

In asking his audience to " Resolve earnestly on Self-culture," Channing observed: " difficulties are meant to rouse, not discourage. The human spirit is to grow strong by conflict." [22] He also announced that he did not despair of progress, declaring: " I conclude with recalling to you the happiest feature of our age, and that is, the progress of the mass of the people in intelligence, self-respect and all the comforts of life." [23]

This enthusiasm for self-culture and the support given the lyceum movement were excellent illustrations of the reality in the United States of the idea of progress. Not the plaything of the cloistered philosopher, the concept was being put into actual

---

19 Thomas Dick, *The Mental Illumination and Moral Improvement of Mankind* (New York, 1836), pp. 3-4, and *passim*.

20 W. E. Channing, " Self Culture " (1838), *Works*, II, 368.

21 *Ibid.*, II, 381.

22 *Ibid.*, II, 408.

23 *Ibid.*, II, 411.

effect in America. That an educated people meant a better society became accepted as almost a national truism. A further
purpose, and perhaps the main point of the lyceums, was to
agitate for a better school system. Lectured to in their mechanics' institutes by lyceum orators, the workingmen themselves, coming to represent a political force during the early
thirties, were foremost in the struggle for public education.[24]
The first volume of the *Working Man's Advocate* of 1830 contained a characteristic article, urging the adoption of a plan of
national and state education as a means of progress. The writer
maintained:

> This has been called the age of improvement, but what im-
> provement is comparable to that of the human mind? All the
> splendid projects of railroads, canals, and manufactories,
> which engage the attention of our statesmen, dwindle into in-
> significance—into mere children's play—when brought into
> comparison with the intellectual and moral improvement of the
> people.[25]

A contributor to the *Free Enquirer,* the organ of Frances
Wright and Robert Dale Owen, argued that universal education
portended the perfection of society. Therefore, wise legislators,
interested in the support of labor, were urged to recognize that

> Progress is the law of humanity, notwithstanding all appar-
> ent or temporary retrogradations. The universality of a state
> of high mental cultivation will be one of the results of that
> great reorganization of society which must take place—which
> has actually commenced.[26]

In the more general literature of the 1830's the relation of
public education to the idea of progress was also developed. In

24 F. T. Carlton, *Economic Influences upon Educational Progress in the
United States, 1820-1850* (Madison, Wisconsin, 1908), ch. 3.

25 " Popular Education " (From the Alabama *Spirit of the Age*), *Working Man's Advoc.*, I (April 10, 1830), 4.

26 B. F. P., " The Progress of Popular Intelligence," *Free Enquirer,* 2nd
ser. IV (Jan. 14, 1832), 89.

speeches and in magazine articles practical, utilitarian education was advocated as the type most appropriate to the progress of the age and to America's own progressive destiny.[27] Walter R. Johnson, one of the founders of free schools in Pennsylvania, advocated state support of education as an indication of state patriotism and progressiveness, and in a pamphlet on this question, published in 1834, he wrote:

> The destiny of man is for activity and improvement; the destiny of *states,* that would maintain a respectable rank, is for activity and improvement. Without this character of progressive advancement, any single State must soon feel its relative degradation, must feel, (if there be a feeling in the community), the mortifying sense of insignificance.[28]

Horace Greeley's *New Yorker,* although alarmed at the failure of some states to advance education, was able to report in 1938:

> Among the aspects of the times most auspicious to the progressive and rapid improvement of mankind in wisdom and virtue, the increased and increasing attention which is every where paid to the subject of Popular Education may be deemed most significant. It forms a striking characteristic of the age—one by no means peculiar to our country, to republics, or to the Anglo-Saxon race.[29]

The following year Robert Rantoul, a reformer and member of the Massachusetts State Board of Education, in his discourse

27 "Appropriation of Public Lands for Schools," *North Am. Rev.,* XIII (Oct., 1821), 337-338; "On the Study of the Natural Sciences," *Illinois Monthly Mag.,* I (April, 1831), 315-330; "Education," *Knickerbocker,* V (June, 1835), 509.

James Gould, *An Oration . . . New Haven before the . . . Phi Beta Kappa Society* (New Haven, 1825), p. 29; J. R. Ingersoll, *An Address . . . Lafayette College* (Phil., 1833), *passim;* James Tallmadge, *Address . . . the University of the City of New York* (New York, 1837), *passim.*

For a different view, see: A. H. Everett, "American Library of Useful Knowledge," *North Am. Rev.,* XXXIII (Oct., 1831), 529-530; "A Chapter on Society," *Knickerbocker,* IV (July, 1834), 25-32.

28 W. R. Johnson, *Remarks on the Duty of the Several States, in Regard to Public Education* (Phil., 1830), p. 7.

29 "Education," *New Yorker,* V (May 5, 1838), 105.

before the American Institute of Instruction called for universal education to enable the United States to achieve its mission of spreading democracy. Believing that Providence had instilled in man the instinct of progress, Rantoul advocated that it be improved by education.[30]

By no means lacking in their enthusiasm over the possibilities of universal education, the new states of the Northwest were among the first to establish systems of public education.[31] Influential in securing the passage of the Ohio School law was the Western Literary Institute, composed of public and private school teachers.[32] Albert Picket, the organizer of the Institute, in his " Opening Address " before its fourth annual meeting in 1834, urged the teachers to participate in and to promote the progress of society. In an age of improvement, he asked, are we " to sit at our desks, and make no effort to advance the progress of moral and scientific light, beyond our school-rooms, and endeavour to spread farther and wider the knowledge we possess?" [33] Speaking before the same meeting, Thomas S. Grimké, a prominent Southern educator, and an advocate of religious and utilitarian training, in urging "A Christian and American Education," noted:

> This is an age, and ours is a country in which educated men are not at liberty to sit down contented with things as they are. Their plain duty is, to enquire and examine constantly, are things as they should be? Their dutys are active not passive.

30 Robert Rantoul, Jr., " The Education of a Free People " (1839), *Memoirs Speeches and Writings*, ed. Luther Hamilton (Boston, 1854), pp. 112-140.

31 On the Western faith in education, see for example: James Hall, " To the Reader," *Western Monthly Mag.*, I (Jah., 1833), 3; and also the article " On the Formation of a National Character," *ibid.*, I (Aug., 1833), 348-355.

32 E. P. Cubberley, *Public Education in the United States* (rev. ed.; Boston and New York, 1934), pp. 169-170, ch. 6.

33 Albert Picket, " Opening Address " (1834), *Transactions of the Fourth Annual Meeting of the Western Literary Institute* (Cincinnati, 1835), p. 26; see also his " Opening Address " (1835), *Transactions* fifth meeting (Cin., 1836), p. 45.

They are responsible for the progress of society in their time . . .[34]

A speaker, at a later meeting of the Institute in 1838, called for federal aid to education in his "Address on the importance of introducing a uniform system of common school education and adapting it to the genius of our republican institutions." Education, it was felt, would advance the public welfare and prevent the evils arising from an increased population. Moreover, the speaker declared:

> History will demonstrate, that in all ages of the world in which mankind were known to have made progress in civilization and in the science of political liberty, that popular instruction in letters and in the arts was by no means neglected.[35]

A most important development in public education was the centralization of the district common schools under the supervision of a state administrator. In 1837 Massachusetts and Ohio both inaugurated this system. In Ohio Samuel Lewis was appointed state superintendent of schools, and Calvin E. Stowe was sent to Europe to make a study of elementary education. Massachusetts gave evidence of a revived interest in its common schools by the establishment of a state board of education and with the appointment of Horace Mann as its executive secretary. Mann, whose commencement oration at Brown had been on the " Progressive Character of the Human Race," [36] on the day he accepted the office, wrote in his diary:

> Henceforth so long as I hold this office I devote myself to the supremest welfare of mankind upon earth . . . I have faith in the improvability of the race—in their accelerating improv-

34 T. S. Grimké, "American Education" (1834), *Transactions* fourth meeting, p. 102.

35 E. Vance, "Address . . . ." (1838), *Transactions* eighth meeting (Cin., 1839), p. 91.

36 Memoir of "Horace Mann," *Am. Journal of Educ.*, V (Dec., 1858), 614; see also on Mann's faith in progress: Merle Curti, *The Social Ideas of American Educators* (New York, 1935), ch. 3, pp. 126-127, 134, 138.

ability. This effort may do, apparently, but little. But mere beginning in a good cause is never little. If we can get this vast
wheel into any perceptible motion, we shall have accomplished
much.[37]

With Mann, education was more than individual matter; it
also involved the progress of society and of future generations.
In his *Common School Journal* for 1840 he denounced the people, who believed public education visionary, as those persons,
" not without worth and influence, who have no faith in the
progress of humanity." And he concluded:

> Often the wisdom of hope is better than the wisdom of ex-
> perience. Never be discouraged by the slow growth of your
> hopes. The greatest effects are often long in ripening. Every
> generation must work in part, for those which will come
> after.[38]

In his magazine for 1848, he noted the presence of two parties
in the world, the Forward-looking and the Backward-looking,
or the Progressives and Retrogressives, and he observed: " It
seems to us that there is great significancy in the arrangement
of nature. The eyes of man look forward, that they may see
where they go; because Progress is the law of the universe." [39]
In Massachusetts, he saw the retrogressive spirit developing
under the slogan of the practical against the theoretical. A
staunch believer in the idea that, *"All intelligent action includes
both theory* AND *practice,"* he warned that resistance to improvement invited revolution by its contradiction of the instinct
of the race and of the law of progress. However, he felt that in
the end " the party of Progress is sure to triumph." [40]

37 Quoted in Cubberley, *Public Education*, p. 223.

38 Horace Mann, " An Appeal to the Citizens of Massachusetts, in Behalf
of Their Public Schools," *Common School Journal*, II (Feb. 15, 1840), 56;
see also his "Annual Report for 1844," *Life and Works*, III, 463-464.

39 Mann, " Practice *against* Theory. Theory And Practice," *Common
School Journal*, X (March 1, 1848), 65.

40 *Ibid.*, pp. 66-71.

Mann believed that God had given human beings the capacity for indefinite progress, and, although he felt this gift was as yet undeveloped, in 1841 he rejoiced: " *Our* attainments are no measure of *their* capacities. The human soul is to be appreciated, not for what it is, but for what it is capable of becoming. Hence its law of expansion and progress is its richest endowment." [41] To develop fully this capacity for progress a sound system of education was absolutely necessary. And when education received the same attention as the useful arts, Mann was confident that

> temperance, liberality, rectitude, and piety, will be extended as far beyond its present limits, as the dominion of civilized man, who converts all the laws of nature into instruments of power, is superior to that of the savage, to whom the most splendid manifestations of those laws are only so many sources of superstition and debasement.[42]

For over a decade Mann devoted himself to the cause of public education, laying the foundations of a strong system in Massachusetts, and securing a nation-wide reputation for himself. Also interested in the other reform movements of his time, Mann was elected to Congress in 1848 as an anti-slavery Whig, giving up his position on the Board of Education and his work as editor of the *Common School Journal*. While Mann was in Congress, his successor as editor of the *Common School Journal* denounced the materialistic, military spirit of the country, the rise of which, he felt, was placing education and progress in the background.[43] Mann himself, defeated as the Free Soiler candidate for the Governorship of Massachusetts in 1852, was persuaded to assume the Presidency of Antioch College in Ohio.

41 "Introduction," *ibid.*, III (Jan. 1, 1841), 13.

42 *Ibid.*, p. 14.

43 *Common School Journal*, XII (Nov. 1, 1850), 336; *ibid.*, XIII (Nov. 15, 1851), 345-347; for another article in which a concern over the progress of education was expressed, see: "What should be America's Example?" *Knickerbocker*, XXXII (Oct., 1848), 347-352.

In his *Inaugural Address* to the college Mann pointed out that the human race had still made but little progress in fulfilling the designs of its Creator.[44] Unsuccessful in his efforts to build a great college at Antioch, Mann in 1859, the year of his death, told his students that he should like to be starting out again, fighting anew for the cause of reform. Mann then closed his address with the advice to his listeners : " *Be ashamed to die until you have won some victory for humanity.*" [45]

The common school, described by Horace Mann as " *the greatest discovery ever made by man,*" [46] was dramatized by Daniel Thompson, a Vermont lawyer, in his popular novel *Locke Amsden, or the Schoolmaster a Tale.* The book described the transformation effected in a village by the establishment there of a solid, useful system of common schooling. In summarizing the happy results of the system, Thompson wrote :

> The village instead of a trifling, has become a reading and a thinking community ; doing every thing for the encouragement of popular education at home, and now yearly sending off, to the academies and colleges abroad, some half-dozen scholars, where one, and oftener none, were sent before. The proportion of vice and crime has already very sensibly decreased, while that of industry, general competence, and rational happiness, has still more sensibly increased. In short, the whole tone of society has changed ; and that change, kind reader, great and beneficial as it is, has been effected by the nobly begun, and, subsequently, the no less nobly sustained efforts of THE COMMON SCHOOLMASTER.[47]

44 Mann, " Dedicatory and Inaugural Address " (1853), *Life and Works,* V, 325.

45 Mann, " Baccalaureate Address " (1859), *ibid.,* V, 524, 503-504.

46 *Common School Journal,* III (Jan. 1, 1841), 15: for two later statements of faith in the common schools and in public education, see: Joseph Henry, " Philosophy of Education," *Am. Journal of Educ.,* I (August, 1855), 17-31 ; H. P. Tappan, *Public Education* (Detroit, 1857), p. 10, and *passim.*

47 D. P. Thompson, *Locke Amsden* (Boston, 1847), p. 231.

Widely used as text books in the common schools, were the Peter Parley readers and histories by Samuel G. Goodrich, who gave his pseudonym " Peter Parley " to over a hundred of these tales written by himself and his assistants. Goodrich believed civilization to be a series of progressive stages with mankind still in the beginning of its development.[48] His standard of progress was the type of civilization enjoyed in Western Europe, and especially in the United States, where " the people are certainly happier than in any other part of this Western Hemisphere." [49] Goodrich admitted that Europe might surpass America in culture and refinement, but he maintained that its monarchical society was decaying, while

> With us, the career of improvement and of glory lies in the near and certain prospect before us. Under these circumstances we may easily hear the gibe of the scoffer; and while he, standing in the midst of decay, points to the splendors of the past, we, in the midst of present prosperity, shall find ennobling inspiration in the cheering anticipations of a happy future.[50]

Against pessimists who feared that civilization was declining, he cited the advances being made in science and in education:

> These are incontestable facts; and how are they to be reconciled with the ideas of retrogradation which have been suggested? The truth is, society is advancing with the force of an irresistible tide in its intellectual career. Already, it has made great progress.[51]

Goodrich also believed that those nations adhering to the Protestant religion made the greatest progress, and he was careful,

48 [S. G. Goodrich]: *Modern History* (Louisville, 1848), p. 477; *The Young American* (8th ed.; New York, 1847), pp. 13-19.

49 [Goodrich], *The First Book of History* (New York, 1831), p. 178; see also his *Peter Parley's Common School History* (6th ed.; Phil., 1839), p. 15.

50 [Goodrich], *Lights and Shadows of American History* (Boston, 1844), p. 14.

51 *Ibid.*, p. 16.

therefore, in his textbooks to stress the religious as well as the practical implications of scientific and material progress.[52]

In reviewing one of these many Peter Parley tales for *Godey's Lady's Book,* Rufus Dawes, the poet, noted the popular connection of the idea of progress with the democratic principle. Dawes however felt that progress was not natural. Man was " designed to be educated to progress," he declared, and he quoted with approval Goodrich's concept of education as the great lever of society.[53] *Godey's* in other articles also embraced this idea with enthusiasm, identifying it especially with the cause of female education. The editors of the *Lady's Book* in 1841, when the country was emerging from a long depression, wrote that " in the increasing attention paid to female education, we see a surer omen of the onward progress of social and moral improvement, than was ever before, in any age exhibited." [54] In the period before the Civil War, however, women did not enjoy the same educational facilities afforded the men. Aware of this discrepancy, the advocates of women's rights argued the cause of more female education. In *Godey's* "Editors' Table " their viewpoint was given a characteristic expression. Declaring in 1854 that " Education is the grand lever to elevate society," the writer predicted:

> When both sexes are allowed equal privileges of instruction, the advancement of the race will be accelerated in more than twofold proportion, because the ignorance of one half the species serves to hinder greatly the influences of intelligence in the enlightened portion. A small cloud can dim the sun.[55]

52 [Goodrich] : *The Wonders of Geology* (Boston, 1845), pp. 286-287; *A Glance at the Physical Sciences* (Boston, 1844), pp. 5-8; *Enterprise, Industry, and Art of Man . . . .* (Boston, 1845), pp. 327-335.

53 Rufus Dawes, " Fireside Education," *Godey's Lady's Book,* XVII (Dec., 1838), 275-277.

54 " Editors' Table," *ibid.,* XXIII (Nov., 1841), 236.

55 " Editors' Table," *ibid.,* XLVIII (June, 1854), 555; see also: X, 22; XVII, 140; XXIII, 93; LII, 370.

For some other statements linking progress with the influence of women, see: Samuel Young, *Suggestions on the Best Mode of Promoting Civilization*

The *Lady's Book,* restrained even in its primary interest, did not allow its enthusiasm for female education to be extended into a crusade for equal rights for women in all fields. The editors rather felt that

> The true arena for woman's awakened intellect is, as we hold, at home, and in promoting the progressive improvement of her own sex.[56]
>
> The greatest triumph of this progression is redeeming woman from her inferior position and placing her where the Creator designed she should stand—side by side with man, a *help-meet* for him in *all* his pursuits and improvements.[57]

The principal concession offered by *Godey's* to women, who desired to put their education to use outside the home, was school teaching, and in 1853 the editors wrote:

> Educate rightly the educators of the world; give to woman the means and opportunities of cultivating her talents, directing these to the moral improvement of the young and the well-being of society; then the true progress will be attained, and, by the blessing of Heaven, soon become universal.[58]

Godey's Lady's Book was one of the most widely-circulated and prosperous magazines in America before the Civil War. In 1846 the editors, anxious to secure a circulation of 50,000, called attention to all that the magazine had done for the cause of female education and urged practical support from its friends because: " We should then feel sure that the ' progression ' of our own sex in this country was rapidly advancing—because

---

and Improvement; or the Influence of Woman on the Social State (Albany, 1837), p. 33, and *passim*; E. D. Sanborn, "The Progress of Society as Indicated by the Condition of Women," *Bib. Repos.*, 2nd ser., VIII (July, 1842), 91-115; J. W. T., "Woman in America," *Q. Rev. of the Meth. Epis. Church South*, XIII (July 1859), 389.

56 "Editors' Table," *Godey's Lady's Book*, XXVI (May, 1843), 249.

57 "Editors' Table," *ibid.*, XXXIII (Nov., 1846), 235.

58 "Editors' Table," *ibid.*, XLVII (Oct., 1853), 368.

those who love and join in this progress would thus generously sustain us." [59]

As the number of students in the various types of schools and colleges of the nation grew, the question of the role which their graduates would take in society became a problem of increasing importance. With the changes symbolized by the term " the rise of the common man," and with the diffusion of political democracy and public education among the people, the prestige of the old aristocratic classes, including the college graduates, was called into question. In danger of being overwhelmed by the era of reform succeeding the Jacksonian revolution, the conservative classes cultivated the colleges as the strongholds of the aristocratic tradition. Some of the leading college educators in their text books and academic addresses expressed a conservative view of the progress of society. Unable to ignore the scientific advances and social reforms of the age, they however urged that a similar regard be directed toward the moral and religious nature of progress.

Jaspar Adams, the New England born President of Charleston College, South Carolina, from 1824 to 1836, in his academic addresses during this period included scientific and material progress among the leading characteristics of the century. However, he was alarmed at the neglect of " the moral causes of the welfare of the nations," and in an address on this subject in 1834, he declared:

> Those nations which have been best educated, which have been the most moral and the most religious; that is, those which have been the most distinguished for the great virtues of industry, temperance, moderation, moral courage, prudence, justice, benevolence, enterprise, foresight and good faith; whose members have habitually regulated their tempers and disciplined their passions; whose energies, physical, moral and intellectual, have been guided by virtue and knowledge, have always possessed an immense superiority in numbers, wealth,

[59] "Editors' Table," *ibid.*, XXXIII (Nov., 1846), 236-237.

power, reputation and influence, over those who have lived in
disregard of these virtues . . .[60]

Adams sought some basis on which to unite the physical and
moral causes of progress. Therefore in his textbook *Elements
of Moral Philosophy,* published in 1837, he proposed the theory
that mankind have advanced in intellectual, social, and moral
improvement, in proportion as their physical condition and circumstances have improved . . ." Then he went on to say " that
the physical improvement of mankind has been accomplished
chiefly by labor-saving machinery . . ." [61]

In New England Mark Hopkins, a Congregational clergyman, and the well-known President of Williams College from
1836 to 1872, conceived of progress in terms of an individual
and religious improvement.[62] In an address, *The Law of Progress of the Race,* delivered in 1843 at the celebration of Williams' semi-centennial anniversary, Hopkins declared that the
world too often mistook commotion for progress. Despite all
the advances made in science and in the diffusion of knowledge,
he believed progress represented something different than material or cultural improvement. " The true idea of progress,
then, is not that of movement, or simply of progression towards
the realization of an idea, but it involves the recognition of the
true end of man as a social being . . ." [63] The real goal of man,
he decided, was his individual improvement and his moral bet-

60 Jaspar Adams, *The Moral Causes of the Welfare of Nations* (Charleston, 1834), p. 20, and *passim*; see also his *An Inaugural Discourse* (Geneva,
1827), *passim*; and *Characteristics of the Present Century* (Charleston,
1836), pp. 4-9.

61 Adams, *Elements of Moral Philosophy* (New York, 1837), p. 468; see
also: S. P. Newman, *Elements of Political Economy* (Andover and New
York, 1835), pp. 72, 13-16.

62 Mark Hopkins: "On Originality," *Bib. Repos.,* VI (Oct., 1835), 482-
497; *The Central Principle* (New York, 1854), pp. 14-19; *Eagles' Wings*
(Boston, 1858), pp. 3-5, 8, 17; *Lectures on Moral Science* (Boston, 1862),
pp. 33-34.

63 Hopkins, *An Address delivered before the Society of the Alumni of
Williams College* .. (Boston, 1843), p. 13.

terment along the path pointed out by his Creator. And because
he felt that the fundamental condition of true progress was a
moral one, he stated: .

> We believe in no *law* of progress that would exclude the
> providence of God, and in no conditions of progress that would
> exclude the religion of Jesus Christ. If men choose voluntarily
> to adopt the ends which God proposes, and to act in coinci-
> dence with the laws which he has instituted, they will make a
> progress individual and social, such as will realize the brightest
> dreams of poetry and of prophecy; but if they pursue any other
> course, their progress can be only progress towards ruin.[64]

No less devout than Hopkins, Francis Wayland, a Baptist
minister, and the President of Brown from 1827 to 1885, was
more interested, however, in a practical, utilitarian sort of education. In his widely-used college texts he defended property and
productive industry as essential elements of the progress of
civilization. And in his tremendously popular *Elements of
Moral Science,* first published in 1835, Wayland upheld the idea
that man was " created, with moral and intellectual powers,
capable of progressive improvement. Hence, if he uses his faculties as he ought, he will progressively improve . . ." [65] An individual having once secured the fruits of his toil, Wayland defended his right to his property as in accord with the will of
God. Moreover, he wrote: " The existence and progress of
society, nay the very existence of our race, depends upon the
acknowledgment of this right." Without this right of property,
he warned:

> Progress would be out of the question; and the only change
> which could take place would be, that arising from the pres-
> sure of heavier and heavier penury, as the spontaneous pro-

---

64 *Ibid.,* pp. 23-24; see also: Francis Bowen, *Lowell Lectures on the
Application of Metaphysical and Ethical Science to the Evidences of Religion*
(Boston, 1849), pp. 245, 379; John Williams, *Academic Studies* (Hartford,
1849), p. 21, and *passim.*

65 Francis Wayland, *The Elements of Moral Science* (New York, 1835),
p. 84.

ductions of the earth became rarer, from improvident consumption, without any corresponding labor for reproduction.[66]

Wayland also translated his views on society into an educational program designed to make the college curriculum attractive to the rising industrial interests in New England. In his *Report to the Corporation of Brown University, on changes in the system of collegiate education, read March 28, 1850,* he advocated a broadened curriculum, designed to draw students from every class and interest in society, and preparing its graduates for business as well as for the professions. Upholding his proposal, he declared that it was expedient because:

> The moral conditions being equal, the progress of a nation in wealth, happiness, and refinement, is measured by the universality of its knowledge of the laws of nature, and its skill in adapting these laws to the purposes of man. Civilization is advancing, and it can only advance in the line of the useful arts. It is, therefore, of the greatest national importance to spread broadcast over the community, that knowledge, by which alone the useful arts can be multiplied and perfected.[67]

The conservative viewpoint was re-echoed in the argument that the true progress of society could only be preserved by the educated classes. Subscribing to this opinion, a large number of academic orators—including prominent educators, clergymen, and statesmen—urged the colleges to exercise their influence against the radical tendencies of the day.[68] During the 1830's a

66 *Ibid.*, pp. 247-248, and 379-380; see also Wayland's *The Elements of Political Economy* (2nd ed.; New York and Boston, 1838), pp. 58-65.

67 Wayland, *Report to the Corporation of Brown University . . .* (Providence, 1850), p. 57; and his *The Education Demanded by the People of the U. States* (Boston, 1855), *passim;* see also: G. R. Russell, *The Merchant* (Boston, 1849), p. 52 and *passim;* H. W. Bellows, *The Ledger and the Lexicon: or, Business and Literature in Account with American Education* (Cambridge, 1853), *passim.*

For a different view, see: Joseph Le Conte, *The Principles of a Liberal Education* (Columbia, S. C., 1859), pp. 4-9, and *passim.*

68 See the study by S. L. Jackson, *America's Struggle for Free Schools* (Washington, D. C. [1942]), *passim.*

considerable group of educators felt impelled to address college audiences on the general subject of the duty of the scholar in an age of material progress and radical reform. The moral and religious aspects of the idea of progress were emphasized in these speeches,[69] and a typical illustration of their conservative treatment of the idea of progress was provided in the academic orations of Caleb Sprague Henry, a clergyman, editor, leader in the peace movement, and a professor of philosophy for fourteen years at New York University. Henry strongly denounced the materialism of the 1830's. " National well-being ", he declared, " consists in the development of the proper humanity of a na- tion—in the cultivation and exercise of the reason and moral nature, and in the subordination to these of all the lower prin- ciples."[70] To combat the " love of money " and " the strife of party politics," Henry called for a learned class or " an intellec- tual High Priesthood " which, he felt, might promote true progress by being one of the " conservative powers " of the na- tion.[71]

In the forties, when many a reform scheme was urged in the name of progress, the college students continued to be warned by a succession of eloquent orators against the radical tendencies of the day. Benjamin F. Tefft, a professor at Indiana Asbury University, and a Methodist minister, addressed an audience at the college in 1845 on the subject, *Inequality in the Condition*

69 B. F. Joslin, *A Discourse on the Privileges and Duties of Man as a Progressive Being* (Schenectady, 1833), p. 15, and *passim*: Henry Vethake, *An Address delivered at his Inauguration as President of Washington College* . . . (Lexington, 1835), p. 6, and *passim*; W. G. Goddard, *An Address to the Phi Beta Kappa Society of Rhode Island* . . . (Boston, 1837), pp. 12-13, and *passim*; Benjamin Hale, *Liberty and Law* (Geneva, 1838), *passim*; G. C. Verplanck, *The Advantages and the Dangers of the American Scholar* (New York, 1836), pp. 5-10, and *passim*.

70 C. S. Henry, " The Importance of Elevating the Intellectual Spirit of the Nation " (1836), in *Considerations on Some of the Elements and Con- ditions of Social Welfare and Human Progress* (New York and London, 1861), p. 7.

71 *Ibid., passim*; see also his " The Position and Duties of the Educated Men of the Country " (1840), *ibid.*, pp. 63-106.

of Men Inevitable. Denouncing all radical attempts to change this inequality, Tefft directed the attention of his listeners to the superior progress secured by a devotion to God and his Gospel.[72] A year later, in 1846, David H. Riddle, President of Jefferson College, Pennsylvania, declared " that *sound and sanctified scholarship is the true conservative principle of our age and country!*" and he called for:

> Men, who will *be the advocates of progress,* without permitting everything, that time has consecrated or use approved, to be turned upside down to appease the insatiable maw of the monster of modern revolution![73]

At Lafayette College in 1847, John M. Krebs, a Presbyterian clergyman and educator, urged the scholars to promote moral and religious progress, instead of following the materialism and radicalism of the age. In concluding his address, Krebs emphasized the gradual nature of true progress, saying:

> Far be it from me, to oppose all progress, or to exhort you to a blind defense of time-honored abuses ... There is a certain arrangement of Divine Providence, under which its own plan of melioration in our fallen world is accomplished by degrees. Creation itself was a gradual process.[74]

The conservatism of these academic addresses was exemplified in *An Oration on the Scholar's Mission,* delivered at Dartmouth College in 1843, by Orestes A. Brownson. Brownson, at this time unenthusiastic over public education and on the verge of his conversion to Catholicism and complete conservatism, noted that no amount of education could overcome the natural inequality between men, and he declared that progress rested on this diversity. Seeing the country characterized by levelling tendency, he told the students: " You are to *withstand this lev-*

72 B. F. Tefft, *Inequality in the Condition of Men Inevitable* (Greencastle, 1845), p. 16, and *passim.*

73 D. H. Riddle, *Sound and Sanctified Scholarship* (Pittsburg 1846), pp. 11, 9.

74 J. M. Krebs, *Education and Progress* (Easton, 1847), p. 36.

elling tendency, so far, but only so far, as it is a tendency to level downwards, and not upwards." [75] Because he recognized that the scholar was often criticized for his exclusiveness, Brownson concluded with the plea:

> Redeem the sacred character of the Scholar, I beseech you, from this reproach, by devoting yourselves heart and soul, to the progress of your race, to the moral, intellectual, and social elevation of all men, especially of the poorer, and more numerous classes. In so doing you will magnify your profession as scholars, fulfil your mission, do honor to your country, and receive the approbation of your God.[76]

Other reformers, whose liberalism was less transient than Brownson's, joined him in his plea, urging the scholar to take up the cause of progress. Like Brownson, the advocate of many reform schemes, Horace Greeley, the editor of the *Tribune,* informed a group at Hamilton College in 1844 that upon " the discipline and duties of the scholar " depends " the progress and well-being of the human race." [77] College orators, who shared some of Greeley's liberalism, counselled the students to judge fairly between the forces of conservatism and reform. Frederic H. Hedge, the Unitarian minister and transcendentalist, told an audience at Bowdoin College in 1843 that the age was marked by a sharp collision between the old and the new, in which

> All progress is judgement. Every new generation is a new verdict on human affairs, and the world's history is the world's tribunal. But the progress of society is never wholly a unanimous movement; its judgement is never a unanimous verdict. Our motion in time, like a motion in space, is subject to a

75 O. A. Brownson, *An Oration on the Scholar's Mission* (Boston, 1843), p. 33; for Brownson's view of public education, see his " Education of the People," *Chr. Ex.,* XX (May, 1836), 153-169.

76 Brownson, *An Oration on the Scholar's Mission,* p. 40.

77 Horace Greeley, *An Address before the Literary Societies of Hamilton College* (Clinton, 1844), p. 40, and *passim.*

contrary power. All civilization is a conflict of opposite forces.[78]

In 1850 Henry B. Stanton, husband of Elizabeth Cady Stanton, close friend of Whittier, and long identified with the anti-slavery cause, spoke at Williams College on the subject, *Ultraists, Conservatives, Reformers*. Seeing progress as a resultant of these three forces, Stanton, one month before the passage of the Compromise of 1850, urged the educated men of the country to promote progress by partiotically supporting the Constitution.[79] In that same year, 1850, Henry J. Raymond, the well-known editor, just entering active politics under the Free Soil banner, discussed *The Relations of the American Scholar to his Country and the Times*. Although he believed that the human race was naturally progressive, he called on all scholars to aid this improvement by using their knowledge to further the progress of society. He deprecated the contemporary fear of radicalism, and went on to denounce the extreme conservatism which would deny all progress, declaring:

> The radical movements which at the present day give alarm to many thoughtful minds, will seem of much less importance when thus considered in the light of this fundamental law of social life and growth . . . What they need, therefore, is not suppression but *guidance*: and this it is the peculiar province of the Scholar to furnish.[80]

Among the orators invited to speak before college audiences, no class was more conservative in their treatment of the idea of progress than those jurists and statesmen whose formal education revolved around the study of the law. And of this group probably no one equaled Daniel Dewey Barnard, lawyer, polit-

78 F. H. Hedge, *Conservatism and Reform* (Boston, 1843), pp. 3-4, 38-39, and *passim*; see also: S. B. Canfield, *An Address on the Power and Progressiveness of Knowledge* (Painesville, [1843]), pp. 26-27, and *passim*.

79 H. B. Stanton, *Ultraists, Conservatives, Reformers* (New York, 1850), *passim*.

80 H. J. Raymond, *The Relations of the American Scholar to his Country and his Times* (New York, 1850), p. 52, and *passim*.

ical figure, and Whig Congressman from New York, in the number of addresses delivered during the 1830's and 1840's on the theme of the duty of the scholar toward the progress of the age. Returning to America in 1831 from a five months vacation abroad, part of which he had spent in a study of the Revolution of 1830, Barnard announced to a group at Williams College:

> A wide field opens before the American scholar and patriot. The physical and moral condition of man—already better than the world has yet seen it—is to be improved and elevated. The political institutions of the country—the best the world has yet known, are to be perfected, preserved, propagated and transmitted. And every thing is to be done by the force of intellect.[81]

Later in the decade, while the Jacksonian upheaval was still active, he delivered a series of addresses urging the educated classes of the country to seek political office.[82] By this means Barnard felt they would temper the effects of majority rule and of political equality, and at the same time preserve American democracy, and promote the progress of society. Barnard was very skillful in using American patriotism and the faith in progress as symbols by which to reassure conservative gatherings alarmed by Jacksonian reform. From 1839 to 1845 he was a member of Congress, and then declining reelection, he returned to the academic platform. In his addresses of the late forties, he called on the educated classes to further real progress by defending established American institutions and the existing social and economic order.[83] He also desired the government to become more active in advancing progress, and in 1846 he declared:

81 D. D. Barnard, *An Address delivered September 6, 1831, before the Adelphic Union Society of Williams College* (Williamstown, 1831), p. 34.

82 Barnard: *An Address ... Rutgers College ...* (Albany, 1837); *A Discourse Pronounced at Schenectady ...* (Albany, 1837); *Discourse Pronounced at ... the University of Vermont ...* (Albany, 1838); *An Address delivered at Amherst ...* (Albany, 1839).

83 Barnard: *A Plea for Social and Popular Repose* (New York, 1845); *The Social System* (Hartford, 1848).

With the active and efficient cooperation of the State, and the Government, we have a right to hope—and assume—that a people may make progress in virtue, morality, and happiness; but that will be on one condition. I mean that there must be a prevalent spirit of subjection and obedience to established law and constituted authority. A rare old virtue this, of Obedience, and not half as much honored, I am afraid, now-a-days, as it ought to be. In all efforts at moral renovation and progress, whether personal or political, men will find they cannot get along without it; and they may as well begin with this, first as last.[84]

A good many jurists, reverencing antiquity, and mindful of the contributions of the past to the progress of civilization, did not surrender themselves to the enthusiasms of their contempories.[85] Alarmed by the conflict occasioned in the Jacksonian era, Joseph Story, a great intellect and scholar, and second only to Marshall as a conservative justice of the Supreme Court, counselled some degree of moderation between the positions of the opposing forces. Story especially feared that the events of the thirties had threatened the influence of the learned classes of the nation. Seeing the predominant danger of the times in the tendency to ultraism, he advised the alumni of Harvard in 1842 that

The main ground, therefore, for apprehension is not from undue reverence for antiquity, so much as it is from dreamy expectations of unbounded future intellectual progress; and, above all, from our gross over-valuation and inordinate exaggeration of the peculiar advantages and excellences of our own age over all others . . . The truth is, that the past is not every thing; nor the future every thing; nor the present everything. The intellect of man is now neither in its infancy, nor in its decrepitude.[86]

84 Barnard, *Man and the State, Social and Political* (New Haven, 1846), pp. 47-48.

85 See for example: Joel Parker, *Progress, An Address...Dartmouth College* (Hanover, 1846); J. P. Bradley, *Progress, Its Grounds and Possibilities* (New Brunswick, 1849).

86 Joseph Story, "Literary Tendencies of the Times" (1842), *Miscellaneous Writings* (Boston, 1852), pp. 747, 745; for a similar expression,

Conservative jurists, in addressing college audiences, also related their concept of progress to the preservation of private property against the danger of a popular revolt. Before the Phi Beta Kappa Society of Union College in 1841, William Kent, son of the famous Chancellor and also a well-known lawyer in his own right, defended hereditary property at a time when the large landed estates in New York were under the attack of the anti-renters. Kent nevertheless saw " a ceaseless progress in the principles of Democracy and equality," and he therefore contented himself with picturing an imaginary, impartial seer, modeled on Bolingbroke's idea of a patriot king, so that,

> Looking around him, he may rank himself with the moderate reformers, not attempting the impossible task of resisting popular will and progress—not desiring to resist it, if he had the power; but endeavoring to guide, to divert, to *moderate* it.[87]

In Rhode Island the dominance of the conservative, propertied interests was also threatened. During the early 1840's this struggle took the form of a demand for a wider suffrage, and culminated in the so-called " Dorr's Rebellion." At Brown, the leading college of the state, several speakers urged the students to take a conservative attitude toward the concept of progress. In the most famous of these speeches Judge Job Durfee, who had presided at Dorr's trial, delivered in 1843 an oration in which he criticized popular opinion as a force in progress. Durfee believed the better minds of the country had discovered the true cause of progress in the natural laws of the universe and in the reality of scientific advance. He further remarked that, in the connection between scientific and social progress, he saw

which cited Story, see: Ezekiel Bacon, *Recollections of Fifty Years Since* (Utica, 1843), p. 32, and *passim*; see also Story's early discourse, " Characteristics of the Age " (1826), *Misc. Writings*, pp. 341 ff.

87 William Kent, *An Address . . . Union College . . .* (New York, 1841), p. 29, and *passim*.

an assurance of progress, not dependent, thank Heaven, upon carrying to their results any political abstractions or any ideas of popular sovereignty drawn from the perversions of revolutionary France; but upon a law of progress, which God has ordained for the government of humanity, and which is as certain and eternal in its operations as any law which governs the material universe.[88]

During the fifties, the academic orators continued to devote their attention to the conservative implications of the idea of progress.[89] However, the attitude of many of these speakers was summed up by Edward Everett, one of the most famous orators of his day. In 1852, at the annual celebration of the Harvard alumni, he denounced those radical programs which claimed to be in accord with the progress of the age. Favoring a conservative as well as a progressive element in society, he declared:

> Heaven knows I am no enemy to progress . . . but let it really be progress. Movement is not necessarily progress; it may be sideways or backward. I doubt that progress which denies that the ages before us have achieved anything worth preserving. I believe in both parts of the apostolic rule,— Prove all things, hold fast to that which is good. True progress is thoughtful, hopeful, serene, religious, onward, and upward.[90]

Distrustful of the times, afraid of reform, reverencing anti-

---

88 Job Durfee, *The Influence of Scientific Discovery and Invention on Social and Political Progress* (Providence, 1843), p. 13, and *passim*; see also: Thomas Kinnicutt, *An Oration . . . Brown University* (Providence, 1840); William Greene, *Some of the Difficulties in the Administration of a Free Government* (Providence, 1851).

89 See for example: Timothy Walker, *The Reform Spirit of the Day* (Boston, 1850), pp. 35-36; Levi Woodbury, "The Right and the Duty of Forming Individual Opinions" (1851), *Writings*, III, 223-247; J. N. Whiting, *Modern Reforms, and the Duty of the Instructed Towards Them* (Geneva, 1852), pp. 14-15; W. F. Morgan, *Conservatism* (Hartford, 1852), *passim*; W. M. Evarts, *An Oration . . . Yale College . . .* (New Haven, 1853), p. 33, and *passim*.

90 Edward Everett, "Festival of the Alumni of Harvard" (1852), *Orations and Speeches*, III, 120.

quity, and skeptical of material progress, a majority of the academic orators of the period urged the rising generation to temper progress by conservatism. With few illusions about stemming the march of progress, these speakers called upon the scholar to take the lead in separating the idea of progress from any radical program considered dangerous to conservative interests. In a reminiscent article, written in 1854, James Russell Lowell, in discusing the conservatism of a former President of Harvard, also gave a good picture of the fate of these rebels against the times when

> the good ship Progress weighs anchor, and whirls them away from drowsy tropic inlets to arctic waters of unnatural ice. To such crustaceous natures, created to cling upon the immemorial rock amid softest mosses, comes the bustling Nineteenth Century and says, " Come, come bestir yourself and be practical! Get out of that old shell of yours forthwith!" Alas, to get out of the shell is to die![91]

On the whole, however, it may be said that universal education was considered a powerful force and evidence of progress in the decades following 1815. To reformers it offered the hope that an educated people would adopt their schemes. To the underprivileged it meant the chance to rise, and to the more favored classes it seemed to preclude the possibility of a violent revolution. It was widely believed that the people must be educated if American democracy was to realize its full promise, while among those who distrusted some of the implications of American democracy in the Middle Period, it was felt that the scholar should assume his duty and insure an aristocratic type of progress. Thus for a variety of reasons, education appealed to various groups as synonymous with the hope offered by the idea of progress.

91 J. R. Lowell, " Cambridge Thirty Years Ago " (1854), *Complete Writings* (Boston and New York, 1904), I, 51.

CHAPTER VIII

THE QUALIFIED AFFIRMATION OF THE SOUTH

WHILE Southerners joined in the formulation of the American conception of the idea of progress, their point of view was in general characterized by a defence of the institution of Negro slavery. In the words of an early writer on the subject: " Slavery has ever been the step-ladder by which civilized countries have passed from barbarism to civilization."[1] Wedded to the institution of slavery and to the production of ever greater quantities of cotton, the South was primarily an agricultural society. Although an occasional Southerner argued the merits of manufacturing or of diversified agriculture, the section on the whole remained only slightly affected by the industrialization taking place in the North. As the gap in the years leading to the Civil War narrowed, the divergence between the economies of the North and of the South widened. The ante-bellum Southern contention that slavery was an agency in the progress of civilization became more and more unacceptable to the North. Pursuing two different ways of life, and adhering to two unlike social and economic systems, the ideals and the concepts of progress entertained in the South and in the North also differed. However, because they found the idea of progress useful to their purposes, both Southern planters and Northern abolitionists adopted it in their arguments over the " peculiar institution."

Deferring for the moment a treatment of the Southern adaptation of the idea of progress to the devices of its own pro-slavery arguments, the use of the idea by the proponents of Southern industrial expansion may be noted. In the South programs for state aid to railroads and for government protection of slavery were advocated along with appeals to American free institutions and to the traditional view that " Free Trade

1 Edward Brown, *Notes on the Origin and Necessity of Slavery* (Charleston, 1826), p. 6.

is the great cause of human improvement." [2] From the North Abbot Lawrence, the Lowell cotton manufacturer, in 1846 advised the people of Virginia to promote internal improvements, manufacturing, and popular education, for, he declared, " from these movements will soon be seen the happiest results, in a healthful prosperity, and a striking improvement in the condition of the people." [3] In their reply to Lawrence, some of the members of the Virginia Legislature rejoiced " that the spirit of improvement is abroad in the State," but they declared that some individual like Lawrence was needed to establish industry in Virginia and thus " unite the North and the South more closely and harmoniusly together in their onward progress to equal rewards and a common destiny." [4]

A pioneer in urging his section to take up the cause of industry was the South Carolinian, William Gregg, the father of Southern cotton manufacturing. In his *Essays on Domestic Industry, or an Inquiry into the Expediency of Establishing Cotton Manufactures in South Carolina,* first published in 1845, Gregg admitted that those who projected new enterprises were subjected to ridicule by men who, he declared, were as wise as those who had predicted the failure of the railroad and the steamboat. With Charleston and South Carolina already behind the age in agriculture, industry, and enterprise, Gregg called for a change in Southern habits and pursuits, declaring that this was more important and desirable than any change in government, laws, or tariffs.[5]

2 Statement made by H. S. Legaré in his " Speech before the Union Party " (1831), *Writings,* I, 273.

3 Lawrence, *Letters from the Hon. Abbott Lawrence to the Hon. William C. Rives, of Virginia* (Boston, 1846), p. 7.

4 Quoted in H. A. Hill, *Memoir of Abbott Lawrence* (Boston, 1884), p. 35.

5 William Gregg, " Essays on Domestic Industry " (1845), pp. 203-240 in D. A. Tompkins, *Cotton Mill, Commercial Features* (Charlotte, N. C., 1899), pp. 214, 216, 208; see also Gregg's Letter in *De Bow's Rev.,* XII (April, 1852), 429-430; and Broadus Mitchell, *The Rise of Cotton Mills in the South* (Baltimore, 1921), ch. I, and *passim.*

Foremost in publicizing the idea that Southern progress depended on a commercial and industrial expansion was James D. B. De Bow, the editor of the famous *De Bow's Review*. Beginning in 1845 with the Southwestern Convention at Memphis, sectional gatherings were held from time to time to discuss the economic rehabilitation of the South and especially the construction of railroads.[6] De Bow, one of the secretaries at the Memphis Convention, presided over by John C. Calhoun, was inspired by its arguments to found his *Review,* which became the leading repository for the presentation of the opinions of the Southern commercial interests. In the first number of his magazine in 1846, De Bow, in summarizing the achievements of the Memphis Convention, contrasted such gatherings with political assembles. He declared that the former " has been an invention of the present age, to carry out its purposes. It has operated as a lever to overcome the strongest resistance, and few can estimate how largely it has contributed to the general progress." [7]

During the period of the Mexican War and the incorporation of California in the Union, the *Commercial Review* devoted articles to the theme that the future progress of the nation would be achieved in the West.[8] To capture the commerce of the West for the South, it was widely urged by De Bow and others that a railroad be constructed from the Mississippi to the Pacific. At a convention held in 1849 to promote this scheme, De Bow and seven others signed an " Address," in

6 See: Herbert Wender, *Southern Commercial Conventions* (Baltimore, 1930), *passim*; R. R. Russel, *Economic Aspects of Southern Sectionalism, 1840-1861* (Urbana, 1924), chs. 2, 5, 12.

7 "Convention of Southern and Western States," *De Bow's Rev.*, I (Jan., 1846), 7.

8 "Cities of the Valley of the Mississippi and Ohio," *ibid.*, I (Feb., 1846), 145; W. L. Hodge, "New Orleans, Its Present Situation and Future Prospects," *ibid.*, II, (July, 1846), 53-64; "Progress of the Great West," *ibid.*, IV (Sept., 1847), 31; B. F. Porter, "The Mission of America," *ibid.*, IV (Sept., 1847), 108-122; Maunsel White, "Destinies of the West and the Union," *ibid.*, VIII (Jan., 1850), 73-75.

which the favorable arguments for a railroad were concluded
with an appeal to the citizens of the United States to realize
that

> the age in which we live is one of great achievements in arts
> and sciences and in human progress. The nations of the world
> are engaged in the great race for position and for empire. It
> becomes our country to aim as high and to realize as soon as
> may be that bright and glorious destiny for which God and
> nature seem to have reserved her.[9]

De Bow, like many other Southerners, was irked by the
economic dependence of his section upon the manufacturing
interests in the North. In 1851, in an " Address to the People
of the Southern and Western States," he declared that the
Southern States, producing " in proportion to population the
greatest amount of exportable commodities," were one of the
wealthiest regions in the world. The West, he went on to say,
was also " full of youth and vigor," and destined to become
" the great manufacturing centre of the world." He was
alarmed, however, at the prospect of the products of the West
being shipped to the North over the recently developed railroads,
and he argued that Western interests would be better served
by a railroad to the South. To help encourage the construction
of such a railroad, he promised that the West " will find us
ready to co-operate heartily in every enterprise which shall
make for her interests and progress." Moreover, although
forced to admit that the Southern, like the Western, markets
paid tribute to the North, he protested:

> It is not true, that we at the South are deficient altogether
> in the spirit of progress and improvement, and can only be fed
> by the labors of our fellows. The South has had triumphs
> enough to satisfy us that the principle of progress is here,
> though latent for the moment, and that it only requires the

9 J. D. B. De Bow, et. al., "Address of the Memphis Convention to the
People of the United States," in *Minutes and Proceedings of the Memphis
Convention, Assembled Oct. 23, 1849* (Memphis, 1850), p. 49 and *passim.*

proper stimulant to be brought into an activity which shall know no rest.[10]

In his enthusiasm for better transportation, De Bow in 1852 urged the legislature of Tennessee not to sleep in an age of progress but to construct those railroads on the tracks of which " revolves the ' car of progress,' carrying with it light, and life and civilization. . . ." [11] In *De Bow's Review* during the early 1850's the cause of a Pacific railroad was further related to the idea of an American political mission and to the general progress of civilization.[12] Then, summing up the work of the commercial and railroad conventions, De Bow himself wrote in 1853 that much of " the amazing development and progressive spirit of the South and West " might be attributed to their stimulus, and he declared:

> Compare these great regions of the Union with what they were in 1845, when rail-road improvement and manufacturing progress began first to be discussed on an enlarged scale among us! The wand of the enchanter seems to have passed over them all.[13]

Some months later De Bow prepared an elaborate article on " The Progress of the Republic," outlining in detail his faith in the future of America's physical resources and conservative institutions.[14]

10 "Address to the People of the Southern and Western States," *De Bow's Rev.*, XI (August, 1851), 154, 142-175.

11 " Railroad Prospects and Progress " (Speech by De Bow), *ibid.*, XII (May, 1852), 507, 492-507.

12 " Department of Internal Improvements " (Speech by James Robb), *ibid.*, XII (May, 1852), 551; " Progress—the Past and the Present," *ibid.*, XIV (May, 1853), 461-470.

13 " The Memphis Convention," *ibid.*, XV (Sept., 1853), 255.

14 De Bow, " The Progress of the Republic," *ibid.*, XVII (August, 1854), 111-129; see also: " Commerce and Finances," *ibid.*, XV (August, 1853), 196-207; W. J. Sasnett, " The United States—Her Past and Her Future," *ibid.*, XII (June, 1852), 614-631; Southron, " Visions of American Progress," *ibid.*, XXIII (August 1857), 203-208; R. H. G. " Monarchy vs. Democracy,"

De Bow's presentation of the industrialization of the South as a patriotic enterprise in accord with the progress of the age met with the favor of other Southerners. James H. Hamond, an ardent secessionist statesman from South Carolina, in 1849 made an appeal to his state to recognize the decline of agriculture and to turn to cotton manufacturing. He felt that in the future national grandeur would be based upon the peaceful development, to the fullest extent, of a nation's resources, and he warned that those states which failed "will fall rapidly behind in the arduous but steady march of progress." [15] Henry W. Hilliard, a conciliatory Alabama Whig, in a speech on "American Industry" delivered in New York in 1850, discussed the favorable prospects for future American progress, but he cautioned: "We must make no war upon your property and industry, and you must make no war upon ours." [16]

An especially strong advocate of commercial expansion was the United States naval officer from Virginia, Matthew Fontaine Maury, who wrote articles in Southern periodicals in which he advocated a ship canal across the isthmus of Panama and a railroad to the Pacific coast. With these accomplished Maury foresaw a great future market for American goods in Asia, and in 1848 he predicted:

> The Islander will cease to go naked—the Chinaman will give up his chop-sticks, and the Asiatic Russian his train oil the moment they shall find that they can exchange the productions of their climate and labor for that which is more pleasing to the taste or fancy.[17]

ibid., XXIV (April, 1858), 312-320; W. S. Grayson, "The Cause of Human Progress," ibid., XXVII (July and Sept., 1859), 168-172, 328-335.

15 J. H. Hammond, An Address delivered before the South Carolina Institute ... 1849 (Charleston, 1849), p. 10, and passim.

16 H. W. Hilliard, "American Industry" (1850), Speeches and Addresses (New York, 1855), p. 353, and passim; see also his "The American Government" (1851), ibid., 357-379.

17 M. F. Maury, "Steam-Navigation to China," S. Lit. Mess., XIV (April, 1848), 253.

Again urging these schemes a few years later, Maury added the Amazon valley in Brazil as a fertile field for Southern expansion, declaring that " there is no colonizer, civilizer, nor Christianizer like commerce.[18]

Largely through Maury's influence, an exploration of the Amazon valley was made by two United States Lieutenants under the direction of the Navy Department.[19] In their report the naval officers depicted the commercial benefits which would result from an opening of the Amazon valley to American trade. " We, more than any other people, are interested in the opening of this navigation," William Lewis Herndon, a young Virginian, and the brother-in-law of Maury, wrote in his part of the report, and he went on to say that " The greatest boon in the wide world of commerce is in the free navigation of the Amazon, its confluents and neighboring streams." [20] Because Brazil and Peru were reluctant to entrust the trade of the river " to the energy and competition of the great commercial nations of the world," Herndon stigmatized their policy as " the progress of a denizen of their own forests—the sloth." [21]

Of course, there was also some dissent from the De Bow thesis that Southern progress depended on the promotion of commerce and on future industrialization. Some felt that agriculture provided the key to prosperity, especially in the newer states. A correspondent from Louisiana confided in the *American Agriculturist* for 1849 that, " The planters of the south are just beginning to put their ' shoulders to the wheel,' and revolutionize all the obsolete ideas in farming. *Progress* has reached us even here, and we are in earnest." [22] In 1854 a planter con-

18 Maury, " The Commercial Prospects of the South," *ibid.*, XVII (Oct. and Nov., 1851), 695.

19 See the article by W. J. Bell, Jr., " The Relation of Herndon and Gibbon's Exploration of the Amazon Valley to North American Slavery, 1850-1855," *Hispanic Am. Hist. Rev.*, XIX (Nov., 1939), 494-503.

20 W. L. Herndon, *Exploration of the Valley of the Amazon*. Part I, 32 Cong., 2 Sess., Senate Ex. Doc. no. 36 (Washington, 1853), pp. 190, 193.

21 *Ibid.*, pp. 365, 190.

22 J. S. Peacocke, "Agricultural Progress South," *Am. Agriculturist*, VIII (July, 1849), 215.

tributed to the *Southern Quarterly Review* an article in which he urged the South to renounce Northern progress and railroad building in favor of its traditional interest in agriculture. The editors appended a note disapproving this part of the argument, but not the part in which the writer criticized the radicalism of the North and its faith in the idea of progress, which he believed was destroying the rights of the individual. Sensitive to the Northern attack upon Southern slavery as an unprogressive institution, the author replied that the South had retrograded because the slave trade had been closed, and he observed with scorn:

> No word in the English language is so much used as the dissyllable progress. In America we use it so much, that we have made a verb of it. This is an age of progress—a country of progress—a people of progress. Progress is synonymous with enlightenment, and he who falls into the rear rank, is considered recreant to the cause of civilization.[23]

During the fifties this planter's defence of slavery was repeated by many Southerners who were not so hostile to the idea of progress, and who even incorporated the concept in their expositions on the "peculiar institution." The acknowledged leader of Southern thought and politics until his death in 1850, John C. Calhoun, the Senator from South Carolina, during a speech in the Senate in 1839, had defended slavery as not an evil but "a good—a positive good." [24] Calhoun, however, was not unreceptive to the needs of his section for commercial expansion. Speaking in 1845 to the Southwestern Convention at Memphis, as its chairman, he warned the materialistically-minded delegates that

> the first step towards the accomplishment of the objects for which we are convened—the development of the resources of

23 "The Prospects and Policy of the South as They Appear to the Eyes of a Planter," *S. Q. Rev.*, XXVI (Oct., 1854), 431, and *passim*.

24 J. C. Calhoun, "Speech on the Reception of Abolition Petitions delivered in the Senate Feb. 7, 1839," *Works*, ed. R. K. Crallé (New York, 1853-1856), II, 631.

the South and West—is the preservation of our liberty and our free popular institutions; and the first step, towards that, is the preservation of our Constitution. To them we owe our extraordinary prosperity and progress in developing the great resources of our country, and on them we must depend for their full and perfect development, which would realize the anticipations of all the founders of our Government, and raise our country to a greatness surpassing all that have gone before us.[25]

A student of the Constitution, Calhoun's concept of progress was presented in its greatest detail in his formal treatises on government, prepared during the late 1840's but not published until after his death in 1850. In his personal correspondence during these years and earlier, Calhoun had expressed the desire for some sort of a progressive reform in society. However, he was at the same time greatly alarmed by the abolitionism and Dorrism prevalent in certain parts of the North, and also by the resurgence of the natural rights philosophy of liberty and equality in the revolutionary movements of 1848 in Europe. Although he declared himself sympathetic with progress, he wrote in April 1848 that it ought never to be forgotten that " *the past is the parent of the present . . .*" [26] Hopeful that this conservative philosophy would pervade Calhoun's forthcoming book on government, his friend James H. Hammond, the ardent advocate of secession, in a letter to Calhoun shortly before the latter's death, wrote:

I trust that you have taken the ground that the fundamental object of Government is to *secure* the fruits of labor and skill —that is to say *property,* and that its forms must be moulded upon the social organization. Life and liberty will then be secured, for these are naturally under the guardianship of So-

25 Calhoun, "Address on Taking the Chair of the Southwestern Convention, Memphis, Nov. 13th, 1845," *ibid.*, VI, 279-280.

26 Calhoun, "To Mrs. T. G. Clemson" (April 28, 1848), in *Correspondence* (Annual Report of the Am. Hist., Assoc. 1899, vol. II; Washington, 1900), p. 753; see also pp. 368, 457, 749-750, 758 (1837-1848).

ciety and that civilization which is the fruit of its progress. " Free Government " and all that sort of thing has been I think a fatal delusion and humbug from the time of Moses. Freedom does not spring from Government but from the same soil which produces Government itself; and all we want from that is a guarantee for property fairly acquired.[27]

In his *Disquisition on Government*, published posthumously in 1851, Calhoun in a large measure attempted to justify a society based upon slavery by the development of the idea that the progresss of civilization depended on an inequality in the condition of men. Although progress was the chief end of liberty, the perpetuation and preservation of the race, Calhoun felt, depended on the protection of government. He believed that in any conflict between these two forces of liberty and protection, the former must yield. Calhoun further warned that the progress of a people to greater liberty " is necessarily slow :—and by attempting to precipitate, we either retard, or permanently defeat it," while to " make equality of *condition* essential to liberty, would be to destroy both liberty and progress." Repudiating the dogma that all men are born free and equal, he declared:

> It is indeed, this inequality of condition between the front and rear ranks, in the march of progress, which gives so strong an impulse to the former to maintain their position, and to the latter to press forward into their files. This gives to progress its greatest impulse. To force the front rank back to the rear, or attempt to push forward the rear into line with the front, by the interposition of the government, would put an end to the impulse, and effectually arrest the march of progress.[28]

In his famous doctrine of the concurrent majority, Calhoun offered the Southern slaveholders a solution to the age-old problem of reconciling the power of government with minority interests. Such a plan, he believed, " must necessarily be more

27 J. H. Hammond to Calhoun (March 5, 1850), *ibid.*, p. 1212.

28 Calhoun, "A Disquisition on Government " (1851), *Works*, I, 53-57.

favorable to progress, development, improvement, and civilization . . ." [29]

In the course of Calhoun's career, Southern thought experienced a profound change.[30] Jeffersonian liberalism was subordinated to Calhoun's emphasis upon inequality as a requisite for the continued progress of civilization. Southern sentiment for gradual abolition all but disappeared, and during the 1850's Negro slavery was widely defended by Southern apologists as the only condition possible for a race which, they argued, was incapable of progress through its own unaided efforts.[31] In a speech on Clay's Compromise Resolutions in 1850, Solomon W. Downs, Senator from Louisiana, declared: " This inferiority is the reason why, when all other races of the world have made some progress, however little, he alone has stood perfectly still, and remained in all his original ignorance and barbarism." [32] Conceiving civilization to be in its death throes before the menaces of barbarism, socialism, and communism, a contributor to the *Southern Quarterly Review* for 1851 announced that Negro emancipation would be a blow to the accumulated progress of eighteen centuries. This writer pointed out that the Negro had not been prevented by slavery from attempting to make progress in his native habitat, and he concluded, therefore, that his lowly status was due to the fact that: " The white man, by his nature, has sought and found improvement. The negro, by *his nature,*

29 *Ibid.*, I, 61 ; see also : E. B. B., " Political Philosophy of South Carolina," *S. Q. Rev.*, XXVI (July, 1854), 37-41, 69-70; T. R. Dew, "An Address," *S. Lit. Mess.*, II (March, 1836), 261-282; George Tucker, " Dangers to be Guarded Against in the Progress of the United States," *Am. (Whig) Rev.*, V (June, 1847), 614-629.

30 Clement Eaton, *Freedom of Thought in the Old South* (Durham, 1940), *passim.*

31 W. S. Jenkins, *Pro-Slavery Thought in the Old South* (Chapel Hill, 1935), *passim*; C. H. Wesley, " The Concept of Negro Inferiority in American Thought," *Journal of Negro Hist.*, XXV (Oct., 1940), 540-560.

For some Northern apologists, see: Nathan Lord, *Letter . . . on Slavery* (Boston, 1854) ; *Second Letter . . . Slavery* (Boston, 1855) ; J. H. Hopkins, *The American Citizen* (New York, 1857), pp. 121-122, 131-134, 159.

32 S. W. Downs, *Cong. Globe*, 31 Cong., 1 Sess., Senate (Feb. 19, 1850), Appendix, p. 174.

has crouched contented in the lowest barbarism."[33] Then in 1854, in a work which passed through many editions, Josiah C. Nott, a Southern ethnologist and physician, attempted to give a scientific basis to the claim of Negro inferiority. Arguing that the world would retrograde if the superior races were further adulterated, he declared: " It is the strictly white races that are bearing onward the flambeau of civilization, as displayed in the Germanic families alone."[34]

Other Southerners also maintained the position that the institution of Negro slavery advanced the progress of white civilization. In 1850 John H. Savage, a Representative from Tennessee, in the debate over the Compromise rejoiced that slavery was " doomed to exist forever," and he announced in Congress:

> With the possession of slaves, the progress of this country has been onward and upward, with a power so mighty and a flight so rapid as to leave no doubt upon my mind but that the approving smiles of an overruling Providence have rested upon us. This fact alone, with sensible men, should outweigh all the sophistry of mere theorists. It stands out upon the dark wave of speculation and fanaticism, a mighty rock of common reason, upon which the mind may repose in peace, security, and sunshine.[35]

That same year, 1850, in a sermon preached at the dedication of a church for colored people, James H. Thornwell, soon to be elected President of South Carolina College, urged the slaves to be content with their humble role in advancing the progress of civilization. However, he also advocated that the masters pro-

[33] L. S. M., " Negro and White Slavery," S. Q. Rev., XX (July, 1851), 130.

[34] J. C. Nott and G. R. Gliddon, Types of Mankind (Phil., 1854), p. 405; see also the translation by H. Hotz of Gobineau, The Moral and Intellectual Diversity of Races (Phil., 1856), with an appendix by J. C. Nott. See especially Hotz's Introduction and Gobineau's ch. 13.

[35] J. H. Savage, Cong. Globe, 31 Cong., 1 Sess., House of Rep. (May 13, 1850), Appendix, p. 558.

For a Northern view sympathetic with this position, see: R. F. Stockton, " Letter on the Slavery Question" (1850), in [S. J. Bayard], Sketch of Stockton, pp. 69-79.

mote the improvement of their charges by giving them opportunities for education and religion.[36] In 1852, under the title of
The Pro-Slavery Argument, the earlier arguments for slavery
as an instrument in the progress of civilization made by Thomas
R. Dew, Chancellor Harper, W. Gilmore Simms, and J. H.
Hammond were gathered into one volume. Commenting upon
one of these essays, the editors pointed out that in their opinion
slavery constituted

> one of the most essential agencies, under the divine plan, for
> promoting the general progress of civilization, and for elevat-
> ing, to a condition of humanity, a people otherwise barbarous,
> easily depraved, and needing the help of a superior condition—
> a power from without—to rescue them from a hopelessly sav-
> age state.[37]

The Negro race was considered, therefore, by the defenders
of slavery as incapable of making any great progress through its
own unaided efforts, and the institution of slavery was exalted,
moreover, as a necessary instrument in the continued progress
of white civilization. To support this pro-slavery argument, a
conservative interpretation of the progress of civilization was
maintained by a group of Southern sociologists. Their viewpoint was presented in characteristic form by the Southern lawyer and sociologist, George Fitzhugh. In his *Sociology for the
South or the Failure of Free Society,* published in 1854, Fitzhugh relegated the dogmas of personal liberty and freedom to
a period of barbarism, while he attributed progress to a society
of government and laws. Skeptical of modern progress, except
in the sciences, he urged the South to cultivate manufacturing
and also to preserve its slave society as a barrier against the
social conflict and revolution rising in the free society of the
North.[38] Then in 1857, in a magazine article, Fitzhugh warned

36 J. H. Thornwell, *The Rights and the Duties of Masters* (Charleston,
1850), *passim.*

37 *The Pro-Slavery Argument* (Charleston, 1852), p. 177.

38 George Fitzhugh, *Sociology for the South* (Richmond, 1854), pp. 29-30,
90-95, 115, 158-160, 222; see also his *Cannibals All: or Slaves without
Masters* (Richmond, 1857), pp. 46, 123, and *passim.*

that the attack on Negro slavery by Northern radicals was also an attack upon the slavery principle itself, a principle which he believed was the basis of property, marriage, and the other bulwarks of civilization and progress. Although he felt that the condition of the Negro had been bettered by slavery, and that the South would listen to ways of further improvement, his foremost appeal for reconciliation was based on his class argument in which he maintained:

> You, conservatives, North and South, must usher in, and inaugurate this new world. Adopt the slavery principle, vindicate the institution in the abstract, screw up the chords of society, tighten the reins of government, restrain and punish licentiousness in every form, scout and repudiate the doctrines of let alone, and " Pas trop gouverner," and govern much and rigorously. This is the only new world that we want.[39]

Fitzhugh was one of a small circle of Southern writers who adapted the sociology of Comte's positive philosophy to the devices of their own pro-slavery arguments. In 1854, the same year in which Fitzhugh published his *Sociology for the South,* his fellow Southerner, Henry Hughes of Mississippi, who had met Comte in his travels abroad, published his own *Treatise on Sociology.* In this work, largely an apology for slavery, Hughes maintained that the labor system of the South had progressed to the extent that it merited the description of his own term of warranteeism. In place of the laissez faire, capitalistic society of the day, he depicted a socialistic society of the future based on Negro labor or warranteeism, under which the slaves or " warrantees shall banquet in PLANTATION-REFECTORIES; worship in PLANTATION-CHAPELS; learn in PLANTATION-SCHOOLS; and after slumbers in PLANTATION-DORMITORIES; . . . rise at

---

39 Fitzhugh, " The Conservative Principle," *De Bow's Rev.,* XXII (April, 1857), 429, 419-430; and: " One of the Evils of the Times," *ibid.,* XXII, (June, 1857), 561-570; " The War Upon Society—Socialism," *ibid.,* XXII (June, 1857), 633-644; " Mr. Bancroft's History and the Inner Light," *ibid.,* XXIX (Nov., 1860), 598-613.

See also the article by Harvey Wish, *George Fitzhugh, Conservative of the Old South* (Charlottesville, 1938), *passim.*

the music-crowing of the morning-conchs, to begin again welcome days of jocund toil . . ." [40] Hughes died in 1862 at an early age, and his *Treatise* was almost completely ignored in his own day.

A more important and influential Southern thinker was the pessimist George Frederick Holmes, who came to the United States from England in 1837 as a young man, and who after pursuing a brief legal career turned to his life work as a history professor in various Southern colleges.[41] Holmes, like Fitzhugh and Hughes, was very critical of the nineteenth-century American, individualistic social system, under which, he believed, material progress had become the chief goal of life. In his reviews of some of the reform literature of the 1850's, he took issue with the radical programs for future progress, especially criticizing Horace Greeley and other Northern socialists, and also the theories of Condorcet and of Spencer's *Social Statics*.[42] Although Holmes admitted the popular appeal of the theories of the perfectibility of man, he rejected any concept of progress which went beyond a mere chronicle of the rise and fall of na-

---

40 Henry Hughes, *Treatise on Sociology, Theoretical and Practical* (Phil., 1854), pp. 291-292, and *passim*; see also: L. L. Bernard, " Henry Hughes, First American Sociologist," *Social Forces*, XV (Dec., 1936), 154-174.

41 Harvey Wish, " George Frederick Holmes and the Genesis of American Sociology," *Am. Journal of Sociology*, XLVI (March, 1941), 698-707; and his " George Frederick Holmes and Southern Periodical Literature of the Mid-Nineteenth Century," *Journal of Southern Hist.*, VII (Aug., 1941), 343-356.

42 See the following articles attributed to Holmes: " Greeley on Reforms," *S. Lit. Mess.*, XVII (May, 1851), 259, 262-263; " Spencer's Social Statics," *Q. Rev. Meth. Epis. Church South*, X (April, 1856), 197-198; " Theory of Political Individualism," *De Bow's Rev.*, XXII (Feb., 1857), 146-149.

Herbert Spencer's *Social Statics* was first published in England in 1851. It was an early volume in Spencer's series of works expounding the philosophy of Darwinism and laissez faire. Although Spencer's philosophy enjoyed a great vogue in the United States, it does not seem to have attracted much attention before the Civil War.

For another review of *Social Statics*, besides that of Holmes, see the article, "At Home and Abroad," *North Am. Rev.*, LXXXVI (Jan., 1858), 80-83.

A brief summary of Spencer's concept of progress may be found in his article, " Progress: Its Law and Cause," *Westminster Rev.*, LXVII (April, 1857), 445-485.

tions. In regard to the United States on the eve of the Civil War, he wrote: "The bright morning of American greatness is shrouded with ominous gloom. The extended Union, which has been the pride, the glory, the security and the power of the American people is threatened with violent disruption." [43]

An especially staunch defender of slavery and of the rights of property was James H. Hammond, the South Carolinian states-man. At the time of the nullification controversy, Hammond strongly supported Calhoun's stand for state rights. Of the opinion that, since the French Revolution, the despotism of the few had been succeeded by the tyranny of the majority, he called for the preservation of the Constitution and of slavery as the last safeguards of the minority.[44] He also repudiated the idea that progress was automatic, noting in an oration of 1849 at South Carolinia College that despite "the progress of the last ten centuries—their brilliant epochs, their illustrious characters—it cannot be denied that we must still look to antiquity for the noblest deeds and grandest thoughts that illustrate the race of men." Hammond therefore concluded that "permanence [was] the starting point of genuine progress." [45]

In a speech before the Senate in 1858, Hammond carried his philosophy to its logical conclusions with a notorious and extra-ordinary apology for the institution of Negro slavery, in which he repeated the Southern argument that cotton insured his sec-tion's progress and prosperity. Moreover, he declared that "the greatest strength of the South arises from the harmony of her political and social institutions," and he went on to explain:

43 Holmes, "The Virginia Colony" (An Address ... 1859), *Virginia Historical Reporter* (vol. II, part 1; Richmond, 1860), p. 25.

44 J. H. Hammond: "An Oration delivered at Barnwell College, S. C., on the 4 July 1833," unpublished Ms. in the J. H. Hammond Papers, vol. III (Library of Congress), pp. 4-11, 19-21; *Register of Debates*, 24 Cong., 1 Sess., House of Rep. (Feb. 1, 1836), pp. 2458-2460; "Hammond's Letters on Slavery" (1845), in *The Pro-Slavery Argument*, pp. 109-111, 149-151.

45 Hammond, *An Oration ... South Carolina College ... 1849* (Charles-ton, 1850), pp. 20, 22, and *passim*.

In all social systems there must be a class to do the menial duties, to perform the drudgery of life. Such a class you must have, or you would not have that other class which leads to progress, civilization, and refinement. It constitutes the very mud-sill of society and of political government; and you might as well attempt to build a house in the air, as to build either the one or the other, except on this mud-sill. Fortunately for the South, she has found a race adapted to that purpose to her hand . . .[46]

Then warning the North that its mud-sill class of wage slaves were rising, Hammond proclaimed:

Transient and temporary causes have thus far been your preservation. The great West has been open to your surplus population, and your hordes of semi-barbarian immigrants, who are crowding in year by year. They make a great movement, and you call it progress. Whither? It is progress, but it is progress towards vigilance committees.[47]

Hammond's warnings were repeated in less extreme form by other Southerners who also argued that the Negroes were incapable of progress. Robert Toombs, the fiery secessionist of Georgia, invaded the North in 1856 to deliver a lecture at the Tremont Temple in Boston, in which he defended white superiority and the slavery system. These were the bulwarks of civilization, he insisted, and the Southern states, where the conflict between labor and capital was minimized, illustrated the further progress that was possible only if Negro slavery continued to be preserved and defended from Federal interference.[48] Toombs' fellow Georgian, Alexander H. Stephens, in the following year told the voters of his congressional district that the Southerners were not the sole ones interested in the continuance of slavery. Noting that the cotton manufacturers of New England also had

46 Hammond, *Cong. Globe*, 35 Cong., 1 Sess., Senate (March 4, 1858), Appendix, p. 68.

47 *Ibid.*, p. 71.

48 Robert Toombs, *A Lecture delivered in the Tremont Temple, Boston ...January, 1856* ([Washington, 1856]), *passim*.

a stake in slavery, Stephens declared: " We emphatically hold the lever that wields the destiny of modern civilization in its widest scope and comprehension; and all we have to do is to realize the consciousness of our power and be resolved to maintain it." [49] *Cotton Is King,* E. N. Elliott, President of Planters College, Mississippi, entitled his anthology of pro-slavery arguments, and he included his own essay, in which he urged that the Negro continue to be enslaved because

> their own happiness and well-being, their duties to the human race, the claims of civilization, the progress of society, the law of nations, and the ordinance of God, require that they should be placed in a subordinate position to a superior race.[50]

In the pro-slavery argument the idea of progress, therefore, played an important role. Even though the Southerners realized that, by the year 1860, most of the civilized world was opposed to slavery, still, in the words of William H. Holcombe, a prominent Southern homeopathic physician, and also a novelist and poet :

> The Southern view of the matter, destined to revolutionize opinion throughout the civilized world, is briefly this: African slavery is no retrograde movement, no discord in the harmony of nature, no violation of elemental justice, no infraction of immutable laws, human or divine—but an integral link in the grand progressive evolution of human society as an indissoluble whole.[51]

49 "Alexander H. Stephens to the Voters of the Eighth Congressional District of Georgia " (From the ' Constitutionalist,' Augusta, Ga., Aug. 18, 1857), in *Correspondence of Toombs, Stephens, and Cobb,* ed. U. B. Phillips (Annual Report of the Am. Hist. Assoc., 1911, vol. II; Washington, 1913), p. 415.

50 E. N. Elliott, " Slavery in the Light of International Law " (1860), in *Cotton is King* (Augusta, Ga., 1860), p. 736. See also: H. A. Washington, " The Races of Men," *S. Lit. Mess.,* XXX (April, 1860), 259; " The Negro Races," *ibid.,* XXXI (July, 1860), 3-4.

51 W. H. Holcombe, *The Alternative: A Separate Nationality, or the Africanization of the South* (New Orleans, 1860), p. 7.

A very different interpretation of progress was advanced by those Negroes who, having secured their freedom, were able to express their sentiments on slavery. Charles Ball, for forty years a slave and also a veteran of the War of 1812, in a volume on his experiences, published in 1837, observed that the majority of the slaves in America had no hope of a peaceful progress toward freedom. Instead they looked forward only to the possibility of a future life after death or to the chance of revenge offered by violence or revolution.[52] Some later Negro writers were more hopeful. William C. Nell, in his work *The Colored Patriots of the American Revolution* (1855), pointed out that the principles of '76 would not be consummated until they achieved the universal brotherhood of both the white and the black races. However, despite the continuance of slavery, he still felt able to rejoice: " So sure as night precedes day, war ends in peace, and winter wakes spring, just so sure will the persevering efforts of Freedom's army be crowned with victory's perennial laurels!" [53]

Most famous of all the escaped slaves was Frederick Douglass, who presented the case for freedom on the lecture platform and in the pages of his own newspaper and autobiography. When the Southerners charged that the Negro as a race was incapable of progress, Douglass accused them of rationalizing their own selfish interests. In a lecture delivered in 1854 he declared: " The evils most fostered by slavery and oppression, are precisely those which slaveholders and oppressors would transfer from their system to the inherent character of their victims." [54] In his widely-circulated autobiography Douglass related how, as a youth, he had been troubled by being a creature of the past and present only, and how he had " longed to have a *future,* a future with hope in it." He then went on to observe:

52 Charles Ball, *Slavery in the United States* (New York, 1837), pp. 218-221.

53 W. C. Nell, *The Colored Patriots of the American Revolution* (Boston, 1855), pp. 378-381.

54 Frederick Douglass, *The Claims of the Negro, Ethnologically Considered* (Rochester, 1854), pp. 15, and 6-7.

> To be shut up entirely to the past and present, is abhorrent to the human mind; it is to the soul—whose life and happiness is unceasing progress—what the prison is to the body; a blight and mildew, a hell of horrors.[55]

In concluding his volume Douglass wrote that he felt able to tell his colored brethren that, despite their low origin in Africa and years of slavery in America, "progress is yet possible . . ."[56]

The Southern adaptation of the idea of progress as a rationalization of slavery was, of course, not generally accepted in the North. There the consciousness of slavery exerted a depressing effect on the optimism of reformers and abolitionists like William Lloyd Garrison, who announced on the Fourth of July, 1829:

> I tremble for the republic while slavery exists therein. If I look up to God for success, no smile of mercy or forgiveness dispels the gloom of futurity; if to our resources, they are daily diminishing; if to all history, our destruction is not only possible, but almost certain.[57]

Garrison and many other Northerners were, however, also confident that the progressive tendencies of the age were opposed to the continuance of slavery. William Jay, a staunch opponent of slavery and war, in a letter to James Fenimore Cooper in 1832, deplored the lack of resentment shown against South Carolina's nullification, but he observed: "The progress of Science and the arts is daily augmenting the superiority of free over slave labour: advancing the prosperity of the North, and subjecting the South to embarrassment and discontent." [58] In

55 Douglass, *My Bondage and My Freedom* (New York, 1855), p. 273.

56 *Ibid.*, p. 405.

57 W. L. Garrison, "The Dangers of the Nation" (An Address . . . July 4, 1829), *Selections from the Writings and Speeches of . . . Garrison* (Boston, 1852), p. 46.

58 William Jay to Cooper (Dec. 11, 1832), in *Correspondence of James Fenimore Cooper*, I, 302; see also: J. Q. Adams: *An Oration to . . . the Town of Quincy . . .* (Boston, 1831), pp. 36, 38; Letter to Edmund Quincy, July 28, 1838, in John Quincy Adams Papers (Library of Congress).

a speech in 1844, on the tenth anniversary of the emancipation of the Negroes in the British West Indies, Ralph Waldo Emerson announced that he saw the American indifference to slavery passing:

> There have been moments, I said, when men might be forgiven who doubted. Those moments are past. Seen in masses, it cannot be disputed, there is progress in human society. There is a blessed necessity by which the interest of men is always driving them to the right; and, again, making all crime mean and ugly. The genius of the Saxon race, friendly to liberty; the enterprise, the very muscular vigor of this nation, are inconsistent with slavery.[59]

In reply to the Southern declarations affirming unity in the defence of slavery, a writer in the abolitionist *Massachusetts Quarterly Review* for 1849 declared that men would unite only in a just cause and that " all human nature, not the North alone, is united against oppression; the very stones cry out against it; the genius of the republic is its foe; the law of progress disowns it." [60]

In the course of the Southern defence of Negro slavery, its proponents pointed to the wage slavery existing among the factory workers of the North. On the other hand, anti-slavery writers contrasted the general unprogressiveness of the South with the material prosperity enjoyed in the North. Such a position was taken by Richard Hildreth, the historian, in his volume *Despotism in America* (1840), an exposition and denunciation of the backwardness of the Southern slave-holding society. Of the opinion that " Density of population, and the existence of towns and cities, are essential to any great degree of social progress," Hildreth asserted that the evidences of progress in the South were derived from its connection with the North.[61] An

59 R. W. Emerson, "Address delivered in Concord ... 1844," *Complete Works*, XI, 147.

60 " Recent Defences of Slavery," *Mass. Q. Rev.*, II (Sept., 1849), 512.

61 [Richard Hildreth], *Despotism in America* (Boston and New York, 1840), ch. 3, p. 39.

especially vocal opponent of slavery, the Kentuckian Cassius M. Clay, editor of the famous paper *The True American,* in his editorials and other writings during the late 1840's depicted the failure of the South to make any progress. Clay, however, continued to believe in the progress of humanity, and on the whole, felt confident that the United States in their entirety would, like the North, rise to a great future if only slavery were abolished.[62] Defending its opposition to Negro slavery against the Southern charge that wage slavery existed in the North, Horace Greeley's *Tribune* in 1851 asserted that with all its miseries wage slavery was to be preferred because:

> Society based on Free, or more exactly speaking on Hireling Labor, is progressive; Society based on Slavery is stagnant, inclining always to decay. The former advances ever more and more rapidly and surely toward a better condition; the latter stands still or tends toward decline, bankruptcy, dissolution. The former improves in spite of the evils attending its imperfections; the latter cannot improve until it has utterly changed its character and ceased to be itself.[63]

Free labor was also defended by Abraham Lincoln in an address before the Wisconsin State Agricultural Society in 1859. Raising his voice against the Southern advocates of the theory that there must be a mud-sill class in society, he defined the free labor system of the North as " the just, and generous, and prosperous system, which opens the way for all, gives hope to all, and energy, and progress, and improvement of condition to all." [64]

62 C. M. Clay: "Address to the People of Kentucky " (1845), *Writings* (New York, 1848), pp. 173-183; excerpts from the *True American* and other journals (1845-1848), *ibid.,* pp. 221-224, 368-369, 373-377, 458-464, 477-479, 488-489; " Hints on Religious and Civil Liberty " (1848), *ibid.,* pp. 17-37.

63 " Slavery and Freedom," *New York Weekly Tribune,* IX (June 29, 1850), 3; for other *Tribune* comments on slavery in its effects on progress, see: " The Danger of the Future," *ibid.,* X (May 10, 1851), 5; " Fillibuster Enterprises," *ibid.,* XIV (May 5, 1855), 4; " The New Year," *ibid.,* XVI (Jan. 3, 1857), 4.

64 Abraham Lincoln, "Annual Address before the Wisconsin State Agricultural Society, at Milwaukee, Wisconsin, September 30, 1859," *Complete Works,* ed. Nicolay and Hay (new ed.; New York, 1905), V, 250.

Further support for the Northern argument that the South was unprogressive and backward because of the blighting effects of slavery, was received from the writings of two intimate observers of the Southern scene, Frederick Law Olmstead and Hinton Rowan Helper. Olmstead, a farmer and landscape architect, born in New England, began in 1850 a series of famous travels which carried him through the South. Stimulated by a discussion with William Lloyd Garrison, he decided to record his impartial impressions of slavery and of the economic conditions in the South. As a result, Olmstead gave it as his considered opinion that slavery was the cause of the Southern inferior and unprogressive condition as compared with the North.[65] He believed that democracy could not exist along with slavery, and he suggested that the progress of the slaves and their masters might be entirely incompatible.[66] In regard to South Carolina, perhaps the leading state in the South, Olmstead concluded: "The amount of it, then, is this: Improvement and progress in South Carolina is forbidden by its present system." [67] Much the same conclusions were reached by Hinton R. Helper, a native born Southerner of the poorer class in North Carolina, who caused a tremendous stir with the publication in 1857 of his book *The Impending Crisis of the South*. Using statistics to show the decline of the South, Helper became famous for his apostasy in placing the blame upon slavery. He denounced it as an expensive and unprofitable institution, and he declared that "slavery, and nothing but slavery, has retarded the progress and prosperity of our portion of the Union . . ." [68] Although Helper was not interested in the welfare of the Negro, he earned fame in the North and obloquy in the South because of his opinion that

65 F. L. Olmsted, *A Journey in the Seaboard Slave States* (New York and London, 1856), pp. 140, 183-185, 489-490, 515-516.

66 *Ibid.*, pp. 214, 298, 367-368.

67 *Ibid.*, pp. 522-523, 497-500; see also the Englishman, Charles Mackay's comments in his *Life and Liberty in America* (New York, 1859), pp. 234, 238.

68 H. R. Helper, *The Impending Crisis of the South: How to Meet It* (New York, 1860), pp. 32, 359, and ch. 1, *passim*.

slavery is a shame, a crime, and a curse—a great moral, social, civil, and political evil—an oppressive burden to the blacks, and an incalculable injury to the whites—a stumbling block to the nation, an impediment to progress, a damper on all the nobler instincts, principles, aspirations and enterprises of man, and a dire enemy to every true interest.[69]

In the decade leading up to the Civil War, the anti-slavery forces made that same extensive use of the idea of progress which was also noted in connection with the pro-slavery arguments during the 1850's. When, in the debate on the Compromise measures of 1850, the North was reminded that its states had once sanctioned slavery and that its merchants had profited in the slave trade, Horace Mann, the famous educator, recently elected to Congress, asked the Southerners if they could " read no lesson, as to the Progress of the Age, from the fact that all those States have since abjured slavery of their own free will . . . ?" [70] Mann predicted a revolution if the South continued to prevent the progress of freedom, but Senator William H. Seward of New York in his speech denied this possibility, and he therefore deprecated the Southern demands for security. To the Southern call for the return of fugitive slaves, Seward replied, " That guaranty you cannot have . . . because you cannot roll back the tide of social progress." [71] Two years later in 1852 Charles Sumner, the Senator from Massachusetts, in speaking for his motion to repeal the Fugitive Slave bill, took issue with the Southern contention that slavery had been finally settled. " Truth alone is final," Sumner declared, and he argued:

To make a law final, so as not to be reached by Congress, is, by mere legislation, to fasten a new provision on the Consti-

69 *Ibid.*, p. 184; for a different view, see T. P. Kettell, *Southern Wealth and Northern Profits* (New York, 1860), *passim.*

70 Horace Mann, *Cong. Globe*, 31 Cong., 1 Sess., House of Rep. (Feb. 15, 1850), Appendix, p. 224.

71 W. H. Seward, *ibid.*, 31 Cong., 1 Sess., Senate (March 11, 1850), Appendix, p. 268; see also the reply to Seward by Lewis Cass, *ibid.*, 31 Cong., 1 Sess., Senate (March 13, 1850), p. 518.

tution. Nay more; it gives to the law a character which the very Constitution does not possess. The wise fathers did not treat the country as a Chinese foot, never to grow after infancy; but, anticipating Progress, they declared expressly that their great Act is not final.[72]

The Fugitive Slave Law particularly aroused Northern opposition. Emerson, in his lectures on the subject, attacked the false notions of patriotism which had acted as a cloak for the bill, but he urged:

> Nothing is impracticable to this nation, which it shall set itself to do.[73]
> Slavery is disheartening; but Nature is not so helpless but it can rid itself at last of every wrong. But the spasms of Nature are centuries and ages, and will tax the faith of short-lived men.[74]

With equal indignation Theodore Parker condemned the enforcement of the Fugitive Slave Law and the idea that the government existed chiefly for the protection of property. While he believed that the spirit of the age was against slavery and that an unjust law could not stop the progress of freedom, he also regretted that the United States neglected their limitless possibilities: " What opportunities—and what a waste of them! Has any nation more deserved rebuke? A Democracy, and every eighth man a slave! Jesus the God of the Church, and not a sect that dares call Slavery a sin!" [75]

In 1854, when the Kansas Nebraska bill was being considered in Congress, Gerritt Smith, a Representative from New York and a well known abolitionist, warned that freedom and prog-

72 Charles Sumner, *ibid.*, 32 Cong., 1 Sess., Senate (August 26, 1852), Appendix, p. 1103.

73 Emerson, " The Fugitive Slave Law" (1851), *Complete Works*, XI, 209.

74 Emerson. " The Fugitive Slave Law" (1854), *ibid.*, XI, 238.

75 Theodore Parker, "A Discourse of the Relations...," in *Proceedings of the Progressive Friends* (1855), p. 95; see also his *The State of the Nation...1850* (Boston, 1851), *passim.*

ress could not exist along with slavery in America.[76] And a writer in a Baptist religious periodical declared: " This barbarism must be abolished by the progress of civilization, or slavery must abolish it." [77] When the passage of the Kansas Nebraska bill resulted in the struggle between the settlers of the North and the South to occupy the territory, Edward Everett Hale, an enthusiastic supporter of the New England Emigrant Aid Company, wrote a long article in the *North American Review* in which he contrasted the conditions of a Kansas under slavery with that of a free Kansas, which " will kindle with its beams the elements of social progress and regeneration in all the surrounding regions, and throughout the world." [78]

Many of these opponents of slavery took comfort from their belief that it was inexorably doomed by the progress of virtue and intelligence. In the words of Joseph Haven, a Congregational clergyman and a professor of philosophy at Amherst, writing in 1859, " Much is to be hoped from the progress of society, and the gradual prevalence of more enlightened views, and of a loftier and purer morality." [79] A more material reason for believing slavery doomed was that set forth by Thomas Ewbank, formerly Commissioner of Patents, who in 1860 published his paper *Inorganic Forces Ordained to Supersede Human Slavery*. Ewbank believed that many " existing evils are incidental to progress, and doomed to disappear as society advances." [80] Although he felt that the white race was the only one aware of the idea of progress, he did not conclude that the black

76 Gerritt Smith, *Cong. Globe*, 33 Cong., 1 Sess., House of Rep. (April 6, 1854), Appendix, pp. 519-530; see also G. W. Curtis' address at Wesleyan University, *The Duty of the American Scholar* ... (New York, 1856), pp. 21-22.

77 " Civilization: Helps and Hindrances," *Freewill Baptist Q.*, II (April, 1854), 207.

78 E. E. Hale, " Kansas and Nebraska," *North Am. Rev.*, LXXX (Jan., 1855), 96.

79 Joseph Haven, *Moral Philosophy* (Boston, 1859), p. 146.

80 Thomas Ewbank, *Inorganic Forces Ordained to Supersede Human Slavery* (New York, 1860), p. 3.

race was doomed to slavery, but he wrote that the Negro " is not to be treated as if the characteristic element of progress was not in him. In this respect, and others, he differs from us only in degree." [81] Of the opinion that slavery would prevail only so long as it was profitable, he predicted that scientific progress would render it obsolete. " For progress," he wrote, " untrammeled and unbounded power is required, and we may have it in the inorganic forces." [82]

The anti-slavery, like the pro-slavery forces, made generous use of the idea of progress in their arguments. While the Southern concept of progress took the form of a conservative defence, the Northern view in large part shared the optimism of the reform movements of the period. Although some, in their extreme pessimism over the institution of slavery, were willing to see the Union dissolved, there was also the widespread hope in the North that, in the words of an English traveller of an earlier period, the abolition of slavery " will not only remove a more tremendous curse than can ever again desolate society, but restore the universality of that generous attachment to their common institutions which has been, and will again be, to the American people, honour, safety, and the means of perpetual progress." [83]

81 *Ibid.*, pp. 15, and 10-15; see also: G. M. Weston, *The Progress of Slavery in the United States* (Washington, 1857), pp. 231-232, and *passim*.

82 Ewbank, *op. cit.*, pp. 31, and 17-30.

83 Harriet Martineau, *Society in America* (New York, 1837), I, 81.

CHAPTER IX

THE SYSTEMATIC EXPLORATION
OF THE IDEA

THE preceding chapters show how the concept of progress pervaded American thought in the decades before the Civil War. Interpreted in the light of the ideas and interests of its sponsors, the dogma of progress was the intellectual force and rational in much of the American life of the period. Widely invoked to give authority to all kinds of arguments, and introduced as a justification for all sorts of schemes and panaceas, it was an idea functional to the American economy and way of life in that era between the War of 1812 and the Civil War. Although no contemporary American philosopher of those decades formulated the idea into an extended treatise in the manner of certain European thinkers, the general literature of the period—the books, periodical articles, private correspondence, academic addresses, Congressional speeches, and patriotic orations—is, as we have seen, full of the supporting data which testify to the role of the concept in an important period of our early history. Much of this material has already been analyzed in the fore-going chapters. However, it is important to devote some attention to those American treatises in which a modest attempt was made to give a formal historical and philosophical interpretation of the idea of progress.

During the decade of the 1830's several works were published in which the authors developed the thesis that progress was the natural state of man, in accord with the principles of the universe and of God. This argument in a way joined the natural rights philosophy of the American Revolution to the perfectibility of man theories of the French Revolution. It also denied both Rousseau's concept of a deterioration from an ideal state of nature and the Malthusian pessimism over the ability of civilization to maintain itself.

An important presentation of this general position was contained in Nathaniel Chipman's *Principles of Government*, published in 1833 as an elaboration of a volume which had first appeared forty years earlier.[1] Chipman, a soldier in the Revolution, a former United States Senator, a Hamiltonian Federalist and prominent Vermont jurist, took issue with Rousseau's thesis that civilization represented a degeneration from an ideal state of nature. He felt that a wider study of human nature would show that civilization represented progress and not degeneration.[2] And in his books, he again and again pointed out that progress was not opposed to the law of nature:

> Perhaps as good a definition as any which has been given of man is, that he is a being capable of improvement, in a progression, of which he knows not the limits. Deity has implanted in his nature the seeds of improvement, furnished him with power and faculties for the cultivation, and to these superadded a sense that the cultivation is a duty.[3]

Chipman strongly defended the authority of government and the rights of property as natural to man.[4] He was of the opinion that the great possibilities inherent in scientific improvement made the corruption and abuse of the power of governments less likely or necessary.[5] He also dissented from Montesquieu's idea that all governments eventually decayed, feeling that the improved experimental techniques in learning made it possible for a perpetual, progressive science of government to be

[1] A comparison of the two editions shows little change in Chipman's statements on progress. The chief addition to the second edition seems to be Chipman's adoption of Bentham's principle of utility as an added authority for his own views on law and property.

See also: B. F. Wright, Jr., *American Interpretations of Natural Law* (Cambridge, Mass., 1931), pp. 249-251.

And for Chipman's belief in education as a means of progress, see: A. O. Hansen, *Liberalism and American Education* (New York, 1926), pp. 89-104.

[2] Nathaniel Chipman, *Principles of Government: A Treatise on Free Institutions* (Burlington, 1833), pp. 1-15.

[3] *Ibid.*, p. 16; see also the earlier edition: *Sketches of the Principles of Government* (Rutland, 1793), p. 33.

[4] Chipman, *Principles of Government*, pp. 51-54, 67, 74.

[5] *Ibid.*, p. 177a.

created. Although all past governments had indeed fallen, he believed that " Under free institutions of government, the state of society will always be progressive. . . ." Because he felt that the Constitution of the United States was based on the principles of the happiness and the sovereignty of the people, and because it provided for its own amendment, he was confident that the American government would survive by progressive improvement and last forever! [6]

During that same year, 1833, Alexander H. Everett, brother of Edward, and at the time an owner and the editor of the *North American Review,* delivered *A Discourse on the Progress and Limits of Social Improvement.* Everett, who had earlier criticized the pessimistic conclusions of Malthus,[7] believed that the interest in the idea of progress was a post-French Revolutionary development, identified with the perfectibility of man theories of Condorcet, Godwin, Robert Owen, and Frances Wright. He noted that this doctrine had been advanced in Germany by Herder and elsewhere by Victor Cousin; while its optimism had evoked the pessimism exemplified by Malthus.[8] Everett took a position between these extremes, holding progress indefinite but not infinite, and maintaining " that there is in our nature a capacity for improvement within certain limits and under certain conditions." [9] He felt that since the nature of men did not change, their advance depended " partly on the will of Providence, which places them in a more or less favorable condition for progress and improvement, but still more, perhaps, on the fidelity with which they respectively take advantage of the talents committed to their trust." [10] Although he found no law

6 *Ibid.,* pp. 298-302; see also B. F. Wright, *op. cit.,* p. 248.

7 A. H. Everett, *New Ideas on Population,* cited in ch. 3, pp. 85-86.

8 Everett, *A Discourse on the Progress and Limits of Social Improvement* (Boston, 1834), pp. 7-11. This discourse was delivered at Amherst College in 1833, and it was also published in the *North Am. Rev.,* XXXVIII (April, 1834), 502-538.

9 Everett, *A Discourse,* p. 13.

10 *Ibid.,* p. 16.

of progress " by which each successive nation or race takes up the work of improvement at the point where it was left by preceding ones," [11] he was, like Chipman, sanguine of the future for America. In the advance and application of the sciences, in its free and practical social and political institutions, and in the favorable location of its vast territories, he saw a guarantee that the United States was destined to equal in a short time the progress of any nation.[12]

Alexander H. Everett was not alone in his interest in the causes of the progress of nations. Alexander Kinmont, a Scotsman attracted by the freedom in America, who eventually settled as a school teacher in Cincinnati, delivered there in 1837 and 1838 a course of lectures on the *Natural History of Man.* Kinmont, like Everett, believed that the laws of nature and of God were fixed but not designed to impede man's free will in the development of his natural faculties or in the use of the material wealth of the universe. Each nation and race, he felt, had a particular period of time and an area in which to flourish. Despite this rise and fall, he believed that there had been a general continuity and progress in civilization. Repudiating all notions of decline and degeneration, from a study of the state of the world in the time of Plato's *Republic,* he announced his conviction that " there has been a progress within the last three thousand years in the science of government, and in the more practical and useful developments of human nature." [13]

Another Ohio school teacher, and also a lawyer, Samuel Eells in 1839 delivered, before an audience at Yale, an *Oration on the Law and Means of Social Advancement.* In his address Eells declared that the " universal and concurring sentiment of all ages that the course of humanity is on an ascending scale . . . is strong and cheering evidence that such will be the result. It proves that the doctrine of social progress has its founda-

11 *Ibid.,* p. 22.

12 *Ibid.,* pp. 39-44.

13 Alexander Kinmont, *Twelve Lectures on the Natural History of Man* . . . (Cincinnati, 1839), pp. 297, and 31-32, 143-144, 155, 170-171, 340-341.

tion in nature." [14] From his knowledge of history he felt certain that the progress of freedom and of Christianity was destined to continue, and he urged

> that all real and permanent improvement must begin from within and work outwardly; that the fountain of all social progress lies in the moral nature of man; and that every civilization which has not its foundation and support here, must decay and come to an end.[15]

Eells, like Kinmont and Everett, stressed the idea that progress was the design of both God and nature, and his oration was widely-noted and favorably commented upon in the periodical press by reviewers who sympathized with his emphasis upon the moral and religious nature of true progress.[16]

Toward the close of the succeeding decade, when the forties reached a climax in the upheavals of 1848, it seemed for a time that progress and democracy might become synonymous terms. From this social ferment came one of the best single treatments of the idea of progress by an American author in the pre-Civil War era. This period also witnessed extended analyses of the concept of progress by writers who propounded visionary reform schemes of their own.

Although completed a few months before the outbreak of the revolutions, Frederick Grimké's *Considerations Upon the Nature and Tendency of Free Institutions* was a product of the age. Grimké, the brother of the South Carolinian educator and reformer Thomas S. Grimké, moved to Ohio as a young man, and after a period in which he was active as a lawyer and a judge, he retired in 1842 to devote himself to study and writing. His *Free Institutions* was an elaborate and sympathetic study

14 Samuel Eells, *Oration on the Law and Means of Social Advancement* (Cincinnati, 1839), p. 7.

15 *Ibid.*, p. 26.

16 See for example: *Godey's Lady's Book*, XX (April, 1840), 191; *West Mess.*, VIII (Sept., 1840), 212-219; *S. Lit. Mess.*, VIII (March, 1842), 209-211.

of the principle of American democracy in its relations to the larger theme of the progress of civilization. Grimké believed that the struggle for equality and the preservation of freedom were both conducive to a good society,[17] but he predicted that the increasing wealth of the United States would sharpen class differences and create an aristocracy of capitalists and of members of the learned professions. Such an aristocracy would represent a threat to the powers of the large middle class in the United States, a class which, he believed, had been responsible for the widespread influence of American free institutions.[18] On the other hand, his confidence in the future was bolstered by his conviction that

> The enlightened of all countries begin to sympathize with one another, in the efforts which each is making to ameliorate the condition of the community to which he belongs. People of different nations are learning to look upon each other as members of one great commonwealth, each of whom is interested in the advancement and prosperity of the others.[19]

In 1856 Grimké published a revised edition of his work, introduced by a new chapter devoted to the idea that " The existence of free institutions presupposes a highly civilized society." [20] Then in an additional concluding chapter, entitled " The Ultimate Destiny of Free Institutions," he adopted an optimistic view of this question, noting that " a visible and marked improvement has taken place in both the social and political organization, within a hundred years." [21] Although perfection was unattainable, he felt certain that the improvement of the existing civilized nations would continue. " The principle of progression is the rule, that of retrogradation the exception," he declared,

17 Frederick Grimké, *Considerations Upon the Nature and Tendency of Free Institutions* (Cincinnati and New York, 1848), pp. 56-57.

18 *Ibid.,* pp. 305-318.

19 *Ibid.,* p. 533.

20 Grimké, . . . *Free Institutions* (2nd ed. corrected and enlarged; New York and Cincinnati, 1856), p. 1.

21 *Ibid.,* p. 649.

concluding that " Free institutions best fall in with the natural desire of improvement. They afford scope and opportunity to a greater number to lift themselves in the scale of physical and intellectual improvement." [22]

Before the Phi Beta Kappa Society of Union College in the summer of 1848, Charles Sumner delivered an oration on *The Law of Human Progress,* giving in all probability the most adequate and significant treatment of the subject of any of his contemporaries in the United States.[23] Sumner regarded the concept of progress as an explanation of history and as the controlling factor in the reform movements of the nineteenth century. Seeking the roots of the idea, he concluded that the law had first been recognized by the Italian professor Vico in the early eighteenth century. In Germany, he acknowledged the contributions of Leibnitz and of Herder, but he felt that the clearest development of the idea had been made in France. Following the influence of Descartes, Pascal, and Fontenelle, Turgot and Condorcet, in the eighteenth century, Sumner noted, had arrived at an explicit formulation of the dogma of progress.[24] However, unlike some of these French philosophers, Sumner did not expect perfection to be attained. " Let me state the law as I understand it," he wrote:

> Man, as an individual, is capable of indefinite improvement. Societies and nations which are but aggregations of men, and, finally, the Human Race, or collective Humanity, are capable of indefinite improvement. And this is the Destiny of man, of societies, of nations, and of the Human Race.[25]

22 *Ibid.,* pp. 661, 663.

23 For an indication of the genesis and reception of the *Oration,* see: Charles Sumner, *Memoir and Letters,* III, 30-32; Weiss, *Life and Correspondence of Theodore Parker,* I, 316; O. B. Frothingham, *George Ripley,* pp. 214-215.

Sumner's *Oration* was also well received by audiences in the West according to an enthusiastic editorial in the Cleveland *Daily True Democrat* (July 21, 1849), quoted in the *Annals of Cleveland* (Cleveland, 1936-1938), XXXII (1849), p. 140, no. 948.

24 Sumner, *The Law of Human Progress* (Boston, 1849), pp. 4, 13-25.

25 *Ibid.,* p. 28.

Like so many of his contemporaries, Sumner assumed the fundamental unity of the human race, and he announced his belief that Christianity, science, and education were all ministers to its progress. Denouncing the conservatism that abhorred all change, but cautioning that progress was gradual, he maintained that the law of progress was both a great comfort and an inspiration. Let " a confidence in the Progress of our race be, under God, our constant faith," he declared, and he went on to tell his youthful audience to

> Cultivate, then, a just moderation. Learn to reconcile order with change, stability with Progress. This is a wise conservatism; this is a wise reform. Rightly understanding these terms, who would not be a conservative? Who would not be a reformer? A conservative of all that is good—a reformer of all that is evil . . .[26]

The title of Sumner's oration was also used by James C. Halsall, an obscure writer, who proposed to discover the key to human progress through a psychological study of human nature and intelligence. He believed that the advantage of the moderns over the ancients was not in a superior absolute intelligence, but in an intelligence more subtle and refined through its descent from generation to generation, according to the theory maintained by Lamarck.[27] Halsall's study also showed a familiarity with the works of other important European thinkers. He hoped that, by extending the theories of Locke's philosophy, scientific discoveries might be made in the field of "psycology," the equal of those made in pure science by Newton, and he proclaimed geology and phrenology the heralds of a new era in the progress of civilization.[28] Then in a *Sequel,* published in 1854, Halsall announced that, in his desire to find a scheme of the mind analogous to the order of the material universe, he had

26 *Ibid.*, p. 47, and *passim.*

27 J. C. Halsall, *The Law of Human Progress* (Charlottesville, 1849), pp. 3, 7, 12-19.

28 *Ibid.*, pp. 48-55, 38.

become satisfied that "Association is in the intellectual world, what attraction is in the physical. . . ." [29]

Another writer whose concept of progress was identified with an unusual Utopian program was J. Stanley Grimes, a lawyer, professor of medical jurisprudence, and an erratic philosopher. Grimes' main interest, however, was in pseudo-science, and in 1851 he published a volume in which he attempted to show that phrenology and geology, combined into a new science called phreno-geology, offered the clue to the limits which he felt nature imposed upon progress. Critical of the phrenological systems of Spurzheim and Combe, Grimes in his own unorthodox theory attempted to link the organization and the functions of the brain with the successive geological epochs. Grimes regarded progress as an evolutionary process and, like Halsall's, his work showed the influence of the Lamarckian theory of development. Although he denied that progress was unlimited, he did believe that man's mental powers and the material resources of the universe would be capable of further development until the goal of the universal brotherhood of man was attained:

> The past is prophetic of the future. The task of consciousness is yet to be accomplished. War, slavery, pauperism, superstition, must yet be conquered. The confederation of mankind, to insure peace, justice, and humanity, is yet to be established. These phreno powers clustered around human consciousness will not pause in their toil until the destiny of man is accomplished.[30]

Much better known than Grimes or Halsall, were those two famous historians of the period, George Bancroft and Richard Hildreth, who each gave a different interpretation to the idea of progress. Hildreth was the author of treatises on the *Theory of Morals* and on the *Theory of Politics,* in which the conservative approach of his *History* was discarded for the philosophy of

29 Halsall, *Sequel to the Law of Human Progress* (Richmond, 1854), p. 53, and *passim.*

30 J. S. Grimes, *Phreno-Geology* . . . (Boston, Cambridge, and London, 1851), p. 130, Preface, and Section XIV.

Jeremy Bentham.[31] In 1844, in the first of these works, Hildreth followed Bentham in asserting that the theory of morals involved the principle of utility. With regard to religion he observed:

> It seems to be at once a characteristic and a cause of stationary civilization, when forms and ceremonies usurp the place of, and rise superior to, the very sentiments of which in their origin they were the expressions and the signs.[32]

He accordingly argued "that the science of morals, like all other sciences, is progressive in its nature, advancing continually as experience extends."[33] Although the progress of civilization relieved society of certain pains it also increased others, thereby arousing protests like that of Rousseau. Therefore, Hildreth concluded: "As yet we have seen only the beginning of the end. Notwithstanding all the beneficial changes that have taken place, a vast deal remains to be done."[34]

In 1853 Hildreth published his *Politics* as a companion volume to his *Theory of Morals*. In this later work he attributed the progress of European civilization to the growth of its cities, fostering the essential elements of political equality and of productive industry.[35] He defined the progress of civilization to include: the spread of knowledge, the accumulation of wealth, the increase of benevolence, and the refinement of sensibility or taste. Through the interaction of these conditions of progress, he felt that human desires might be elevated and satisfied.[36] Hildreth also attempted to discover what type of government best fulfilled his four conditions of progress. If a civic aristocracy promoted knowledge and wealth, it was indifferent to the masses of the people, and so he decided that democratic govern-

31 On this subject see: A. M. Schlesinger, Jr., "The Problem of Richard Hildreth," *New Eng. Q.*, XIII (June, 1940), 223-245.

32 Hildreth, *Theory of Morals* ... (Boston, 1844), pp. 241-242.

33 *Ibid.*, p. 252.

34 *Ibid.*, pp. 270-272.

35 Hildreth, *Theory of Politics* ... (New York, 1853), pp. 120-125.

36 *Ibid.*, pp. 230-231.

ments, by permitting a spirit of freedom, best guaranteed progress.[37] In his final chapter, " Hopes and Hints as to the Future," Hildreth predicted a coming age of the people, of the working class. He called for an increase in the productiveness of human labor by the use of the powers of science, and he declared that the socialist agitation for the distribution of wealth would some day have to be considered.[38]

Less interested than Hildreth in the economic and legal aspects of history, George Bancroft in his writings combined the background of his study in Germany with a lively partisanship for the Democratic party in the United States and for the ideal of democracy at large. Bancroft gave a clear expression to his identification of the democratic faith and the idea of progress in his oration, " The Office of the People in Art, Government, and Religion," which he delivered at Williams College in 1835, and which he subsequently revised for publication in the *Boston Quarterly Review.* Convinced that every individual possessed the capacity for progress, he also believed that this natural faculty of man could be further developed if the true office of government were recognized as its duty to promote the public welfare and to provide for the happiness of the mass of the people. " The exact measure of the progress of civilization is the degree in which the intelligence of the common mind has prevailed over wealth and brute force; in other words, the measure of the progress of civilization is the progress of the people." [39]   However, before man could achieve his destiny, it was necessary that he be emancipated from the curse of ignorance and allowed to enjoy " the natural right of every human being to moral and intellectual culture."

From his strong belief in democracy, Bancroft developed the conception of the idea of progress which he presented at length

37 *Ibid.,* pp. 236-246, 261-266.

38 *Ibid.,* pp. 267-274.

39 Bancroft, " The Office of the People in Art, Government, and Religion " (1835), *Literary and Historical Miscellanies* (New York, 1855), pp. 426 ff.; see also: " On the Progress of Civilization," *Boston Q. Rev.,* I (Oct., 1838), 388-407; and his *Oration ... before the Democracy of Springfield* (Springfield, 1836), p. 5.

in his famous oration before the New York Historical Society, assembled to celebrate a half-century " unequalled in its discoveries and its deeds." Since neither human nature nor truth varied, he declared, " The progress of man consists in this, that he himself arrives at the perception of truth. The Divine mind, which is its source, left it to be discovered, appropriated and developed by finite creatures." [40] Firmly convinced that " each individual is to contribute some share toward the general intelligence," and that " the many are wiser than the few," he concluded, in true democratic fashion, that progress was dependent upon " the totality of contemporary intelligence." [41] Bancroft, however, also recognized that man's quest for an ideal state divided him into the classes of conservatives and idealists, with a conciliatory group between these two. While all three of these groups were necessary to progress, he argued that wise men should accept the present as a natural result of the past, and then strive for constant betterment in the future.[42] After summarizing the past progress of liberty and of science in the history of the world, Bancroft closed his address with a patriotic and religious appeal for the United States to fulfill its Divine mission—spreading the principles of Freedom, and achieving the unity of the human race.[43] And in a letter to a friend, written some months after the delivery of his Oration, Bancroft, the historian of American democracy, wrote:

> Happy man, that you are to be so young. You will live to see great things achieved in your country. The men of your day will go far beyond those of mine; America is destined through your generation and the next to take the highest place in the empire of mind. I feel myself at most to be but a pioneer; and rest my hopes on those who come after me.[44]

40 Bancroft, " The Necessity, the Reality, and the Promise of Progress of the Human Race" (1854), *Literary and Historical Miscellanies*, p. 484.

41 *Ibid.*, pp. 484-485.

42 *Ibid.*, pp. 486-487.

43 *Ibid.*, pp. 493-517; see also the article, " Bancroft on the Progress of Society," *Chr. Rev.*, XX (April, 1855), 190-202.

44 Bancroft to Evert Duyckinck (May 26, 1855), in the Duyckinck Papers (New York Public Library).

Much less confident of the future progress of American democracy was Caleb Sprague Henry, an Episcopalian clergyman, professor of philosophy, leader in the peace movement, and an influential editor and author. Beginning with the third American edition in 1842, Henry contributed to Guizot's *General History of Civilization* its ' occasional notes ' in which he expressed a general agreement with the Guizot thesis that civilization was progressive.[45] However, Henry also cautioned that progress could not be attained without the aid of God and of Christianity, and in 1854 he devoted an article in *The Churchman* to showing how God intervenes in history.[46] That same year, in an editorial for the *New York Daily Times,* Henry urged the radicals of " Young America " to remember that progress had to be considered in reference to the end to be reached:

> It must not be ignorant of the past, nor despise it, much less hate it. The spirit of true progress is an organizing, not a destroying spirit. It is a spirit of love, not of hatred. It is wise and reverent, not ignorant and arrogant.[47]

In the following year, 1855, Henry delivered a discourse on progress to the New Jersey Historical Society, and he contributed to the *Church Review* a critical notice of Bancroft's Oration of the previous year. In his own address he confronted the believers in progress with the spectacle of the current Crimean War, with the failure of science to check poverty, and with the corruption by wealth of American democracy. The progress of this type of civilization, he felt, would not achieve the millennium. " On the contrary, *the progressive development of such a civilization in the same line, would be the intensification of all the irrational aspects it now presents—*" [48] In his review of

45 Guizot, *General History of Civilization*, footnotes by C. S. Henry, pp. 18, 30-31.

46 C. S. Henry, " The Providence of God the Genius of Human History " (*The Churchman*, May 20, 1854), in Henry's, *Considerations on ... Human Progress* (New York and London, 1861), p. 195.

47 Henry, " Young America.—The True Idea of Progress " (*New York Daily Times*, May 2, 1854), *ibid.*, p. 201.

48 Henry, " The Historical Destination of the Human Race " (1855), *ibid.*, p. 225, and *passim*.

Bancroft's Oration, he expressed his strong disagreement with its optimistic mirroring of the future in terms of the present, and he observed:

> Progress in civilization in science and in knowledge, in the subjugation of the tremendous forces of nature to man's earthly uses, has not been a proportional progress of humanity in true rational, moral and spiritual development. On the contrary it has intensified some of the worst physical, social and moral evils which the aspect of society presents. The greater the development of civilization, the worse the moral aspects of the extremities of the social scale; the greater luxury and corruption at one end, and the greater misery and degradation at the other end; and throughout the whole scale the tendency to hard worldliness in place of true spiritual development.[49]

Also critical of Bancroft's faith in the masses and in democracy, Henry on the contrary believed that, until " the moral spirit of Christianity " became " the *actuating priniciple* in the heart of humanity," there could be no " true progress of the human race in the line of its proper development." [58]

Caleb Sprague Henry was not alone in his skepticism over the tendencies of modern civilization. A decade before the bulk of Henry's writings were published, a contrast to the sympathetic interpretations of the idea of progress was provided in the *Lecture on the Philosophy of History,* delivered in 1844, by Severn Teackle Wallis, an individualist in politics and a leader of the Maryland bar for almost half a century. Wallis denounced the self-glorification of the age and the attempt to identify the history of the world with the philosophy of material progress. Admitting the unanimity of belief in the idea of progress, he pointed out that the difference of opinion was over the means of its achievement. From an examination of the contemporary claims of progress, he concluded:

49 Henry, "Remarks on Mr. Bancroft's Oration on Human Progress" (*Church Review*, July, 1855), *ibid.*, pp. 270-271.

50 *Ibid.*, p. 271; see also: R. V. Wells, *Three Christian Transcendentalists* (New York, 1943), p. 94.

It is then a bold proposition, to say, that because nations are great, and prosperous, and wise, their people are, therefore, happy, or high in their moral standard. I am as far removed as any one, from the absurd belief, that happiness and moral excellence are necessarily attendant upon the ruder stages of society, or that a complicated and advanced social system drives them, of necessity, to groves and sheepwalks. I only mean to say, that a brilliant, ostensible social progression may be accompanied by a low stage of individual welfare, physical and moral. I have proven, I think, that the " civilization " of the nineteenth century, is a sad exemplification of this sad truth.[51]

" Not in enthusiastic, wild anticipations," he declared, " but in grave, and careful, and deliberate deductions, will the philosophy of true progress find its realization." [52] Years later, in 1859, in the course of another lecture, Wallis condemned the materialistic, utilitarian passion of the country. He defended culture and leisure as worthy objects of life, and he denounced the false philosophy of the age under which

The theory of our social progress, in its relation to individuals, is a mere delusion. We have taken fever for high health, and intoxication for happiness. We are sacrificing ourselves to our work. We are bartering life for the appliances of living.[53]

These formal treatises were, for the most part, scholarly efforts dealing with the concept of progress in its historical and philosophical implications. The writers of the thirties shared Chipman's faith that the idea of progress was in agreement with natural law. In the following decade, Sumner and some of the other writers on the subject considered the idea in its connec-

51 S. T. Wallis, *Lecture on the Philosophy of History* (Baltimore, [1844]), p. 21, and *passim*; see also his *Address before ... Saint Mary's College ...* (Baltimore [1841]), *passim*.

52 Wallis, *Lecture on the Philosophy of History*, p. 29.

53 Wallis, *Leisure: Its Moral and Political Economy* (Baltimore, 1859), p. 14, and *passim*.

tions with the age of liberal reform which seemed to be sweeping over the world. Aware of the European philosophy of progress, the American thinkers were, however, always conscious of the relations of the idea to the American scene. Over-boastful in the spirit of Bancroft, their nationalism aroused the criticism of men like Henry and Wallis, who voiced the conservative implications of the concept of progress.

Although it was not always indicated by these formal treatments of the idea of progress, the underlying note in much of the American concept was the secure feeling derived from an observation of man's conquest and control of the immense forces of nature. With the presence of a vast reservoir of lands in the West, and with the tremendous power made available through technological advancement, there seemed to be every reason for faith in the physical progress of America, and the idea was therefore most widely considered in its material, not in its philosophical, aspects. For those intellectual or religious persons who caviled at the ruthlessness of American expansion and exploitation, its defenders could point to the evidences of cultural and educational improvement. Generalizing from the results of this material and cultural advancement, the American people made the idea of progress both a law of history and the will of a benign Providence. After the Civil War, the minority opposition offered by the South was crushed, and the way was open for the triumph of those forces which had enjoyed their youth in the period of our survey. With the rise of an industrialized, urbanized society, science, with its theory of evolution and its law of thermodynamics, became the chief authority for a belief in the idea of progress. However, even before the Civil War, science was the magic power by which it was felt that progress, if not inevitable, could at least be made highly probable. Confining ourselves to the period covered by this analysis, we may safely conclude that the idea of progress was the most popular American philosophy, thoroughly congenial to the ideas and interests of the age.

BIBLIOGRAPHY

PRIMARY SOURCES

MANUSCRIPTS

NOTE: In an effort to ascertain whether or not the optimistic sentiments expressed in their published works and public speeches also prevailed in their private letters, the correspondence of some of the important figures of the Middle Period was searched for evidences of a belief in progress. Although the fruits were small in proportion to the labor involved in examining some of the manuscript collections, the results justify the conclusion that the faith in progress was sincerely held and not entertained merely for popular consumption.

Library of Congress: The following manuscript collections were examined: John Quincy Adams (one vol. of letters and speeches); Joseph Blunt; Caleb Cushing (large coll. examined for period of this study); Horace Greeley; James Henry Hammond (Mss. of early orations, and letters from William Gilmore Simms and Francis Lieber); George Frederick Holmes; Francis Lieber (especially letters to Samuel B. Ruggles); William H. Seward; William Gilmore Simms; Letters of American Clergymen (1719-1873; examined for the period of this study).

New York Public Library: Bryant-Godwin Papers (especially Parke Godwin's letters to Charles A. Dana, and also letters from George Bancroft, Orville Dewey, William Gilmore Simms, and Charles Sumner); Duyckinck Papers (literary correspondence).

COLLECTED WRITINGS

NOTE: The titles in most every case are arranged in the order of the authors of the original material and not according to the names of the editors or compilers of the particular work.

Adams, John. Works, ed. Charles Francis Adams. 10 vols. Boston, Little Brown, 1850-1856.

Adams, John Quincy. Writings, ed. Worthington C. Ford. 7 vols. New York, Macmillan, 1913-1917.

——. Ten Unpublished Letters of John Quincy Adams, 1796-1837, ed. Edward H. Tatum, Jr. *Huntington Library Quarterly,* IV (April, 1941), 369-388.

American Library of Useful Knowledge, pub. by ... the Boston Society for the Diffusion of Useful Knowledge, vol. I, Boston, Stimpson and Clapp, 1831.

Armstrong, William J. Memoir and Sermons, ed. Rev. Hollis Read. New York, M. W. Dodd, 1853.

Bancroft, George. Literary and Historical Miscellanies. New York, Harpers, 1855.

Benthamiana; or, Select Extracts from the Works of Jeremy Bentham, ed. John Hill Burton. Phil., Lea and Blanchard, 1844.

Blunt, Joseph. Speeches, Reviews, Reports, etc. New York, Van Norden, 1843.

Bottomley, Edwin. An English Settler in Pioneer Wisconsin: The Letters of Edwin Bottomley, 1842-1850, ed. Milo M. Quaife (State Hist. Society of Wisconsin *Collections*, vol. XXV). Madison, The Society, 1918.

Brownson, Orestes A. Works, ed. Henry F. Brownson. 20 vols. Detroit, Nourse, 1882-1887.

Bryant, William Cullen. Life and Works, ed. Parke Godwin. 6 vols. New York, Appleton, 1883-1884.

Burnap, George W. Miscellaneous Writings. Baltimore, John Murphy, 1845.

——. Discourses on the Rectitude of Human Nature. Boston, Crosby and Nichols, 1850.

Burritt, Elihu. Miscellaneous Writings, 2nd ed. Worcester, Drew, 1850.

——. Thoughts and Things at Home and Abroad. Boston and New York, Sampson and Derby, 1854.

Calhoun, John C. Works, ed. Richard K. Crallé. 6 vols. New York, Appleton, 1853-1856.

——. Correspondence, ed. J. F. Jameson (Annual Report of the Am. Hist. Assoc. 1899, vol. II). Washington, Govt. Printing Office, 1900.

Channing, William Ellery. Works. 6 vols. 14th ed. Boston, Am. Unitarian Assoc. 1855.

——. Memoir... with extracts from his correspondence and manuscripts, ed. W. H. Channing. 3 vols. Boston, Crosby and Nichols; London, Chapman, 1848.

Clarke, James Freeman. Autobiography, Diary and Correspondence, ed. Edward Everett Hale. Boston and New York, Houghton Mifflin, 1891.

Clay, Cassius M. Writings, ed. Horace Greeley. New York, Harpers, 1848.

Congressional Globe (1830-1860), Washington.

Cooper, James Fenimore. Works (Mohawk Edition). 32 vols. New York and London, Putnam, [1896-1897].

——. Correspondence, ed. James Fenimore Cooper. 2 vols. New Haven, Yale Univ. Press, 1922.

Correspondence of Robert Tombs, Alexander H. Stephens, and Howell Cobb, ed. U. B. Phillips (Annual Report of the Am. Hist. Assoc., 1911, vol. II). Washington, Govt. Printing Office, 1913.

Elliott, E. N. ed. Cotton Is King, and Pro-Slavery Arguments: comprising the writings of Hammond, Harper, Christy, Stringfellow, Hodge, Bledsoe, and Cartwright... with an essay on slavery in the light of international law by the editor. Augusta, Pritchard, Abbott and Loomis, 1860.

Emerson, Ralph Waldo. Complete Works (Centenary Edition). 12 vols. Boston and New York. Houghton Mifflin, 1903-1906.

——. Journals... with annotations, ed. E. W. Emerson and W. E. Forbes. 10 vols. Boston and New York, Houghton Mifflin, 1909-1914.

Everett, Edward. Orations and Speeches on Various Occasions. 3 vols. (vols. I and II, 2nd ed.), Boston, Little Brown, 1850-1859.

Franklin, Benjamin. Writings, ed. Albert H. Smythe. 10 vols. New York and London, Macmillan, 1905-1907.

Freneau, Philip. Poems, ed. Fred Lewis Pattee. 3 vols. Princeton, The Univ. Library, 1902-1907.

Garrison, William Lloyd. Selections from the Writings and Speeches. Boston, Wallcut, 1852.

Godwin, Parke. Political Essays. New York, Dix, Edwards, 1856.

——. Out of the Past: Critical and Literary Papers. New York, Putnam, 1870.

Greeley, Horace. Hints toward Reforms in Lectures, Addresses, and other Writings. New York, Harpers, 1850.

Hawthorne, Nathaniel. Complete Writings (Old Manse Edition). 22 vols. Boston and New York, Houghton Mifflin, 1903.

Hedge, Frederic H. ed. Prose Writers of Germany. 4th ed. New York and London, Francis and Low, 1856.

Henry, Caleb Sprague. Considerations on Some of the Elements and Conditions of Social Welfare and Human Progress. New York and London, Appleton, 1861.

Hilliard, Henry W. Speeches and Addresses. New York, Harpers, 1855.

Hughes, John. Complete Works, ed. Lawrence Kehoe. 2 vols. New York, Kehoe, 1866.

Jefferson, Thomas. Writings, ed. Paul L. Ford. 10 vols. New York and London, Putnam, 1892-1899.

——. Writings, ed. Albert Ellery Bergh (Definitive Edition). 20 vols. Washington, Thomas Jefferson Memorial Assoc., 1907.

King, Thomas Starr. Patriotism and Other Papers. Boston, Tompkins, 1864.

Legaré, Hugh Swinton. Writings, ed. by his sister. 2 vols. Charleston, Burges and James, 1845-1846.

Leggett, William. A Collection of the Political Writings, ed. Theodore Sedgwick, Jr. 2 vols. New York, Taylor and Dodd, 1840.

Lieber, Francis. Reminiscences, Addresses, and Essays (Miscellaneous Writings, vol. I). Phil., Lippincott, 1881.

——. Life and Letters, ed. Thomas S. Perry. Boston, Osgood, 1882.

Lincoln, Abraham. Complete Works, ed. Nicolay and Hay. 12 vols. New York, Tandy, 1905.

Lindsley, Philip. Works, ed. Le Roy J. Halsey. Phil., Lippincott, 1866.

Lowell, James Russell. Complete Writings (Elmwood Edition). 16 vols. Boston and New York, Houghton Mifflin, 1904.

Mann, Horace. Life and Works. 5 vols. Boston, Lee and Shepard, 1891.

Meek, Alexander B. Romantic Passages in Southwestern History; including orations, sketches, and essays. 3rd ed. Mobile and New York, Goetzel, 1857.

Morse, Samuel F. B. Letters and Journals, ed. Edward Lind Morse. 2 vols. Boston and New York, Houghton Mifflin, 1914.

Nicholas, S. Smith. Conservative Essays, Legal and Political. Phil., Lippincott, 1863.

Norwegian-American Historical Association, *Studies and Records*, vols. I-III, Minneapolis, pub. by the Assoc., 1926-1928.

——. *Travel and Description Series*, vol. III, Minneapolis, Univ. Minnesota Press, 1929.

Orvis, Marianne Dwight. Letters from Brook Farm, 1844-1847, ed. Amy L. Reed. Poughkeepsie, Vassar College, 1928.

Ossoli, Margaret Fuller. Memoirs, ed. R. W. Emerson, W. H. Channing, and J. F. Clarke, 3 vols. London, Bentley, 1852.

Paine, Thomas. Writings, ed. Moncure Daniel Conway. New York and London, Putnam, 1894-1896.

Parker, Theodore. Sermons of Theism, Atheism, and the Popular Theology. 2nd ed. Boston, Little Brown, 1856.

——. Lessons from the World of Matter and the World of Man (selected from notes of unpublished sermons by Rufus Leighton). Boston, Slack, 1865.

——. [Works] (Centenary Edition). [15 vols.] Boston, Am. Unitarian Assoc. [1907-1915?].

Proceedings of the Pennsylvania Yearly Meetings of Progressive Friends, 1853, 1855-1860. New York, Trow, 1853-1860.

Pro-Slavery Argument; as maintained by the most distinguished writers of the southern states, containing the several essays, on the subject, of Chancellor Harper, Governor Hammond, Dr. Simms, and Professor Dew. Charleston, Walker, Richards, 1852.

Rantoul, Robert, Jr. Memoirs Speeches and Writings, ed. Luther Hamilton. Boston, Jewitt, 1854.

Register of Debates in Congress (1824-1837), Washington.

Richardson, James D. ed. A Compilation of the Messages and Papers of the Presidents, 1789-1897. 10 vols. Washington, Govt. Printing Office, 1896-1899.

Ripley, George. Philosophical Miscellanies, tr. from the French of Cousin, Jouffroy, and B. Constant (Specimens of Foreign Standard Literature, vols. I and II). 2 vols. Boston, Hilliard Gray, 1838.

Schurz, Carl. Speeches, Correspondence, and Political Papers, ed. Frederic Bancroft. 6 vols. New York and London, Putnam, 1913.

Seward, William H. Works, ed. George E. Baker. 5 vols. new ed. Boston and New York, Houghton Mifflin, 1884.

Simms, William Gilmore. Views and Reviews in American Literature, History and Fiction. New York, Wiley and Putnam, 1845.

Story, Joseph. Miscellaneous Writings, ed. William W. Story. Boston, Little Brown, 1852.

Sumner, Charles. Memoir and Letters, ed. Edward L. Pierce. 4 vols. Boston, Roberts, 1877-1893.

Thoreau, Henry David. Writings (Manuscript Edition). 20 vols. Boston and New York, Houghton Mifflin, 1906.

United States Patent Office, Reports of the Commissioners: 1829, 1831, 1837-1860. Washington.

Webster, Daniel. Writings and Speeches (National Edition). 18 vols. Boston, Little Brown, 1903.

Weiss, John. Life and Correspondence of Theodore Parker. 2 vols. New York, Appleton, 1864.

Western Literary Institute, Transactions of the fourth to the tenth annual meetings, 1834-1840. Cincinnati, 1835-1841.

Whitman, Walt. The Gathering of the Forces (material written by Whitman as editor of the *Brooklyn Daily Eagle* in 1846 and 1847), ed. Cleveland Rodgers and John Black. 2 vols. New York and London, Putnam, 1920.

——. I Sit and Look Out: Editorials from the Brooklyn Daily Times, ed. Emory Holloway and Vernolian Schwarz. New York, Col. Univ. Press, 1932.

Wilson, James. Works, ed. Bird Wilson. 3 vols. Phil., Bronson and Chauncey, 1804.

Woodbury, Levi. Writings. 3 vols. Boston, Little Brown, 1852.

Wright, Frances. Course of Popular Lectures. 3rd ed. New York, Free Enquirer, 1830.

MAGAZINES AND PERIODICALS

NOTE: In the case of title variations the attempt is made to cite the magazines by their most usual or convenient title. The place of publication is placed in parentheses followed by the inclusive dates, indicating the years of the periodical file examined. Occasionally, however, a few volumes or numbers within these years were unavailable. Although not magazines, it was thought best to include the *Annals of Cleveland* and the *New York Weekly Tribune* in this section of the bibliography.

American Agriculturist. (New York), 1842-1860.

American Journal of Education. (Barnard's; Hartford), 1855-1861.

American Museum of Science, Literature, and the Arts. (Baltimore), 1838-1839.

American (Whig) Review. (New York), 1845-1852.

Annals of Cleveland; digest and index of the newspaper record of events and opinions. (Cleveland, 1936-1938), 1818-1860.

Arcturus; a Journal of Books and Opinion. (New York), 1840-1841.

Biblical Repertory and Princeton Review. (Phil., and Princeton), 1825-1860.

Biblical Repository. (Andover, New York, Boston), 1831-1850.

Bibliotheca Sacra. (Andover), 1843-1860.

Boston Quarterly Review. (Boston), 1838-1842.

Boston Recorder. (Boston), 1837-1849. Continued as the Puritan Recorder, see below.

Brownson's Quarterly Review. (Boston and New York), 1844-1860.

Christian Examiner. (Boston), 1824-1860.

Christian Review. (Boston, Baltimore, New York), 1836-1860.

Church Review. (New Haven), 1848-1860.

Common School Journal. (Boston), 1839-1851.

De Bow's Review. (New Orleans and Washington), 1846-1860.

Democratic Review. See below under U. S. Mag. and Dem. Rev.

The Dial. (Boston), 1840-1844.

Free Enquirer. (New York), 1829-1835. A continuation of the New Harmony Gazette, see below.

Freewill Baptist Quarterly. (Providence and Dover), 1853-1860.

Godey's Lady's Book. (Phil.), 1830-1860.

Graham's Magazine. (Phil.), 1840-1860.

The Harbinger. (New York and Boston), 1845-1849.

Harper's New Monthly Magazine. (New York), 1850-1860.

Herald of the New Moral World. (New York), 1841-1842.

Holden's Dollar Magazine. (New York), 1848-1851.

Home Missionary. (New York), 1828-1860.

Hunt's Merchants' Magazine. (New York), 1839-1860.

Illinois Monthly Magazine. (Vandalia and Cincinnati), 1831-1832. Continued as the Western Monthly Mag., see below.

Independent Beacon. (New York), 1849.

Knickerbocker Magazine. (New York), 1833-1860.

Ladies' Repository. (Cincinnati), 1841-1860.

Massachusetts Quarterly Review. (Boston), 1848-1850.

Methodist Quarterly Review. (New York), 1818-1860.

Missionary Herald. (Boston), 1821-1860.

New Constitution. (Columbus, Ohio), 1849.

New England Farmer. (Fessenden's; Boston), 1822-1843.

New Englander. (New Haven and New York), 1843-1860.

New Harmony Gazette. (New Harmony and New York), 1825-1829. Continued as the Free Enquirer, see above.

New-York Mirror. (New York), 1823-1846.

New-York Weekly Tribune. (New York), 1842-1860.

New-Yorker. (quarto ed.; New York), 1836-1841.

Niles' Register. (Baltimore, Washington, Phil.), 1814-1849.

Nineteenth Century. (Phil.), 1848-1849.

North American Review. (Boston), 1815-1860.

The Pathfinder. (New York), 1843.

The Phalanx. (New York), 1843-1845.

Portland Magazine. (Portland, Me.), 1834-1836.

Practical Christian. (Milford, Mass.), 1850-1852.

Presbyterian Quarterly Review. (Phil.), 1852-1861.

The Present. (New York), 1843-1844.

Puritan Recorder. (Boston), 1849-1860. A continuation of the Boston Recorder, see above.

Putnam's Monthly Magazine. (New York), 1853-1857.

Quarterly Christian Spectator. (New Haven), 1829-1838.

Quarterly Journal and Review. (Cincinnati), 1846.

Quarterly Review of the Methodist Episcopal Church South. (Richmond and Nashville), 1852-1860.

The Regenerator. (Fruit Hills, Ohio), 1847-1848.

Scientific American. (New York), 1845-1860.

Southern Literary Messenger. (Richmond), 1834-1860.

Southern Quarterly Review. (New Orleans and Charleston), 1842-1857.

Southern Review. (Charleston), 1828-1832.

Spirit of the Age. (New York), 1849-1850.

Spirit of the Nineteenth Century. (Baltimore), 1842-1843.

The Subterranean. (New York), 1845-1847.

United States Catholic Magazine. (Baltimore), 1842-1848.

United States Magazine and Democratic Review. (Washington and New York), 1837-1859.

Western Messenger. (Cincinnati), 1835-1841.

Western Monthly Magazine. (Cincinnati), 1833-1837. A continuation of the Illinois Monthly Mag., see above.

Western Monthly Review. (Cincinnati), 1827-1830.

Working Man's Advocate. (New York), 1830, 1835, 1844-1845.

BOOKS AND PAMPHLETS

Adams, Jaspar. Elements of Moral Philosophy. New York, Wiley and Putnam, 1837.

The American Society for the Diffusion of Useful Knowledge. Prospectus. New York, 1837.

Andrews, Stephen Pearl. The True Constitution of Government in the Sovereignty of the Individual as the Final Development of Protestantism, Democracy, and Socialism (The Science of Society, no. 1). New York, Fowlers and Wells, 1852.

——. Cost the Limit of Price: A Scientific Measure of Honesty in Trade, as One of the Fundamental Principles in the Solution of the Social Problem (The Science of Society, no. 2). New York, Fowlers and Wells, 1852.

Arnold, Thomas. Introductory Lectures on Modern History. New York and Phil., Appleton, 1845.

Baird, Robert. The Christian Retrospect and Register: A Summary of the Scientific, Moral and Religious Progress of the First Half of the XIXth Century. New York, Dodd, 1851.

——. View of the Valley of the Mississippi; or The Emigrant's and Traveller's Guide to the West. Phil., Tanner, 1832.

Bakewell, Robert. An Introduction to Geology... 2nd Am. from the 4th London edition, ed. Benjamin Silliman. New Haven, Howe, 1833.

Ball, Charles. Slavery in the United States: A Narrative of the Life and Adventures of Charles Ball. New York, Taylor, 1837.

Ballou, Adin. Practical Christian Socialism: A Conversational Exposition of the True System of Human Society. Hopedale and New York, Fowlers and Wells, 1854.

Bancroft, George. History of the United States. 10 vols. Boston, Little Brown, 1834-1874.

Barlow, Joel. The Vision of Columbus: A Poem in Nine Books. Hartford, Hudson and Goodwin, 1787.

——. Two Letters to the Citizens of the United States, and One to General Washington, written from Paris in the Year 1799, on our Political and Commercial Relations. New Haven, Sidney, 1806.

——. The Columbiad, a Poem. 2 vols. Phil., Conrad, 1809.

[Bayard, Samuel John]. A Sketch of the Life of Com. Robert F. Stockton. New York, Derby and Jackson, 1856.

Beecher, Lyman. A Plea for the West. 2nd ed. Cincinnati and New York, Truman and Smith, Leavitt and Lord, 1835.

Bentham, Jeremy. Principles of Legislation...ed. John Neal. Boston, Wells and Lilly, 1830.

——. Theory of Legislation...ed. Richard Hildreth. 2 vols. Boston, Weeks Jordan, 1840.

Bigelow, Jacob. Elements of Technology, taken chiefly from a course of lectures delivered at Cambridge, on the application of the sciences to the useful arts. Boston, Hilliard, Gray, Little, and Wilkins, 1829.

Bowen, Francis. Lowell Lectures, on the Application of Meta-Physical and Ethical Science to the Evidences of Religion. Boston, Little Brown, 1849.

——. The Principles of Political Economy applied to the Condition, the Resources, and the Institutions of the American People. Boston, Little Brown, 1856.

Bremer, Fredrika. The Homes of the New World; Impressions of America, tr. by Mary Howitt. 2 vols. New York, Harpers, 1853.

Briggs, Charles F. and Maverick, Augustus. The Story of the Telegraph, and a History of the Great Atlantic Cable. New York, Rudd and Carleton, 1858.

Brisbane, Albert. Social Destiny of Man: or, Association and Reorganization of Industry. Phil., Stollmeyer, 1840.

——. Albert Brisbane, A Mental Biography with a character study by his wife Redelia Brisbane. Boston, Arena, 1893.

Brougham, Henry. Practical Observations on Popular Education, from the 20th London edition. Boston, Mass. Journal, 1826.

Brown, Edward. Notes on the Origin and Necessity of Slavery. Charleston, Miller, 1826.

[Brown, Paul]. The Radical; and Advocate of Equality...Albany, Stone and Munsell, 1835.

Brownlee, William C. Popery: An Enemy to Civil and Religious Liberty; and Dangerous to Our Republic. New York, Bowne and Wisner, 1836.

Brownlow, William G. Americanism Contrasted with Foreignism, Romanism, and Bogus Democracy, in the light of reason, history, and scripture. Nashville, 1856.

Brownson, Orestes A. New Views of Christianity, Society, and the Church. Boston, Munroe, 1836.

Buckle, Henry Thomas. History of Civilization in England. 2 vols. New York, Appleton, 1858-1861.

Burton, Warren. Cheering Views of Man and Providence, drawn from a Consideration of the Origin, Uses, and Remedies of Evil. Boston, Carter Hendee, 1832.

Bush, George. Anastasis: or the Doctrine of the Resurrection of the Body, rationally and scripturally considered. New York and London, Wiley and Putnam, 1845.

Byllesby, L. Observations on the Sources and Effects of Unequal Wealth. New York, Nichols, 1826.

Calvert, George H. Introduction to Social Science; a Discourse in Three Parts. New York, Redfield, 1856.

Camp, George Sidney. Democracy. New York, Harpers, 1841.

Carey, Henry C. Principles of Political Economy. 4 parts in 3 vols. Phil., Carey, Lea and Blanchard, 1837-1840.

———. The Past, the Present, and the Future. Phil., Carey and Hart, 1848.

———. The Harmony of Interests, Agricultural, Manufacturing, and Commercial, first pub. 1851; New York, Finch, 1856.

———. Principles of Social Science. 3 vols. Phil., Lippincott, 1858-1859.

Chipman, Nathaniel. Principles of Government; a Treatise on Free Institutions. Burlington, Smith, 1833. (a revision of his earlier work, Sketches of the Principles of Government. 1793).

Claibourne, J. F. H. Life and Correspondence of John A. Quitman. 2 vols. New York, Harpers, 1860.

Claxton, Timothy. Memoir of a Mechanic, being a sketch of the life of Timothy Claxton, written by himself. Boston, Light, 1839.

[Colwell, Stephen]. Politics for American Christians: A Word upon our Example as a Nation, our Labour, our Trade, Elections, Education, and Congressional Legislation. Phil., Lippincott Grambo, 1852.

Combe, George. Notes on the United States of North America during a phrenological visit in 1838-9-40. 2 vols. Phil., Carey and Hart, 1841.

Comte, Auguste. The Positive Philosophy, freely translated and condensed by Harriet Martineau. 3rd ed. New York, Blanchard, 1856.

Condorcet, Marquis de. Outlines of an Historical View of the Progress of the Human Mind. Phil., Lang and Ustick, 1796.

Cooper, James Fenimore. Notions of the Americans: Picked up by a Travelling Bachelor. 2 vols. Phil., Carey, Lea and Carey, 1828.

———. The American Democrat (first pub. 1838). New York, Knopf, 1931.

Cooper, Thomas. On the Connection between Geology and the Pentateuch, in a Letter to Professor Silliman. Boston, Hall, 1833.

Cousin, Victor. Introduction to the History of Philosophy, tr. from the French by Henning Gotfried Linberg. Boston, Hilliard, Gray, Little and Wilkins, 1832.

———. Course of the History of Modern Philosophy, tr. by O. W. Wright. 2 vols. New York, Appleton, 1852.

Curtiss, Daniel S. Western Portraiture, and Emigrants' Guide: A Description of Wisconsin, Illinois, and Iowa; with remarks on Minnesota and other territories. New York, Colton, 1852.

[Davis, Charles A.]. Letters of J. Downing, Major, ... to his old friend, Mr. Dwight, of " The New York Daily Advertiser." New York, Harpers, 1834.

Davis, Emerson. The Half-Century; or, a History of Changes that have taken place, and events that have transpired, chiefly in the United States, between . 1800 and 1850, with an introd. by Mark Hopkins. Boston, Tappan and Whittemore, 1851.

Dick, Thomas. On the Improvement of Society by the Diffusion of Knowledge. New York, Harpers, 1833.

——. The Mental Illumination and Moral Improvement of Mankind (The Christian Library, vol. II). New York, George, 1836.

Douglas, James. The Advancement of Society in Knowledge and Religion, first Am. from the second Edinburgh ed. Hartford, Cooke, 1830.

Douglass, Frederick. My Bondage and My Freedom. New York and Auburn, Miller, Orton and Mulligan, 1855.

[Dove, Patrick Edward]. The Theory of Human Progression, and Natural Probability of a Reign of Justice. Boston, Mussey, 1851.

Dwight, Timothy. Travels in New-England and New-York. 4 vols. New Haven, Converse, 1821-1822.

Edger, Henry. The Positivist Calendar: or, Transitional System of Public Commemoration Instituted by Augustus Comte. Modern Times, Thompson, 1856.

Etzler, J. A. The Paradise within the Reach of All Men, without Labour, by Powers of Nature and Machinery. London, Brooks, 1836.

——. The New World; or, Mechanical System, to Perform the Labours of Man and Beast by Inanimate Powers. Phil., Stollmeyer, 1841.

Everett, Alexander H. New Ideas on Population: with Remarks on the Theories of Malthus and Godwin. Boston, Oliver Everett, 1823.

——. Europe: or a General Survey of the . . . Principal Powers with Conjectures on Their Future Prospects. Boston, Oliver Everett, 1822.

——. America: or a General Survey of the... Several Powers of the Western Continent with Conjectures on Their Future Prospects. Phil., Carey and Lea, 1827.

Ewbank, Thomas. The World a Workshop; or, the Physical Relationship of Man to the Earth. New York, Appleton, 1855.

——. The Position of our Species in the Path of its Destiny; or the Comparative Infancy of Man and of Earth as His Home. New York, Scribner and Richardson, [1860?].

——. Inorganic Forces Ordained to Supersede Human Slavery (originally read before the American Ethnological Society). New York, Everdell, 1860.

Ferguson, Adam. An Essay on the History of Civil Society. first pub. 1767; 7th ed. Boston, Hastings, Etheridge and Bliss, 1809.

Fisher, Richard Swainson. The Progress of the United States of America, from the earliest periods; geographical, statistical, and historical. New York, Colton, 1854.

Fitzhugh, George. Sociology for the South, or the Failure of Free Society. Richmond, Morris, 1854.

——. Cannibals All! or, Slaves without Masters. Richmond, Morris, 1857.

Flint, Timothy. Lectures upon Natural History, Geology, Chemistry, the Application of Steam and interesting discoveries in the Arts. Boston and Cincinnati, Lilly, Wait, Colman and Holden; F. H. Flint, 1833.

Gérando, Joseph Marie de. Self-education; or the Means and Art of Moral Progress, tr. from the French by Elizabeth Palmer Peabody. Boston, Carter and Hendee, 1830.

Gobineau, Count A. de. The Moral and Intellectual Diversity of Races, with particular reference to their respective influence in the civil and political history of mankind... with an analytical introduction... by H. Hotz to which is added an appendix... by J. C. Nott. Phil., Lippincott, 1856.

Godwin, Parke. Democracy, Constructive and Pacific. New York, Winchester, 1844.

——. A Popular View of the Doctrines of Charles Fourier. New York, Redfield, 1844.

Godwin, William. Enquiry Concerning Political Justice, and its Influence on Morals and Happiness (first Am. from the second London ed.), 2 vols. Phil., Bioren and Madan, 1796.

[Goodrich, Samuel G.]. The First Book of History. New York, Collins and Hannay, 1831.

——. Peter Parley's Common School History. 6th ed. Phil., Marshall, 1839.

——. The Young American. 8th ed. New York, Newman, 1847.

——. Lights and Shadows of American History. Boston, Bradbury Soden, 1844.

——. The Wonders of Geology. Boston, Bradbury Soden, 1845.

——. A Glance at the Physical Sciences. Boston, Bradbury Soden, 1844.

——. Enterprise, Industry, and Art of Man. Boston, Bradbury Soden, 1845.

——. Modern History. Louisville, Morton and Griswold, 1848.

Greeley, Horace. Association Discussed (Pamphlet of series of articles by Greeley and Henry J. Raymond in the *Tribune* and *Courier and Enquirer*, Nov. 20, 1846 to May 20, 1847). New York, Harpers, 1847.

——. Art and Industry as represented in the exhibition at the Crystal Palace, New York 1853-4, showing the progress and state of the various useful and esthetic pursuits, from the New York Tribune. New York, Redfield, 1853.

——. Recollections of a Busy Life. New York, Ford, 1868.

Gregg, William. "Essays on Domestic Industry, or an Inquiry into the Expediency of Establishing Cotton Manufactures in South Carolina" (1845), in Tompkins, D. A. Cotton Mill, Commercial Features. Charlotte, 1899. pp. 203-240.

Grimes, J. Stanley. Phreno-Geology: The Progressive Creation of Man. Boston, Cambridge, and London, Munroe and Whitfield, 1851.

Grimké, Frederick. Considerations upon the Nature and Tendency of Free Institutions. Cincinnati and New York, Derby and Barnes, 1848.

——. *Ibid.*, 2nd ed. corrected and enlarged. New York and Cincinnati, Derby and Jackson; H. W. Derby, 1856.

Grund, Francis J. The Americans in their Moral, Social, and Political Relations Boston, Marsh, Capen and Lyon, 1837.

——. Aristocracy in America, from the sketch-book of a German nobleman. 2 vols. London, Bentley, 1839.

Guizot, Francois, P. G. General History of Civilization in Europe, 3rd Am. from the 2nd English ed., with occasional notes by C. S. Henry. New York, Appleton, 1842.

Guyot, Arnold. The Earth and Man: Lectures on Comparative Physical Geography, in its Relation to the History of Mankind, tr. from the French by C. C. Felton. Boston, Gould and Lincoln, 1857.

Hall, James. Letters from the West. London, Colburn, 1828.

——. Notes on the Western States. Phil., Hall, 1838.

——. The West: Its Commerce and Navigation. Cincinnati, Derby, 1848.

Halsall, James C. The Law of Human Progress, or the Science of the Mind. Charlottesville, Allen, 1849.

——. Sequel to the Law of Human Progress. Richmond, Colin and Nowlan, 1854.

Haven, Joseph. Moral Philosophy, including theoretical and practical ethics. Boston, Gould and Lincoln, 1859.

Helper, Hinton Rowan. The Impending Crisis of the South: How to Meet It. New York, Burdick, 1860.

Herndon, William Lewis. Exploration of the Valley of the Amazon... Part I. (32nd Cong. 2nd Sess., Senate Ex. Doc. no. 36) Washington, Armstrong, 1853.

[Hildreth, Richard]. Despotism in America: or An Inquiry into the Nature and Results of the Slave-Holding System in the United States. 2nd ed. Boston and New York, Massachusetts and American Anti-Slavery Societies, 1840.

——. Theory of Morals: An Inquiry concerning the Law of Moral Distinctions and the Variations and Contradictions of Ethical Codes. Boston, Little Brown, 1844.

——, Theory of Politics: An Inquiry into the Foundations of Government, and the Causes and Progress of Political Revolutions. New York, Harpers, 1853.

——. The History of the United States of America. 6 vols. rev. ed. New York, Harpers, 1856.

Hitchcock, Edward. The Religion of Geology and Its Connected Sciences. new ed. Boston, Phillips Sampson, 1859.

Holcombe, William H. The Alternative: A Separate Nationality, or the Africanization of the South. New Orleans, 1860.

Hopkins, John Henry. The American Citizen: His Rights and Duties, according to the spirit of the Constitution of the United States. New York, Pudney and Russell, 1857.

Hopkins, Mark. Lectures on Moral Science (delivered before the Lowell Institute, Boston). Boston, Gould and Lincoln, 1862.

Hughes, Henry. Treatise on Sociology, theoretical and practical. Phil., Lippincott Grambo, 1854.

Humboldt, Alexander von. Cosmos: A Sketch of a Physical Description of the Universe, tr. from the German by E. C. Otté. 2 vols. New York, Harpers, 1850.

Johnson, Walter R. Remarks on the Duty of the Several States, in Regard to Public Education. Phil., Sharpless, 1830.

Kellogg, Edward. Labor and other Capital: The Rights of Each Secured and the Wrongs of Both Eradicated. New York, 1849.

[Kennedy, John P.]. Quodlibet. Phil., Lea and Blanchard, 1840.

Kettell, Thomas P. Southern Wealth and Northern Profits. New York, Wood, 1860.

Kinmont, Alexander. Twelve Lectures on the Natural History of Man, and the Rise and Progress of Philosophy. Cincinnati, James, 1839.

Lawrence, Abbott. Letters from the Hon. Abbott Lawrence to the Hon. William C. Rives of Virginia. Boston, Eastburn, 1846.

Lewis, Tayler. The Six Days of Creation: or the scriptural cosmology, with the ancient idea of time-worlds, in distinction from worlds in space. Schenectady and London, Bogert and Chapman, 1855.

Lieber, Francis. Letters to a Gentleman in Germany, written after a trip from Philadelphia to Niagara. Phil., Carey, Lea and Blanchard, 1834.

——. Manual of Political Ethics. 2 vols. Boston, Little Brown, 1838-1839.

——. Essays on Property and Labour as connected with Natural Law and the Constitution of Society. New York, Harpers, 1841.

——. On Civil Liberty and Self-Government. 2 vols. Phil., Lippincott Grambo, 1853.

Lord, Nathan. Letter of Inquiry to the Ministers of the Gospel of all Denominations on Slavery. Boston, Fetridge, 1854.

——. A Northern Presbyter's Second Letter to Ministers of the Gospel of all Denominations on Slavery. Boston and New York, Little Brown; Appleton, 1855.

Lyell, Charles. Principles of Geology: or, the Modern Changes of the Earth and Its Inhabitants, considered as illustrative of Geology. 3 vols. from the 6th English ed. Boston, Hilliard Gray, 1842.

——. Travels in North America; with Geological Observations on the United States, Canada, and Nova Scotia. 2 vols. London, Murray, 1845.

Mackay, Charles. Life and Liberty in America: or Sketches of a Tour in the United States and Canada in 1857-8. New York, Harpers, 1859.

Maclure, William. Opinions on Various Subjects dedicated to the Industrious Producers. 2 vols. New Harmony, 1831-1837.

Magoon, Elias L. Republican Christianity: or, True Liberty, as exhibited in the life, precepts, and early disciples of the Great Redeemer. Boston, Gould, Kendall and Lincoln, 1849.

——. Westward Empire: or the Great Drama of Human Progress. New York, Harpers, 1856.

Martineau, Harriet. Society in America. 2 vols. 4th ed. New York, Saunders and Otley, 1837.

Mayer, Frank Blackwell. With Pen and Pencil on the Frontier in 1851; The Diary and Sketches of Frank Blackwell Mayer, ed. Bertha I. Heilbron. (Publications of the Minnesota Historical Society, Narratives and Documents, vol. I). Saint Paul, The Society. 1932.

McCosh, James. The Method of the Divine Government, Physical and Moral (first pub. in Edinburgh, 1850; 8th ed. same as 4th ed. of 1855), New York, Carter, [186].

Melville, Herman. Mardi and a Voyage Thither. 2 vols. (Works, Constable Edition, vols. III-IV), London, Constable, 1922.

Minutes and Proceedings of the Memphis Convention, Assembled Oct. 23, 1849. [Memphis], Enquirer Office, 1850.

Morgan, Lewis H. League of the Ho-Dé-No-Sau-Nee or Iroquois. Rochester, Sage and Brother, 1851.

Morse, Jedidiah. A Report to the Secretary of War ... on Indian Affairs ... New Haven, Converse, 1822.

[Morse, Samuel F. B.]. Foreign Conspiracy against the Liberties of the United States: The number of Brutus, originally published in the New-York Observer. New York and Boston, Leavitt Lord, 1835.

Murdock, James. Sketches of Modern Philosophy, especially among the Germans. Hartford, Wells, 1842.

Nell, William C. The Colored Patriots of the American Revolution. Boston, Wallcut, 1855.

Newhall, John B. Sketches of Iowa, or the Emigrant's Guide. New York, Colton, 1841.

Newman, Samuel P. Elements of Political Economy. Andover and New York, Gould and Newman; H. Griffin, 1835.

Nichols, Thomas Low. Forty Years of American Life. 2 vols. London, Maxwell, 1864.

[Norton, Charles Eliot]. Considerations on Some Recent Social Theories. Boston, Little Brown, 1853.

Nott, Josiah C. and Gliddon, George R. Types of Mankind. Phil., Lippincott Grambo, 1854.

Nourse, James D. Remarks on the Past and its Legacies to American Society. Louisville, Morton and Griswold, 1847.

Olmsted, Frederick Law. A Journey in the Seaboard Slave States, with remarks on their economy. New York and London, Dix and Edwards; Sampson Low, 1856.

Owen, Robert. A New View of Society: or Essays on the Formation of the Human Character, preparatory to the development of a plan for gradually ameliorating the condition of mankind (first Am. from the 3rd London ed.). New York, Bliss and White, 1825.

——. The Book of the New Moral World, containing the rational system of society, founded on demonstrable facts, developing the constitution and laws of human society (first Am. ed.). New York, Vale, 1845.

Owen, Robert Dale. Wealth and Misery. (Popular Tracts, no. 11; extracted from the New Harmony Gazette, 1826). New York, Free Enquirer, [1830?].

Parker, Nathan H. Iowa as It Is in 1856; A Gazetteer for Citizens, and a Hand-Book for Emigrants. Chicago and Phil., Keen and Lee; Desilver, 1856.

——. The Minnesota Handbook for 1856-7. Boston, Jewett, 1857.

Peck, John M. A Guide for Emigrants, containing sketches of Illinois, Missouri, and the adjacent parts. Boston, Lincoln and Edmands, 1831. (A 2nd and 3rd ed. were pub. in 1837 under the title, A New Guide for Emigrants to the West).

——. A Gazetteer of Illinois. 2nd ed. Phil., Grigg and Elliot, 1837.

Perry, Matthew C. Narrative of the Expedition of an American Squadron to the China Seas and Japan, performed in the years 1852, 1853, 1854 ... compiled by Francis L. Hawks. 3 vols. (33rd Cong. 2nd Sess., House of Rep. Ex. Doc. no. 97). Washington, Nicholson, 1856.

Pickering, John. The Working Man's Political Economy, founded upon the principles of immutable justice, and the inalienable rights of man; designed for the promotion of national reform. Cincinnati, Varney, 1847.

Price, Richard. Observations on the Importance of the American Revolution, and the Means of Making it a Benefit to the World. London, Cadell, 1785.

Priestly, Joseph. An Essay on the First Principles of Government, and on the Nature of Political, Civil, and Religious Liberty. 2nd ed. London, Johnson, 1771.

Rogers, George. An Address on Our Destiny; with Remarks. New York, [1846?].

Sasnett, William J. Progress: Considered with Particular Reference to the Methodist Episcopal Church, South. Nashville, Stevenson and Owen, 1855.

[Saunders, Frederick]. The Progress and Prospects of America. New York, Walker, 1855. (also pub. in New York with the title, A Voice to America).

Schoolcraft, Henry R. Notes on the Iroquois. (New York Senate Doc. no. 24). New York, Bartlett and Welford, 1846.

——. Information Respecting the History, Condition, and Prospects of the Indian Tribes of the United States; collected and prepared under the Bureau of Indian Affairs. (pub. by authority of Congress; vol. VI of the Archives of Aboriginal Knowledge, 1851-1857). Phil., Lippincott, 1860.

Seaman. Ezra C. Essays on the Progress of Nations, in productive industry, civilization, population, and wealth. Detroit, Geiger, 1846.

Simpson, Stephen. The Working Man's Manual: A New Theory of Political Economy, on the principle of production the source of wealth. Phil., Bonsal, 1831.

Skidmore, Thomas. The Rights of Man to Property. New York, Ming, 1829.

Spencer, Herbert. Social Statics; or the conditions essential to human happiness specified, and the first of them developed (first pub. in England in 1851). New York, Appleton, 1865.

Taylor, William Cooke. The Natural History of Society in the Barbarous and Civilized State: An Essay towards discovering the origin and course of human improvement. 2 vols. New York, Appleton, 1841.

Thompson, Daniel P. Locke Amsden or the Schoolmaster: a Tale. Boston, Lothrop, Lee and Shepard, 1847.

Tocqueville, Alexis de. Democracy in America, tr. by Henry Reeve. 2 vols. 4th ed. from the 8th Paris ed. New York, Langley, 1841.

Tucker, George. Progress of the United States in Population and Wealth in fifty years, as exhibited by the decennial census. New York, Hunt's Merchants' Mag., 1843.

Tyler, Samuel. A Discourse of the Baconian Philosophy (first pub. in 1844). 3rd ed. Washington and Baltimore, Morrison and Murphy, 1877.

United States Census. Population of the United States in 1860; compiled from the original returns of the eighth census. Washington, Govt. Printing Office, 1864.

Walker, Robert J. Letter from the Secretary of the Treasury, transmitting his Annual Report on the state of the finances, Dec. 9, 1847. (30th Cong., 1st Sess., House Ex. Doc. no. 6, pp. 1-35).

Warren, Josiah. Equitable Commerce: A New Development of Principles, for the harmonious adjustment and regulation of the pecuniary, intellectual, and moral intercourse of mankind, proposed as elements of new society. New Harmony, 1846.

Wayland, Francis. The Elements of Moral Science. New York, Cooke, 1835.

——. The Elements of Political Economy. 2nd ed. New York and Boston, Robinson and Franklyn; Crocker and Brewster, 1838.

——. Report to the Corporation of Brown University, on Changes in the System of Collegiate Education, read March 28, 1850. Providence, Whitney, 1850.

Webster, Noah. An American Dictionary of the English Language. (Composite title of various editions of period).

Wells, David A. Annual of Scientific Discovery; or, Year-Book of Facts in Science and Art, for 1852. Boston, Gould and Lincoln, 1852.

——. The Yearbook of Agriculture; or, the Annual of Agricultural Progress and Discovery, for 1855 and 1856. Phil., Childs and Peterson, 1856.

Weston, George M. The Progress of Slavery in the United States. Washington, 1857.

Williams, William R. Religious Progress: Discourses on the Development of the Christian Character. Boston and New York, Gould and Lincoln; Sheldon, Lamport and Blakeman, 1854.

Worcester, Joseph E. A Comprehensive . . . Dictionary of the English Language. (Composite title of various editions of period.)

Young America! Principles and Objects of the National Reform Association, or Agrarian League. (Young America Extra no., [1845?]; pamphlet in the New York Public Library).

UNCOLLECTED ADDRESSES, ORATIONS, AND SERMONS

Adams, Jaspar. An Inaugural Discourse, delivered in Trinity Church, Geneva, New-York, Aug. 1, 1827. Geneva, Bogert, 1827.

——. The Moral Causes of the Welfare of Nations. (An Oration, The College of Charleston, Nov., 1834), Charleston, Burges, 1834.

——. Characteristics of the Present Century. (A Baccalaureate Address, The College of Charleston, Oct., 1834), Charleston, Burges and Honour, 1836.

Adams, John Quincy. An Address ... at the City of Washington on the
    Fourth of July, 1821 ... 2nd ed. Cambridge, Hilliard and Metcalf, 1821.
——. An Oration addressed to the Citizens of the Town of Quincy, on the
    Fourth of July, 1831. Boston, Richardson, Lord and Holbrook, 1831.
——. An Oration delivered before the Cincinnati Astronomical Society, ...
    on the 10th of November, 1843. Cincinnati, Shepard, 1843.
Adams, William. Christianity the End and Unity of all Sciences and Pursuits.
    (An Address, Yale College, Sept., 1847), New York, Leavitt and
    Trow, 1847.
Andrews, John W. An Oration before the ... Phi Beta Kappa Society at
    Yale College, New Haven, August 14, 1850. New Haven, Hamlen, 1850.
Austin, Samuel. An Oration pronounced at Worcester on the Fourth of
    July, 1798. Worcester, L. Worcester, 1798.
Bacon, Ezekiel. Recollections of Fifty Years Since ... (Lecture, the Young
    Men's Assoc. of Utica, Feb., 1843), Utica, Roberts, 1843.
Bacon, Leonard. Christianity in History. (A Discourse, Yale College,
    August, 1848), New Haven, Hamlen, 1848.
Bailey, Gamaliel, Jr. American Progress. (A Lecture, the Young Men's
    Mercantile Library Assoc. of Cincinnati, Dec., 1846), Cincinnati,
    Shepard, 1846.
Bancroft, George. An Oration delivered before the Democracy of Spring-
    field, ... July 4, 1836. Springfield, Merriam, 1836.
Barnard, Daniel Dewey. An Address delivered September 6, 1831, before the
    Adelphic Union Society of Williams College ... Williamstown, Bannister,
    1831.
——. An Address ... Rutgers College ... July 18, 1837. Albany, Hoffman
    and White, 1837.
——. A Discourse pronounced at Schenectady, before the ... Society of
    Phi Beta Kappa, July 25, 1837. Albany, Hoffman and White, 1837.
——. Discourse ... the University of Vermont, August 1st, 1838 ... Albany,
    Hoffman and White, 1838.
——. An Address delivered at Amherst ... August 27, 1839. Albany, Hoff-
    and White, 1839.
——. A Plea for Social and Popular Repose. (An Address, the Univ. of
    the City of New York, July, 1845), New York, The Tribune, 1845.
——. Man and the State, Social and Political. (An Address, Yale College,
    August, 1846), New Haven, Hamlen, 1846.
——. The Social System. (An Address, Trinity College, August, 1848),
    Hartford, Hamner, 1848.
Barnes, Albert. An Oration on the Progress and Tendency of Science. (Yale,
    Phi Beta Kappa, August, 1840), Phil., Ashmead, 1840.
Bartlett, Samuel C. The Duty and Limitations of Civil Obedience. (A
    Discourse preached at Manchester, N. H., on the day of Public
    Thanksgiving, Nov. 24, 1853), Manchester, Abbott Jenks, 1853.
Beecher, Henry Ward. A Discourse delivered at the Plymouth Church,
    Brooklyn, N. Y., upon Thanksgiving Day, November 25th, 1847. New
    York, Cady and Burgess, 1848.

Beecher, Lyman. The Memory of Our Fathers (A Sermon, Plymouth, December, 1827), Boston, Marvin, 1828.

Bellows, Henry W. The Ledger and the Lexicon: or, Business and Literature in account with American Education. (An Oration, Phi Beta Kappa Society of Harvard Univ., July, 1853), Cambridge, Bartlett, 1853.

Beman, Nathan S. S. Characteristics of the Age. (A Discourse, First Presbyterian Church, Troy, N. Y., Thanksgiving Day, Dec. 12, 1850), Troy, Young and Hartt, 1851.

Bigelow, Jacob. Inaugural Address, ... the University at Cambridge, December 11, 1816. Boston, Wells and Lilly, 1817.

Blanchard, Jonathan. A Perfect State of Society. (Address, Oberlin Collegiate Institute, Sept., 1839), Oberlin, Steele, 1839.

Boutwell, George S. Address delivered at Concord, September 18, 1850, before the Middlesex Society of Husbandmen and Manufacturers. Boston, Forbes, 1850.

Bradley, Joseph P. Progress—Its Grounds and Possibilities. (An Address, Rutgers College, July, 1849), New Brunswick, 1849.

Breckinridge, Robert J. A Discourse on the Formation and Development of the American Mind. (Lafayette College, Sept., 1837), Baltimore, Matchett, 1837.

Brooks, Erastus. American Citizenship and the Progress of American Civilization. (An Oration before the Order of United Americans, Feb., 1858), New York, Gildersleve, 1858.

Brownson, Orestes A. A Discourse on the Wants of the Times, ... Boston, Sunday, May 29, 1836. Boston, Munroe, 1836.

——. Babylon Is Falling. (A Discourse, The Society for Christian Union and Progress, May, 1837), 2nd ed. Boston, Butts, 1837.

——. An Oration before the Democracy of Worcester, ... July 4, 1840. Boston and Worcester, Littlefield and Phillips, 1840.

——. An Oration on the Scholar's Mission. (Dartmouth College, July, 1843: Univ. of Vermont, August, 1843), Boston, Greene, 1843.

Bruce, James Cole. An Address ... the University of North Carolina, ... June 3, 1841. Raleigh, 1841.

Bushnell, Horace. An Oration, pronounced before the Society of Phi Beta Kappa, at New Haven, on the Principles of National Greatness, August 15, 1837. New Haven, Herrick and Noyes, 1837.

——. A Discourse on the Moral Uses of the Sea. (Delivered on board the packet-ship Victoria, July, 1845), New York, Dodd, 1845.

——. The Day of Roads. (A Discourse delivered on the annual Thanksgiving, 1846), Hartford, Geer, 1846.

——. Barbarism the First Danger—A Discourse for Home Missions. (Delivered in New York, Boston, etc.), New York, Osborn, 1847.

——. The Age of Homespun. (A Discourse, Litchfield, Conn., on the occasion of the Centennial Celebration, 1851), in "Litchfield County Centennial Celebration, held at Litchfield, Conn., 13th and 14th August, 1851." Hartford, Hunt, 1851. pp. 101-130.

——. Society and Religion. (A Sermon for California, San Francisco, July, 1856), San Francisco, Sterett, 1856.

Caldwell, Charles. Thoughts on the Spirit of Improvement... (An Address, Nashville Univ., April, 1835), Nashville, Nye, 1835.

Canfield, Sherman B. An Address on the Power and Progressiveness of Knowledge,... Willoughby University, Wednesday, February 22, 1843. Painesville, Smythe and Hanna, 1843.

Caruthers, William A. A Lecture delivered before the Georgia Historical Society,... March, 1843. Savannah, Locke and Davis, 1843.

Cass, Lewis. Address... before the Association of the Alumni of Hamilton College,... August 25, 1830. Utica, Williams, 1830.

——. A Discourse... before the American Historical Society, Jan. 30, 1836. Washington, Thompson, 1836.

Channing, William Henry. The Christian Church and Social Reform. (A Discourse delivered before the Religious Union of Associationists), Boston, Crosby and Nichols, 1848.

Clarke, James Freeman. The Well-Instructed Scribe, or Reform and Conservatism. (A Sermon preached... in Waltham, Mass., Oct. 27, 1841). Boston, Greene, 1841.

Curtis, George William. The Duty of the American Scholar to Politics and the Times. (An Oration, Wesleyan Univ., Aug. 1856), New York, Dix Edwards, 1856.

Cushing, Caleb. An Oration pronounced before the Literary Societies of Amherst College, August 23, 1836. Boston, Light and Stearns, 1836.

——. An Oration on the Material Growth and Territorial Progress of the United States, delivered at Springfield, Mass. on the Fourth of July, 1839. Springfield, Merriam Wood, 1839.

——. The Nation's Progress. (Speech at Baltimore, Md. July 11, 1853), in "A Library of American Literature," ed. E. C. Stedman and E. M. Hutchinson. vol. VI, New York, Webster, 1888, pp. 31-32.

Dana, James Dwight. Address before the American Association for the Advancement of Science, August, 1855. Cambridge, Lovering, 1855.

Dewey, Orville, The Laws of Human Progress and Modern Reforms. (A Lecture, the Mercantile Library Assoc., New York), New York and Boston, Francis; Crosby and Nichols, 1852.

Dix, John A. Address... Geneva College, on the 7th of August, 1839. Albany, Packard, Van Benthuysen, 1839.

Douglass, Frederick. The Claims of the Negro, Ethnologically Considered. (An Address, Western Reserve College, July, 1854), Rochester, Daily Am. Office, 1854.

Durfee, Job. The Influence of Scientific Discovery and Invention on Social and Political Progress. (Oration, Brown Univ., Sept., 1843), Providence, Cranston, 1843.

Eells, Samuel. Oration on the Law and Means of Social Advancement. (Delivered before the Alpha Delta Phi Society, New Haven, August 1839), Cincinnati, Kendall and Henry, 1839.

Evarts, William M. An Oration... delivered before the Linonian Society of Yale College... New Haven, The Linonian Society, 1853.

Everett, Alexander H. An Oration... before the Citizens of Boston on the 5th of July, 1830. Boston, Eastburn, 1830.

——. A Discourse on the Progress and Limits of Social Improvement; including a general survey of the history of civilization. (Addressed to the Literary Societies of Amherst College, August, 1833), Boston, Bowen, 1834.

Fowler, John W. Society: Its Progress and Prospects. (A Lecture, the Young Men's Assoc., Utica, April, 1843), Utica, Roberts and Curtiss, 1843.

Gallagher, William D. Facts and Conditions of Progress in the North-West. (Annual Discourse before the Historical and Philosophical Society of Ohio, April, 1850), Cincinnati, Derby, 1850.

Goddard, William G. An Address to the Phi Beta Kappa Society of Rhode Island... 1836. Boston, Eastburn, 1837.

Gould, James. An Oration... before the Connecticut Alpha of the Phi Beta Kappa Society, September 13, 1825. New Haven, Woodward, 1825.

Greeley, Horace. An Address before the Literary Societies of Hamilton College, July 23, 1844. Clinton, 1844.

——. The Crystal Palace and Its Lessons, A Lecture. New York, 1851. (Private copy in the New York Public Library).

Green, William Henry. The Destiny of Man. (An Oration, Lafayette College, July, 1853), Phil., Martien, 1853.

Greene, Albert G. An Oration in Commemoration... of the Declaration of American Independence. Providence, Miller, 1823.

Greene, William. Some of the Difficulties in the Administration of a Free Government. (A Discourse, the Rhode Island Alpha of the Phi Beta Kappa Society, July, 1851), Providence, Moore, 1851.

Greenough, William W. The Conquering Republic. (An Oration, Boston, July 4, 1849), Boston, Eastburn, 1849.

Grimké, Thomas S. An Address on the Character and Objects of Science. (Delivered before the Literary and Philosophical Society of South Carolina, May, 1827), Charleston, Miller, 1827.

Haddock, Charles B. The Patriot Scholar. (An Oration, the Phi Beta Kappa Society of Yale College, August, 1848). New Haven, Hamlen, 1848.

Hale, Benjamin. Liberty and Law. (A Lecture, Young Men's Assoc. Geneva, N. Y., Nov., 1837), Geneva, Merrill, 1838.

Hall, Willis. An Address delivered August 14, 1844, before the Society of Phi Beta Kappa in Yale College. New Haven, Hamlen, 1844.

Hammond, James H. An Address delivered before the South Carolina Institute,... on the 20th November, 1849. Charleston, Walker and James, 1849.

——. An Oration, delivered before the two Societies of the South-Carolina College, on the fourth of December, 1849. Charleston, Walker and James, 1850.

Harrington, Henry F. The Responsibleness of American Citizenship. (A Sermon preached on occasion of the 'anti-rent' disturbances, Sunday, December 22, 1844), Albany, Little, 1845.

Hawley, Charles. The Advantages of the Present Age. (Sermon, Presbyterian Church, Lyons, N. Y., Dec. 2, 1849), Rochester, Daily American Office, 1850.

Headley, Joel Tyler. The One Progressive Principle. (Delivered before the Literary Societies of the Univ. of Vermont, August, 1846), New York, Taylor, 1846.

Hedge, Frederic H. An Oration pronounced before the Citizens of Bangor, on the Fourth of July, 1838. Bangor, Smith, 1838.

——. Conservatism and Reform. (An Oration, Bowdoin College, Sept., 1843), Boston, Little Brown, 1843.

Hickok, Laurens P. A Nation Saved from Its Prosperity only by the Gospel. (A Discourse in behalf of the Am. Home Missionary Society, preached in the cities of New York and Brooklyn, May, 1853), New York, Am. Home. Miss. Society, 1853.

Hitchcock, Edward. The Highest Use of Learning. (An Address delivered at his inauguration to the Presidency of Amherst College), Amherst, Adams, 1845.

Holmes, George F. The Virginia Colony. (An Address, the Virginia Historical Society, at Richmond, Dec., 1859), in the "Virginia Historical Reporter," vol. II, part 1, Richmond, Wynne, 1860.

Hopkins, Mark. An Address delivered before the Society of the Alumni of Williams College, ... August 16, 1843. Boston, Marvin, 1843.

——. The Central Principle. (An Oration, The New England Society of New York, Dec., 1853), New York, French, 1854.

——. Science and Religion. (A Sermon, Albany, August 24, 1856, during the session of the Am. Assoc. for the Advancement of Science), Albany, Van Benthuysen, 1856.

——. Eagles' Wings. (A Baccalaureate Sermon, Williamstown, August, 1858), Boston, Marvin, 1858.

Humphrey, Edward P. An Address delivered before the Literary Societies of Centre College, Ky. June 25, 1850. Louisville, Courier-Job-Office, 1850.

Ingersoll, Joseph R. An Address delivered before the Literary Societies of Lafayette College, at Easton, Pa. July 4, 1833. Phil., [Harding], 1833.

Johnson, Herschel V. The Probable Destiny of Our Country ... (An Address, Mercer Univ., July, 1847), Penfield, Temperance Banner Office, 1847.

Jones, P. Franklin, National Prosperity, secured by a proper regard for the divine being, and the institutions of the gospel. (A Sermon, Thanksgiving Day, Earlville, N. Y.), Utica, Northway, 1852.

Joslin, Benjamin F. A Discourse on the Privileges and Duties of Man as a Progressive Being, delivered before the New York Alpha of the Phi Beta Kappa Society, July 23, 1833. Schenectady, Riggs, 1833.

Junkin, George, Jr. The Progress of the Age. (An Address, Washington College, Lexington, Virginia, June, 1851), Phil., 1851.

Kent, William. An Address, pronounced before the Phi Beta Kappa Society of Union College,... July 27th, 1841. New York, Van Norden, 1841.

King, Thomas Starr. The Railroad Jubilee: Two Discourses delivered in Hollis-Street Meeting-House, Sunday, Sept. 21, 1851. Boston, Greene, 1851.

Kinnicutt, Thomas. An Oration, delivered before The Society of United Brothers, of Brown University, September 1, 1840. Providence, Knowles and Vose, 1840.

Krebs, John M. Education and Progress. (An Address, Lafayette College, Sept., 1847), Easton, 1847.

Le Conte, Joseph. The Principles of a Liberal Education. (An Address, the Euphradian and Clariosophic Societies, April 20, 1859), Columbia, Gibbes, 1859.

Lewis, Taylér, Faith the Life of Science. (An Address, the Phi Beta Kappa Society of Union College, July, 1838), Albany, Hoffman and White, 1838.

——. The Revolutionary Spirit. (A Discourse, the Phi Beta Kappa Society of Wesleyan University), New York, Benedict, 1848.

——. Nature, Progress, Ideas. (A Discourse, the Phi Beta Kappa Society of Union College, July, 1849), Schenectady, Debogent, 1850.

Lincoln, Frederic W., Jr. An Address delivered before the Massachusetts Charitable Mechanic Association on... October 2nd, 1845. Boston, Dutton and Wentworth, 1845.

Lord, Nathan. The Improvement of the Present State of Things. (A Discourse, Dartmouth College, November, 1852), Hanover, Dartmouth Press, 1853.

Lunt, William P. The Union of the Human Race. (A Lecture, the Quincy Lyceum, Feb., 1850), Boston, Ticknor, Reed and Fields, 1850.

Luther, Seth. An Address to the Working Men of New England, on the State of Education, and on the Condition of the Producing Classes in Europe and America... 3rd ed., Phil., 1836.

McCay, Charles F. Inaugural Address of Charles F. McCay, Professor of Mathematics and Mechanical Philosophy in the South Carolina College. (Delivered in the State House, Dec., 1854), Columbia, 1855.

Marsh, George P. The Goths in New-England. (A Discourse, Middlebury College, August, 1843), Middlebury, Cobb, 1843.

——. Address before the Agricultural Society of Rutland County, Sept. 30, 1847. Rutland, The Herald Office, 1848.

Morgan, William F. Conservatism: Its True Signification, and Appropriate Office. (An Address, Trinity College, Hartford, July 1852), Hartford, Hanmer, 1852.

North, Simeon. Anglo-Saxon Literature. (An Oration, the Conn. Alpha of the Phi Beta Kappa Society, New Haven, August, 1847), Utica, Roberts, Sherman and Colston, 1847.

Ogden, James De Peyster. Lecture on National Character. (Delivered at the Jamaica Lyceum, L. I., April, 1843), New York, Wright, 1843.

Olmsted, Denison. An Oration on the Progressive State of the Present Age. (Delivered before the Phi Beta Kappa Society of Yale, Sept., 1827), New Haven, Howe, 1827.

Owen, Robert. Two Discourses on a New System of Society; as delivered in the Hall of Representatives of the United States,... on the 25th of February, and 7th of March, 1825. Pittsburgh, Eichbaum and Johnson, 1825.

Paine, Charles. An Oration pronounced July 4, 1801 at the Request of the Inhabitants of the Town of Boston. Boston, Manning and Loring, [1801?].

Palmer, Elihu. The Political Happiness of Nations. (An Oration, the Fourth of July, New York), New York, [1800]. (photostat of original; in the Columbia Univ. Library).

Parker, Joel. Progress. (An Address, the Phi Beta Kappa Society of Dartmouth College, July, 1846), Hanover, 1846.

Parker, Theodore. The Public Education of the People. (An Oration, The Onondaga Teachers' Institute, at Syracuse, N. Y., Oct., 1849), Boston, Crosby and Nichols, 1850.

——. The State of the Nation, considered in a Sermon for Thanksgiving Day, preached at the Melodeon, Nov. 28, 1850. Boston, Crosby and Nichols, 1851.

Penney, Joseph. Claims of the Missionary Enterprise. (A Discourse at the Ordination of the Rev. F. D. W. Ward and the Rev. Henry Cherry, as Missionaries to Southern India), New York, Osborn, 1836.

Pinckney, Henry Laurens. The Spirit of the Age. (An Address, the University of North Carolina), Raleigh, Gales, 1836.

Poinsett, Joel R. An Inquiry into the Received Opinions of Philosophers and Historians, on the Natural Progress of the Human Race from Barbarism to Civilization. (Read on the Anniversary of the Literary and Philosophical Society, May 14, 1834), Charleston, Burges, 1834. (photostat of original; in the Columbia Univ. Library).

——. Discourse on the Objects and Importance of the National Institution for the Promotion of Science, established at Washington, 1840, delivered at the first anniversary. Washington, Force, 1841.

Porter, Benjamin F. The Past and the Present. (A Discourse, the Univ. of Alabama), Tuscaloosa, Slade, 1845.

Price, Richard. The Evidence for a Future Period of Improvement in the State of Mankind... (A Discourse, London, April 25, 1787), London, Cadell and Johnson, 1787.

Quincy, Josiah. Address, delivered at the Fifth Anniversary of the Massachusetts Peace Society, December 25th, 1820. Cambridge, Hilliard and Metcalf, 1821.

Raymond, Henry J. The Relations of the American Scholar to His Country and His Times. (An Address, the Univ. of Vermont, August, 1850), New York, Baker and Scribner, 1850.

Riddle, David H. Sound and Sanctified Scholarship. (An Address, Western Univ. of Penna., Sept., 1846), Pittsburg, Commercial Journal, 1846.

Ripley, George. The Claims of the Age on the Work of the Evangelist. (A Sermon, Northampton, May, 1840), Boston, Weeks Jordan, 1840.

Robinson, Frederick. An Oration delivered before The Trades Union of Boston and Vicinity,... on the Fifty-Eighth Anniversary of American Independence. Boston, Douglas, 1834.

Royston, S. Watson. An Address delivered at Cumming, Georgia, February, 1844 on the Rise and Progress of Society, and the Formation of Government. New Haven, 1844.

Russell, George R. The Merchant. (An Oration before the Rhode Island Alpha of the Phi Beta Kappa Society, at Providence, Sept., 1849), Boston, Ticknor, Reed and Fields, 1849.

——. An Address before the Norfolk Agricultural Society, at Dedham, September 24, 1851. [Boston, Hewes, 1851.]

Sedgwick, Charles B. An Oration delivered before the United Chapters of the Sigma Phi Fraternity, at their General Convention, held in Geneva, N. Y. August 20th, 1850. New York, Kneeland, 1850.

Sergeant, John. An Address delivered at the Request of the Managers of The Apprentices' Library Company of Philadelphia, 23 November, 1832. Phil., Kay, [1832].

Shute, Samuel M. The Progress of the Race. (An Address, the Young Men's Christian Assoc. of York, Penna., Feb., 1856), Baltimore, Woods, 1856.

Simms, William Gilmore. The Social Principle: The True Source of National Permanence. (An Oration, the Univ. of Alabama, Dec., 1842), Tuscaloosa, The Erosophic Society, 1843.

——. Self-Development. (An Oration, Oglethorpe Univ., Nov., 1847), Milledgeville, The Thalian Society, 1847.

Skinner, Thomas H. Progress, the Law of Missionary Work. (A Sermon, the American Board of Commissioners for Foreign Missions, Rochester, Sept., 1843), Boston, Crocker, and Brewster, 1843.

Snodgrass, William D. An Address delivered before the Alumni Association of Washington College, at Washington, Pa., Sept. 23d, 1845. New York, Ludwig, 1845.

Stanton, Henry B. Ultraists, Conservatives, Reformers. (An Address, Williams College, August, 1850), New York, Baker and Scribner, 1850.

Stillman, Samuel. An Oration delivered, July 4, 1789, at the Request of the Inhabitants of the Town of Boston. Boston, Edes, 1789.

Sumner, Charles. The True Grandeur of Nations. (An Oration delivered before the Authorities of the City of Boston, July 4, 1845), Boston, Eastburn, 1845.

——. The Law of Human Progress. (An Oration, the Phi Beta Kappa Society of Union College, July, 1848), Boston, Ticknor, 1849.

Tallmadge, James. Address delivered May 20, 1837, in the Chapel of the University of the City of New-York, on Occasion of the Dedication of the Building to the Purposes of Science, Literature, and Religion. New York, Fanshaw, 1837.

Tappan, Henry P. Public Education. (An Address, the Hall of the House of Rep., in the Capitol at Lansing, Jan., 1857), Detroit, Barnes, 1857.

Tefft. Benjamin F. Inequality in the Condition of Men Inevitable. (A Sabbath Evening Lecture, Indiana Asbury Univ., March, 1845), Greencastle, The Western Visitor, 1845.

Thornwell, James H. The Rights and the Duties of Masters. (A Sermon, Charleston, S. C., May, 1850), Charleston, Walker and James, 1850.

Toombs, Robert. A Lecture delivered in the Tremont Temple, Boston, Massachusetts, on the 24th January, 1856. [Washington, Towers, 1856].

Ullman, Daniel. The Course of Empire. (An Oration, the Order of United Americans, New York, Feb. 22, 1856), New York, Weiss, 1856.

Verplanck, Gulian C. A Lecture Introductory to the Course of Scientific Lectures before The Mechanics' Institute of the City of New York, delivered November 27, 1833. New York, Scott, 1833.

——. The Advantages and the Dangers of the American Scholar. (A Discourse, Union College, July, 1836), New York, Wiley and Long, 1836.

Vethake, Henry. An Address, delivered at his Inauguration, as President of Washington College, Lexington, February 21st, 1835. Lexington, Baldwin, 1835.

Wadsworth, Charles, America's Mission. (A Sermon, Thanksgiving Day, Phil., Nov. 22, 1855), Phil., [Peterson], 1855.

Walker, Timothy. The Reform Spirit of the Day. (An Oration, the Phi Beta Kappa Society of Harvard Univ., July, 1850), Boston and Cambridge, Munroe, 1850.

Wallis, Severn Teackle. Address delivered before the Reading Room Society of Saint Mary's College, Baltimore, at the Annual Commencement, July 20th, 1841. Baltimore, Murphy, [1841].

——. Lecture on the Philosophy of History, and Some of the Popular Errors which are Founded on It. (Delivered before the Calvert Institute, January 24th, 1844), Baltimore, Murphy, [1844].

——. Leisure: Its Moral and Political Economy. (A Lecture, the Mercantile Library Assoc., Baltimore, March, 1859), Baltimore, Rose, 1859.

Wayland, Francis. The Dependence of Science upon Religion. (A Discourse, Brown Univ., Feb., 1835), Providence, Marshall Brown, 1835.

——. The Education Demanded by the People of the U[nited] States. (A Discourse, Union College, July, 1854), Boston, Phillips Sampson, 1855.

Wheaton, Eber. Oration delivered July 4, 1828, before the Several Civic Societies of New York. New York, Von Pelt, 1828.

Whiting, John N. Modern Reforms, and the Duty of the Instructed Towards Them. (An Address, Hobart College, July, 1852), Geneva, Parker, 1852.

Williams, John. Academic Studies. (An Inaugural Discourse, Trinity College, Hartford, 1849), Hartford, Hanmer, 1849.

Williams, William R. The Conservative Principle in Our Literature. (An Address, the Hamilton Literary and Theological Institution, Madison County, N. Y., June, 1843), New York, Gray, 1844.

Young, Samuel. Suggestions on the Best Mode of Promoting Civilization and Improvement; or the Influence of Woman on the Social State. (A Lecture, the Young Men's Assoc. for Mutual Improvement, Albany, Jan., 1837), Albany, Hoffman and White, 1837.

——. Lecture on Civilization, delivered before the Young Men's Association of Saratoga Springs, March 8th, 1841. Saratoga Springs, Davison, 1841.

——. A Discourse delivered at Schenectady, July 25, 1826, before the New-York Alpha of the Phi Beta Kappa. Ballston Spa, Comstock, 1826.

SECONDARY WORKS

NOTE: The biographical information necessary for this study was taken, for the most part, from the usual compilations and from the standard biographies. Only a few of the latter have been listed, and of the former, the most important is the *Dictionary of American Biography*, ed. by Allen Johnson and Dumas Malone. 20 vols. (New York, Scribners, 1928-1936).

Adams, Henry. History of the United States of America. 9 vols. New York, Scribners, 1889-1891.

Allibone, S. Austin. A Critical Dictionary of English Literature, and British and American Authors. 3 vols. Phil., Lippincott, 1882.

Arvin, Newton. Whitman. New York, Macmillan, 1938.

Baker, Thomas S. Lenau and Young Germany in America. Phil., Stockhausen, 1897.

Barnes, Harry Elmer. An Intellectual and Cultural History of the Western World. rev. ed. New York, Reynal Hitchcock, 1941.

Barnes, H. E. and Howard Becker. Social Thought from Lore to Science. vol. I, Boston and New York, Heath, 1938.

Barzun, Jacques. Darwin, Marx, Wagner: Critique of a Heritage. Boston, Little Brown, 1941.

Beard, Charles A. and Mary R. The Rise of American Civilization. new ed. 2 vols. in one; New York, Macmillan, 1933.

——. The American Spirit: A Study of the Idea of Civilization in the United States. New York, Macmillan, 1942.

Beard, Charles A. ed. A Century of Progress. New York, Harpers, 1933.

Becker, Carl L. "Kansas," in Essays in American History dedicated to Frederick Jackson Turner. New York, Holt, 1910, pp. 85-111.

——. The Heavenly City of the Eighteenth-Century Philosophers. New Haven, Yale Univ. Press, 1932.

——. Progress and Power. Stanford, Stanford Univ. Press, 1936.

Bell, Whitfield J., Jr. "The Relation of Herndon and Gibbon's Exploration of the Amazon to North American Slavery, 1850-1855," *Hispanic American Historical Review*, XIX (Nov., 1939), 494-503.

Bernard, L. L. "Henry Hughes, First American Sociologist," *Social Forces*,

XV (Dec., 1936), 154-174.

Billington, Ray Allen. The Protestant Crusade, 1800-1860: A Study of the Origins of American Nativism. New York, Macmillan, 1938.

Blegen, Theodore C. Norwegian Migration to America, 1825-1860. Northfield, Norwegian-American Historical Assoc., 1931.

Boodin, John Elof. "The Idea of Progress," *Journal of Social Philosophy*, IV (Jan., 1939), 101-120.

——. The Social Mind: Foundations of Social Philosophy. New York, Macmillan, 1939.

Brailsford, H. N. Shelley, Godwin, and their Circle. New York and London, Holt, [1913].

Brinton, Crane. The Political Ideas of the English Romanticists. [London], Oxford Univ. Press, 1926.

——. English Political Thought in the Nineteenth Century. London, Benn, 1933.

Bury, J. B. The Idea of Progress: An Inquiry into Its Origin and Growth. (first pub. in England in 1920), New York, Macmillan, 1932.

——. Selected Essays, ed. Harold Temperley. Cambridge, The Univ. Press, 1930.

Cady, George Johnson. "The Early American Reaction to Malthus," *Journal of Political Economy*, XXXIX (Oct., 1931), 601-632.

Carlton, Frank Tracy. Economic Influences upon Educational Progress in the United States, 1820-1850. Madison, 1908.

Charvat, William. "American Romanticism and the Depression of 1837," *Science and Society*, II (Winter, 1937), 67-82.

Codman, John T. Brook Farm: Historic and Personal Memoirs. Boston, Arena, 1894.

Commager, Henry Steele. Theodore Parker. Boston, Little Brown, 1936.

Crane, Ronald S. "Anglican Apologetics and the Idea of Progress, 1699-1745," *Modern Philology*, XXXI (Feb., and May, 1934), 273-306, 349-382.

Cubberley, Ellwood P. Public Education in the United States. rev. ed. Boston and New York, Houghton Mifflin, 1934.

Cuningham, Charles E. Timothy Dwight, 1752-1817: A Biography. New York, Macmillan, 1942.

Curti, Merle. "Young America," *American Historical Review*, XXXII (Oct., 1926), 34-55.

——. The Social Ideas of American Educators. New York, Scribners, 1935.

——. The Learned Blacksmith: The Letters and Journals of Elihu Burritt. New York, Wilson-Erickson, 1937.

——. "The Great Mr. Locke, America's Philosopher, 1783-1861," *Huntington Library Bulletin*, no. 11 (April, 1937), 107-151.

——. "Francis Lieber and Nationalism," *Huntington Library Quarterly*, IV (April, 1941), 263-292.

——. The Growth of American Thought. New York and London, Harpers, 1943.

Delvaille, Jules. Essai sur l'Histoire de l'Idée de Progres jusqu' a la fin du XVIII⁰ siecle. Paris, Felix Alcan, 1910.

Demaree, Albert L. The American Agricultural Press, 1819-1860. New York, Col. Univ. Press, 1941.

Eaton, Clement. Freedom of Thought in the Old South. Durham, Duke Univ. Press, 1941.

Elsbree, Oliver W. The Rise of the Missionary Spirit in America, 1790-1815. Williamsport, 1928.

Flint, Robert. The Philosophy of History in France and Germany. New York, Scribner, Welford and Armstrong, 1875.

——. Historical Philosophy in France. New York, Scribners, 1894.

Foreman, Grant. The Five Civilized Tribes. Norman, Univ. of Oklahoma Press, 1934.

Frothingham, Octavius B. Transcendentalism in New England: A History. New York, Putnam, 1897.

——. George Ripley. Boston and New York, Houghton Mifflin, 1882.

Fuess, Claude M. The Life of Caleb Cushing. 2 vols. New York, Harcourt Brace, 1923.

Gabriel, Ralph Henry. The Course of American Democratic Thought: An Intellectual History Since 1815. New York, Ronald, 1940.

Gazley, John G. American Opinion of German Unification, 1848-1871. New York, 1926.

Gibbens, V. E. "Tom Paine and the Idea of Progress," *Pennsylvania Magazine of History and Biography*, LXVI (April, 1942), 191-204.

Girard, William. Du Transcendantalisme Considéré Essentiellement dans Sa Definition et Ses Origines Françaises. Berkeley, Univ. of Calif. Press, 1908.

Goddard, Harold C. Studies in New England Transcendentalism. New York, Col. Univ. Press, 1908.

Goodykoontz. Colin B. Home Missions on the American Frontier. Caldwell, Caxton, 1939.

Halévy, Elie. The Growth of Philosophic Radicalism, tr. by Mary Morris. New York, Macmillan, 1928.

Handlin, Oscar. Boston's Immigrants, 1790-1865. Cambridge, Harvard Univ. Press, 1941.

Hansen, Allen Oscar. Liberalism and American Education in the Eighteenth Century. New York, Macmillan, 1926.

Hansen, Marcus Lee. The Atlantic Migration, 1607-1860: A History of the Continuing Settlement of the United States, ed. Arthur M. Schlesinger. Cambridge, Harvard Univ. Press, 1940.

——. The Immigrant in American History, ed. Arthur M. Schlesinger. Cambridge, Harvard Univ. Press, 1940.

Hawkins, Richmond Laurin. August Comte and the United States, 1816-1853. Cambridge, Harvard Univ. Press, 1936.

——. Positivism in the United States, 1853-1861. Cambridge, Harvard Univ. Press, 1938.

Hayes, Cecil B. The American Lyceum: Its History and Contribution to Education. (United States Dept. of Interior Office of Educ. Bull. no. 12, 1932), Washington, Govt. Printing Office, 1932.

Hertzler, Joyce O. Social Progress: A Theoretical Survey and Analysis. New York and London, Century, 1928.

Hill, Hamilton A. Memoir of Abbott Lawrence. 2nd ed. Boston, Little Brown, 1884.

Howard, Leon. The Connecticut Wits. Chicago, Univ. of Chicago Press, 1943.

Inge, W. R. The Idea of Progress. Oxford, Clarendon Press, 1920.

Jackson, Sidney L. "Some Ancestors of the 'Extension Course,'" *New England Quarterly*, XIV (Sept., 1941), 505-518.

——. America's Struggle for Free Schools: Social Tension and Education in New England and New York, 1827-1842. Washington, American Council on Public Affairs, [1942].

Jenkins, William Sumner. Pro-Slavery Thought in the Old South. Chapel Hill, Univ. of North Carolina Press, 1935.

Johnstone, Paul H. "Old Ideals versus New Ideas in Farm Life," in Farmers in a Changing World: The Yearbook of Agriculture, 1940, by the U. S. Dept. of Agric. [Washington], Govt. Printing Office, [1940].

Jones, Howard Mumford. America and French Culture, 1750-1848. Chapel Hill, Univ. of North Carolina Press, 1927.

——. "The Influence of European Ideas in Nineteenth-Century America," *American Literature*, VII (Nov., 1935), 241-273.

Jones, Richard F. Ancients and Moderns: A Study of the Background of the *Battle of the Books* (Washington Univ. Studies, n. s. Lang. and Lit. no. 6), St. Louis, 1936.

Kelley, Maurice. Additional Chapters on Thomas Cooper. Orono, Univ. of Maine Press, 1930.

Laski, Harold J. Political Thought in England from Locke to Bentham. New York, Holt, 1920.

Leary, Lewis. That Rascal Freneau: A Study in Literary Failure. [New Brunswick], Rutgers Univ. Press, [1941].

Lehmann, W. C. Adam Ferguson and the Beginnings of Modern Sociology. New York, 1930.

Leighton, Walter L. French Philosophers and New England Transcendentalism. Charlottesville, Univ. of Virginia, 1908.

Leopold, Richard William. Robert Dale Owen: A Biography. Cambridge, Harvard Univ. Press, 1940.

Long, Orie William. Literary Pioneers: Early American Explorers of European Culture. Cambridge, Harvard Univ. Press, 1935.

Lovejoy, Arthur O. The Great Chain of Being: A Study of the History of An Idea. Cambridge, Harvard Univ. Press, 1936.

—— and George Boas. Primitivism and Related Ideas in Antiquity. Baltimore, Johns Hopkins Press, 1935.

Martin, Edwin Thomas. Thomas Jefferson and the Idea of Progress. (Ph. D. Thesis, Univ. of Wisconsin, 1941), Ms. in the Univ. of Wisconsin Library, Madison, Wisconsin.

Martin, Kingsley. French Liberal Thought in the Eighteenth Century. London, Benn, 1929.

Matthiessen, F. O. American Renaissance: Art and Expression in the Age of Emerson and Whitman. New York, Oxford Univ. Press, 1941.

May, Arthur James. Contemporary American Opinion of the Mid-Century Revolutions in Central Europe. Phil., 1927.

Mims, Helen Sullivan. "Early American Democratic Theory and Orestes Brownson," Science and Society, III (Spring, 1939), 166-198.

Mitchell, Broadus. The Rise of Cotton Mills in the South. Baltimore, Johns Hopkins Press, 1921.

Mode, Peter G. The Frontier Spirit in American Christianity. New York, Macmillian, 1923.

Morley, John. Critical Miscellanies. vol. II, London, Macmillan, 1886.

Mott, Frank Luther. A History of American Magazines, 1741-1850. Cambridge, Harvard Univ. Press, 1939.

———. A History of American Magazines, 1850-1865. Cambridge, Harvard Univ. Press, 1938.

Muirhead, J. H. "How Hegel Came to America," Philosophical Review, XXXVII (May, 1928), 226-240.

Mumford, Lewis. Technics and Civilization. New York, Harcourt Brace, 1934.

Nevins, Allan. The Gateway to History. Boston and New York, Heath, 1938.

Noyes, John Humphrey. History of American Socialisms. Phil. Lippincott, 1870.

Palmer, Paul A. "Benthamism in England and America," American Political Science Review, XXXV (Oct., 1941), 855-871.

Parrington, Vernon Louis. The Romantic Revolution in America, 1800-1860. (Main Currents in American Thought, vol. II), New York, Harcourt Brace, 1927.

Paxson, Frederic L. When the West Is Gone. New York Holt, 1930.

Riley, Woodbridge. American Thought from Puritanism to Pragmatism and Beyond. 2nd ed. New York, Holt, 1923.

Rippy, J. Fred. Joel R. Poinsett, Versatile American. Durham, Duke Univ. Press, 1935.

Ross, John F. The Social Criticism of Fenimore Cooper. Berkeley, Univ. of Calif. Press, 1933.

Russell, Robert Royal. Economic Aspects of Southern Sectionalism, 1840-1861. Urbana, Univ. of Illinois, 1924.

Schapiro, J. Salwyn. Condorcet and the Rise of Liberalism. New York, Harcourt Brace, 1934.

Schlesinger, Arthur M., Jr. Orestes A. Brownson: A Pilgrim's Progress. Boston, Little Brown, 1939.

———. "The Problem of Richard Hildreth," New England Quarterly, XIII (June, 1940), 223-245.

Schneider, Herbert Wallace. Science and Social Progress, Lancaster, 1920.

——. "The Intellectual Background of William Ellery Channing," *Church History*, VII (March, 1938), 3-23.

Schuster, Eunice M. Native American Anarchism: A Study of Left-Wing American Individualism. Northampton, Dept. of History of Smith College, [1932].

Sears, Clara Endicott. Bronson Alcott's Fruitlands. Boston and New York, Houghton Mifflin, 1915.

Sedgwick, W. T. and H. W. Tyler. (rev. by Tyler and R. P. Bigelow). A Short History of Science. New York, Macmillan, 1939.

Silver, Mildred. "Emerson and the Idea of Progress," *American Literature*, XII (March, 1940), 1-19.

Smallwood, W. M. in collab. with M. S. C. Smallwood. Natural History and the American Mind. New York, Col. Univ. Press, 1941.

Smith, Edgar F. Priestly in America, 1794-1804. Phil., Blakiston, 1920.

Smith, Preserved. A History of Modern Culture. 2 vols. New York, Holt, 1930-1934.

Stephen, Leslie. History of English Thought in the Eighteenth Century. 2 vols. 3rd ed. New York, Putnam, 1927.

Stern, Bernhard J. Lewis Henry Morgan: Social Evolutionist. Chicago, Univ. of Chicago Press, 1931.

Stoddard, Paul W. The Place of The Lyceum in American Life. (M. A. Thesis, Faculty of Educ., Columbia Univ., 1929), Ms. in the Teachers College Library, Columbia Univ., New York City.

Strong, Gordon Bartley. Adam Smith and the Eighteenth Century Concept of Social Progress. Chicago, Univ. of Chicago Libraries, 1932.

Swift, Lindsay. Brook Farm: Its Members, Scholars and Visitors. New York and London, Macmillan, 1900.

Teggart, Frederick J. Theory of History. New Haven, Yale Univ. Press, 1925.

Thomas, Macklin. The Idea of Progress in the Writings of Franklin, Freneau, Barlow and Rush. (Ph. D. Thesis, Univ. of Wisconsin, 1938), Ms. in the Univ. of Wisconsin Library, Madison, Wisconsin.

Thonissen, J. J. Quelques Considérations sur la Théorie du Progrès Indéfini ... (Mémoires Couronnés et Autres Mémoires, Publiés par L'Académie Royale des Sciences, des Lettres et des Beaux-Arts de Belgique, Tome IX), Bruxelles, Hayez, 1859.

Turner, Frederick Jackson. Rise of the New West, 1819-1829. (The American Nation: A History, vol. XIV), New York and London, Harpers, 1906.

——. The United States, 1830-1850. New York, Holt, 1935.

Turner, John Roscoe. The Ricardian Rent Theory in Early American Economics. New York, New York Univ. Press, 1921.

Wallis, Wilson D. Culture and Progress. New York, Whittlesey House, 1930.

Waterman, William R. Frances Wright. New York, 1924.

Weinberg, Albert K. Manifest Destiny: A Study of Nationalist Expansionism in American History. Baltimore, Johns Hopkins Press, 1935.

Wells, Ronald Vale. Three Christian Transcendentalists; James Marsh, Caleb Sprague Henry, Frederic Henry Hedge. New York, Col. Univ. Press, 1943.

Wender, Herbert. Southern Commercial Conventions, 1837-1859. Baltimore, Johns Hopkins Press, 1930.

Wesley, Charles H. "The Concept of Negro Inferiority in American Thought," *Journal of Negro History*, XXV (Oct., 1940), 540-560.

Whitney, Lois. Primitivism and the Idea of Progress in English Popular Literature of the Eighteenth Century. Baltimore, Johns Hopkins Press, 1934.

Wiltse, Charles Maurice. The Jeffersonian Tradition in American Democracy. Chapel Hill, Univ. of North Carolina Press, 1935.

Wish, Harvey. George Fitzhugh, Conservative of the Old South. Charlottesville, 1938.

——. George Frederick Holmes and the Genesis of American Sociology," *American Journal of Sociology*, XLVI (March, 1941), 698-707.

——. "George Frederick Holmes and Southern Periodical Literature of the Mid-Nineteenth Century," *Journal of Southern History*, VII (August, 1941), 343-356.

Wright, Benjamin F., Jr. American Interpretations of Natural Law: A Study in the History of Political Thought. Cambridge, Harvard Univ. Press, 1931.

Zahler, Helene Sara. Eastern Workingmen and National Land Policy, 1829-1862. New York, Col. Univ. Press, 1941.

Zunder, Theodore A. The Early Days of Joel Barlow, A Connecticut Wit. New Haven, Yale Univ. Press, 1934.

INDEX